FUGITIVE POLITICS

Fugitive Politics explores the intersection between politics and ecology, between the requirements for radical change and the unprecedented challenges posed by the global crisis, a dialectic which has rarely been addressed in academia.

Across eight chapters, Carl Boggs explores how systemic change may be achieved within the current system, while detailing attempts at achieving change within nation-states. Boggs states that any notion of revolution seems fanciful in the current climate, contending that controlling elites have concentrated their hold on corporate power along three self-serving fronts: technology (Big Tech) and the surveillance order, militarism and the warfare state, and intensification of globalized power. Combined with this Boggs cites the fundamental absence of revolutionary counter-forces, arguing that after decades of subservice relevant, allied to the rise of identity politics and social movements, the Marxist theoretical legacy is now exhausted and will not provide an exit from the crisis. Boggs concludes that the only possibility for fundamental change will come from an open style of politics, in the Jacobin tradition, operating within the overall structures of the current democratic state.

Written for both an academic and a general readership, in the U.S. and beyond, *Fugitive Politics* will be of vital importance to those studying political theory, political philosophy, political history, Marxism and Marxist theory, authoritarian politics, ecology, environmental politics, and climate politics.

Carl Boggs has been professor of social science at National University in Los Angeles for more than 30 years. He has written 25 books in the areas of critical social theory, European politics, American politics, U.S. foreign and military policy, and film studies. For the past 25 years he has been a regular contributor to the online magazine *CounterPunch*. He is a member of the editorial boards of *New Political Science*, *Theory and Society*, and the Global Studies Association. He is recipient of the Charles McCoy Award for career achievement from the American Political Science Association.

"In *Fugitive Politics*, Boggs returns to his days as a campus radical, yolking together two influential yet seemingly disparate narratives in order to fashion a fugitive politics repurposed to challenge the misplaced ontological confidence of much of today's academic left. In so doing he proves that today's algorithmic understanding of politics often serves as an ontological block to capturing the analogue experience of political repression that Boggs and his contemporaries lived on a daily basis. Blending the prehensive nature of political activism with his pathfinding theoretical work on Gramsci, Lenin, and Marx, and his prescient forays into ecosocialism, Boggs creates new zones of contestation, sites of scholarly outlawry, enclaves of political insurgency and fugitive deploys that are equipped to challenge the arc of historical struggle that could not be anticipated by the political sages of yesteryear. This book is vintage Boggs, fearless and forward-looking, at the cutting edge of the political discourse of the day, a beacon of light in these dark times."

Peter McLaren, *Distinguished Professor in Critical Studies, Chapman University, USA*

FUGITIVE POLITICS

The Struggle for Ecological Sanity

Carl Boggs

NEW YORK AND LONDON

First published 2022
by Routledge
605 Third Avenue, New York, NY 10158

and by Routledge
2 Park Square, Milton Park, Abingdon, Oxon OX14 4RN

Routledge is an imprint of the Taylor & Francis Group, an informa business

© 2022 Carl Boggs

The right of Carl Boggs to be identified as author of this work has been asserted by him in accordance with sections 77 and 78 of the Copyright, Designs and Patents Act 1988.

All rights reserved. No part of this book may be reprinted or reproduced or utilised in any form or by any electronic, mechanical, or other means, now known or hereafter invented, including photocopying and recording, or in any information storage or retrieval system, without permission in writing from the publishers.

Trademark notice: Product or corporate names may be trademarks or registered trademarks, and are used only for identification and explanation without intent to infringe.

Library of Congress Cataloging-in-Publication Data
A catalog record for this title has been requested

ISBN: 978-1-032-05416-2 (hbk)
ISBN: 978-1-032-05414-8 (pbk)
ISBN: 978-1-003-19746-1 (ebk)

DOI: 10.4324/9781003197461

Typeset in Bembo
by Taylor & Francis Books

This book is dedicated to my Ventura College amici:
Anne, Bill C., Cyndie, Gerry, Jaimee, Julie, Kim, Michael W.

CONTENTS

Preface ix

    Introduction 1

1 Marxism and Early Capitalism 9

    Marxism and Ecology 11
    In Search of an Ecological Marx 12
    Capitalism and the Natural World 16

2 Capitalism: From Marx to Weber 23

    The Logic of Economic Rationalization 24
    Modernity and State-Capitalism 30
    The Rise of Corporate Globalization 34
    The War on Nature 36

3 From Lenin to Gramsci 44

    Breaking the Theoretical Impasse 44
    The Retrieval of Politics 48
    Marxism in History 49
    The Problem of Revolution 52
    Gramsci's Jacobinism 56

4 Authoritarian State, Mass Society   63

   Sources of Domination 63
   Rise of the Authoritarian State 67
   The Problem of Mass Culture 71

5 Mills: Beyond Marx and Weber   77

   The Authoritarian State Revisited 79
   The "Higher Immorality" 82
   The Mass Society 86

6 Capitalism, Technology, Power   96

   Capitalism and Technology 97
   The McDonaldized Society 100
   The Mass-Surveillance Order 102
   Big Tech Oligarchy 108

7 The Military Behemoth   115

   The New Imperial State 117
   The Doomsday Threat 120
   Permanent War? 124
   The Age of Technowar 127

8 The Road to Ecosocialism?   133

   The New Global Landscape 133
   A Modern Jacobinsm? 137
   Gramsci's Politics Revisited 139
   The Grand Illusion 141
   Traversing the Modern Impasse 142

   Sheldon Wolin: A Tribute   146

Index   151

PREFACE

The title of this book, *Fugitive Politics*, has its rather unusual origins in a bizarre confluence of personal narratives – one going back to an intellectual mentor during graduate-student years, the other involving a friend engaged in antiwar politics at the time of the Vietnam War. The mentor was Sheldon Wolin, whose last (and posthumous) book was titled *Fugitive Democracy*, a lengthy collection of brilliant essays on political theorists ranging from Thomas Hobbes to Karl Marx, Max Weber, the Frankfurt School, and more recent writers such as John Rawls. As professor of political science at U.C., Berkeley during the 1960s, Wolin would exert a profound impact on my intellectual and political development extending well past that turbulent decade. *Fugitive Democracy* would be the final work of a prolific career that included such classics as *Politics and Vision* (1960) and *Democracy, Inc.* (2007).

The activist friend is Howard Mechanic, author of the recently published *The Fugitive Candidate*, which traces the lengthy history of Mechanic's protests against the Vietnam War as a student at Washington University in St. Louis (where I taught in the 1970s), his improbable arrest and prison sentence, his underground years in Arizona, his ultimate detection and arrest while running for Scottsdale city council, and his final pardon in 2000 by President Bill Clinton. I was honored to be able to write the foreword to Mechanic's fascinating book, its appearance coinciding with a documentary on his remarkable saga.

Viewed through the lens of both experiences, the term "fugitive" takes on special meaning – simultaneously open-ended and transgressive, transitory and exotic, fragmentary and radical. Put differently, the reference captures a dynamic element of politics embedded in an ongoing process of deconstruction, where the outer surface of historical reality is increasingly penetrated and revealed. The seminal though quite diverse contributions of Wolin and Mechanic would seem to follow this arc. Wolin writes: "Politics centers around the unmasking of the various disguises of oppression regardless of whether the alleged act has occurred yesterday, or in the distant past, or in an ancient text of philosophy, a nursery fable, a textbook, a modern novel, or a Senate confirmation hearing." The observable world of politics is, from all appearances, rather precarious, unsettled, chaotic, yet must at some point yield to orderly conceptualization – "orderly," however, within perpetually changing historical conditions.

It turns out, further, that the "fugitive" element is innately hostile to sacred (or conventional) forms of thought and action – something, it seems to this writer, central to what both Wolin and Mechanic, in different ways, came to embellish in their personal lives. Wolin comments: "Revolution might be defined for our purpose as the wholesale transgression of inherited forms." Nothing would seem more appropriate to the requirements of confronting the global crisis we presently face, for that crisis poses a range of challenges that demand new modes of understanding. Given such challenges, the old formulas and concepts appear stale and obsolete, as (in Wolin's apt framing) "revolutions activate the demos and destroy boundaries that bar access to the political experience."

A daunting problem today is that, without newer strategic directions for winning political power, hopes for genuine change are virtually sure to be extinguished. Today, on the one hand, the complex dynamics of globalized corporate-state power tend to overwhelm even the most creative theoretical imagination, not to mention the capacity to act with political efficacy. Along with the tightening convergence of economic and governmental power at the very summits of human experience, human beings everywhere face an increasingly concentrated system of rule, strong oligarchical forces, expanded technological domination, frightening new surveillance capabilities, and out-of-control corporate globalization. This trajectory differs radically from that anticipated by Marx and Weber, theorists of the Frankfurt School, and even C. Wright Mills.

Never in history have ruling elites been able to assemble such unbridled power over economic development, state governance, social life, the global environment. These earlier theorists could hardly have foreseen the degree to which later (now contemporary) fortresses of domination would impede popular struggles for a more egalitarian, democratic, sustainable world system. This widening matrix of power – explored in the following chapters – currently unfolds along four interrelated fronts: technology and the surveillance state, militarism and the war-making apparatus, intensification of globalized capitalism, the war against nature. Nowhere are there visible signs of erosion. Attempts to fundamentally break with such a behemoth will sooner or later demand new, highly imaginative ("fugitive"?) forms of insurgency – that is, transcendence of the familiar, the comfortable, the "sacred."

Viewed thus, central to the modern (or postmodern) failure of politics is the sharply declining relevance of the Marxist tradition, in all its variants, to provide theoretical clarity for any potential anti-system opposition. The obvious gravity of what humanity now faces – not only global warming but a world of shrinking natural resources, food shortages, and mounting geopolitical conflict – suggests that time for making sense of remaining political options is quickly running out. The conundrum worsens once the new imperatives are fully taken into account: a revitalized politics, an ecological path of development, popular shifts in cultural behavior and (especially) natural relations. Unfortunately, in the world we inhabit there are no movements, parties, or governments that can even remotely satisfy these epic imperatives.

The challenge ahead inevitably forces historical protagonists to enter new cultural or ideological "zones" – space all-encompassing enough to accommodate what might be described as a "fugitive" state of affairs. Within such an ensemble of relations the idea of *fugitive politics* takes on an intellectual, if not also psychological, meaning consistent with the aforementioned challenges going forward. Toward this end I wish to salute the combined legacies of Sheldon Wolin and Howard Mechanic.

Carl Boggs
Los Angeles, California
March, 2021

INTRODUCTION

This book explores the intersection between politics and ecology, between the requirements for radical change and unprecedented challenges posed by the global crisis. For many reasons, this dialectic has rarely been addressed, even among progressives and leftists. One dimension of this failure – central to the key arguments that follow – is declining relevance of the Marxist tradition, in all of its variants, to provide intellectual substance for any future anti-system politics. The extreme gravity of what humanity now faces – not only global warming but a world of shrinking natural resources and drastic food shortages – means that time for creating a viable strategy is running out. The problem worsens once the momentous tasks at hand are taken into account: a revitalized politics, sustainable economic development, popular shifts in both cultural behavior and natural relations. Sadly, in the world to date we encounter no movements, parties, or governments that even remotely meet this challenge.

For at least a century after the deaths of Karl Marx and Friedrich Engels – that is, the end of the nineteenth century – Marxism in one expression or another was viewed as foundational to any prospects for a transition from capitalism to socialism. Central to that transition was always faith in a proletarian-based revolution, the logical outcome of industrializing (but crisis-ridden) capitalist systems. Historical development was expected to generate deepening systemic contradictions ultimately leading to economic breakdown and social upheaval, though the distinctly *political* elements of this process usually remained vague, ill-defined; strategy was always a point of intense difference across the entire trajectory of Marxism. For reasons nowadays abundantly clear, however, the potential linkage of theory and action within the tradition – the source of political agency – has essentially vanished. Marxism no longer shapes or informs any viable opposition to capitalism, in any locale. Indeed it has been a full century since the last widespread working-class insurgency against capitalist power, the 1919–20 *Biennio Rosso* in Italy, which ended in crushing failure.

Prospects for overcoming the modern crisis will depend on the capacity of counterforces to build and carry forward an ecologically sustainable world system, and that means effective social control over the instruments of economic and political power. Without a concrete *strategy* for winning such power, however, there can be no hopes for revolutionary change. This great conundrum revolves around the question of *power* pure and simple. And today the dynamics of power are shaped, more and more, by the incessant (seemingly irreversible) process of capitalist rationalization first thoroughly charted by Max Weber roughly a century ago. Among its vast consequences, rationalization serves to recast the entire realm of politics, or governance, in ways widely familiar into the present. Those consequences are nothing short of epic: convergence of economic and governmental power, an increasingly state-centered system of rule, strong oligarchical tendencies, expanded technological rationality, corporate globalization. One result of this process has been ongoing solidification of corporate-state capitalism that prevails in the United States and a few other industrialized countries – a rather different pattern from that anticipated by Marx or even Weber. Never in history have ruling elites been able to exercise such overwhelming power over economic development, state governance, social life, and the global ecology.

Neither Weber, leading Marxists of the early twentieth century, or later theorists of capitalist power such as C. Wright Mills could have foreseen the degree to which later fortresses of domination would impede prospects for revolutionary change. The broadened matrix of power explored in the following chapters has been (especially in the U.S.) concentrated along three fronts: technology and the surveillance order, militarism and the warfare state, intensification of globalized power. None of these dynamic historical forces was ever seriously analyzed in tandem by Marx or Weber, nor indeed by most other twentieth-century theorists.

The recent dramatic growth of technological enterprises, centered in North America, Europe, and Asia, can hardly be exaggerated. What is best described as a Big Tech oligarchy – Microsoft, Google, Facebook, Amazon, Twitter, Apple, etc. – now amounts to the largest, most powerful assemblage of capitalist giants in history, its influence over communications, the economy, government, and culture without parallel. Its power is all-encompassing, dwarfing that of many important nations in the world. Google alone, its income surpassing any of more than 70 countries, has accumulated power far greater than any corporate structure ever. Ostensibly forums of free speech, social interaction, and diversity of views, these bastions of technological modernity have become just the opposite: centers of ideological monoculture where much-celebrated diversity and inclusion rarely extends to the domain of thought or ideology, where censorship is more and more common. While social media has virtually overnight become indispensable to public life in the U.S. and elsewhere, communication flows are increasingly governed by algorithms generally congruent with elite opinion.

By the 1950s Mills had identified yet another component of postwar American state-capitalism, a prelude to President Dwight Eisenhower's 1961 warning about the "military-industrial complex." That "complex" has grown steadily throughout the decades, now comprising several enlarged sectors: the Pentagon, CIA, NSA, law enforcement, Homeland Security. For the world's leading superpower since World War II, this apparatus has been rooted in several interrelated phenomena – pursuit of global supremacy, endless wars, military Keynesianism, empire of bases, a massive nuclear complex. In the U.S., at least, we have seen how this institutionalized order has become a state within the state, largely outside the routine flow electoral politics. It is guided by what Mills called the "higher immorality," a power structure attached to ruthless, violent modes of conducting business, largely unaccountable. As a clear roadblock to oppositional politics, this could not have been imagined by Marx or Weber, or even Mills.

Aligned with Big Tech, the intelligence apparatus, and warfare state, a vast global network of corporate and financial interests that has taken a life of its own. Transnational capitalism has seamlessly given rise to such international organizations as the World Bank, IMF, World Trade Organization, G20, and NATO, all presiding over a system of concentrated wealth and power, including 17 financial enterprises in control of more than $40 trillion of wealth.[1] As of 2020 this staggering accumulation of power appeared fully out of reach of the local populations, national communities, labor unions, and social movements. Peter Phillips writes: "Transnational power elites hold a common ideological identity of being the engineers of global capitalism, with a firm belief that their way of life and continuing capital growth is best for all humankind."[2]

At this moment in history anyone concerned about the future of planetary life faces a pressing question: could such a globalized behemoth possibly be transformed into a sustainable world order? The system as presently constituted controls such enormous material, technological, natural, and human resources that the very notion of revolution seems entirely fanciful, illusory. That problem is compounded, as suggested, by the worldwide absence of counter-forces possessing a strategy of fundamental change. At this juncture political opposition is fully integrated into the sphere of electoral and parliamentary activity. During 2020, moreover, elites in many countries have moved to further consolidate (and centralize) power by wielding lockdowns during the COVID-19 pandemic to their full advantage. Could the structural and ideological barriers to deep change now be any more daunting?

As I argue throughout this book, the great Marxist theoretical legacy is mostly exhausted after decades of subversive relevance; those seeking an exit from the crisis will have to look elsewhere. Against the seemingly impenetrable fortress of corporate-state power, the deficits are many and imposing: ongoing capitalist stabilization, proletarian decline numerically and ideologically, deradicalization of parties and governments labeled "Socialist" or "Communist"; an upsurge in identity struggles over class politics, relegation of Marxist theory to the margins.

Here various efforts to "save" or "reconstitute" Marxism, to refashion Marx himself as an "ecosocialist," are destined to meet with despair. None of these efforts manages to address the crucial issue of political strategy, or take into account the vast transformations in modern class and power relations. Reliance on theoretical categories derived from classical Marxism – oriented to early liberal capitalism – only worsens matters.

Viewed against the larger historical backdrop, Marxism inevitably winds up diminished as a political force – a predicament that is unlikely to vanish, Aronson commenting: "From the beginning Marxism depended on events. When a historical project is no longer reflected in the existing forces and secular trends, what else can we say but that the project no longer exists."[3] A proletarian revolution today, however defined, seems more out of reach today than it did a century ago. Among three strategic alternatives within Marxist politics – social democracy, Leninism, council communism – only Leninism ever gave rise to what might be viewed as successful revolutions, starting with Russia at the end of World War I. The ultimate fate of Leninism in that country, however, was Stalinism which eventually led to ideological decline before the final collapse in 1991. Other Communist regimes (China, Vietnam, Cuba, North Korea) currently exist as harsh authoritarian departures from anything Marx (or indeed Lenin!) had in mind. Neither social democracy (an appendage of liberal capitalism) nor the council tradition has generated anything close to a proletarian revolution or transition to socialism.

Could something akin to Leninist strategy make sense today as a political mechanism bringing about the transition to a new order consistent with ecosocialist values – or is that strategy more likely to reproduce authoritarian outcomes? What is often forgotten about Lenin's classic theory of revolution, in my opinion rather distinct from its later Stalinist deformation, is its actual rejection of classical Marxism, starting with its assertion of the "primacy of politics" over the earlier "primacy of economics." Seeing that workers and other subordinate groups would never achieve revolutionary consciousness through everyday material struggles, Lenin's well-known impatience led him to embrace the vanguard party as agency of both mass mobilization and conquest of state power. To succeed, the Bolsheviks would need crucial political advantages: centralized organization, a coherent ideology, strong leadership from a stratum of intellectuals, readiness to win state power and attack the main centers of established resistance. This very approach had been dismissed by Marx and Engels, who believed any form of "Jacobinism" or "Bonapartism" – a premature seizure of power – was ultimately doomed.

In the aftermath of the October Revolution, Antonio Gramsci in Italy responded in terms somewhat consistent with Marx – this time, however, with praise rather than censure. Lenin and the Bolsheviks had approvingly seized the moment, taking advantage of what Georg Lukacs would later call the "actuality of revolution." In fact Lenin's gambit marked an historic "revolution against *Capital*," affirming the subjective or psychological dimension of politics over supposed "laws" or material forces of history. Wrote Gramsci:

Events have exploded the critical schema determining how the history of Russia would unfold according to the canons of historical materialism. The Bolsheviks reject Karl Marx, and their explicit actions and conquests bear witness that the canons of historical materialism are not so rigid as might have been and has been thought.

Gramsci added: "In Russia, Marx's *Capital* was more the book of the bourgeoisie than of the proletariat."[4] Just two years later, Gramsci would follow Lenin's epic initiative, co-founding the Italian Communist Party and joining the Third International – the source, had it succeeded on the verge of a fascist upsurge, of a Jacobin-style revolution in Italy.

At the same time, certain differences between Lenin and Gramsci – between the two modes of Jacobinism—would be noteworthy: the Bolshevik Revolution occurred in a poorly industrialized society dominated by foreign capital, whereas Italy was much further along the path to European-style modernization. Gramsci's more complex Jacobinism, theorized at length in the *Prison Notebooks*, was oriented toward a broader cultural transformation that expected to lead, ultimately, toward a socialist conquest of state power (or "war of maneuver"). Soviet-style Communism, meanwhile, would furnish the strategic framework for later revolutions in China, Vietnam, Yugoslavia, and Cuba – all relatively poor countries subjected to imperialist wartime dislocations. In neither case, however, would the Marxist classics be a guide to successful upheavals in settings mostly bereft of a large, class-conscious proletariat.

The crucial point here is that historical forms of Jacobinism were invoked to seize upon the moment of crisis to carry out a revolutionary mission. Whether Leninist or Gramscian, the strategy was one that refused the limits of electoral reformism on the one hand and restricted local struggles on the other, thus embracing the "actuality of revolution." Worth noting here is that the great challenges faced by earlier vanguard parties (economic collapse, war, imperialism) might well be transcended by the very immensity of the present ecological crisis. Could Jacobinism, facing prospects of planetary collapse, now constitute something of a moral imperative, especially when taking into account the bankruptcy of modern electoral politics?

Something like this proposition has been taken up by Geoff Mann and Joel Wainwright in their provocative book *Climate Leviathan*, where the concept of "planetary sovereign" is suggested as an exit from the crisis. The authors recognize that even the most ambitious reform efforts, including those of the 2015 Paris Accords, will do little to impact the carbon footprint or ecological downturn. They further acknowledge that anti-system movements dedicated to fundamental change are nowhere in sight. They argue for a "planetary green Keynesianism, the only kind that might have a hope of confronting the problem in its scale and magnitude ..." This in turn requires the emergence of one nation-state, or a small set of nation-states, that arrogate to themselves the impossible institutional capabilities that come with an interest in supranational "ecological stimulus". This is Climate Leviathan that can bear the burden required of a planetary Keynesian subject, capable of coordinating investment, distributing productive and destructive capacity, and managing free riders.[5]

While Mann and Wainwright are laudably driven by a sense of ecological urgency, the difficulties with *Climate Leviathan* are several – the first being that the articulated goal, vague as it is, has not been connected to any workable *political strategy*. In fact one cannot locate a politically transformative dimension to their work; vehicles of social transcendence are never elucidated. Further, the very concept of Keynesianism remains embedded in capitalist development, that is, continuation (in reformist mode) of a system of domination and exploitation itself responsible for sustaining the crisis. Finally, the reference to "Leviathan" associated with the theories of Thomas Hobbes seems rather opaque. After all, whereas the concept of Jacobinism signifies dramatic change or rupture, Leviathan as counter to the "state of nature" has always meant something altogether different—a political *arbiter*, a rule-giver and enforcer.

In the end, Jacobinism could offer a distinctly political solution, one way out of the crisis, but that would pose a huge threat to liberals, social democrats, and others fearful of genuine change. Communist parties in the West that once might have been regarded as agencies of anti-system change long ago succumbed to the pressures of deradicalization, and there is probably no reversing that outcome. A similar dynamic has overtaken other erstwhile oppositional forces, most recently social democrats and Greens. In this context it is more difficult to retain faith in an enlightened, sustainable ecological path forward. We know that the behemoth of corporate-state power will always be hostile to meaningful change, even where such change is advertised to "save the planet." One alternative would be to build a Gramsci-style Jacobinism from the ground, bypassing the failed counter-forces inherited from the past. Another prospect might be a tectonic radicalization of larger Green parties in Europe, which have (in varying degrees) already subscribed to a project of ecological rationality. Whatever the path ahead, we know (or should know) that time is running short. A future global food calamity alone, rendered likely by shrinking land and water resources, ought to be warning enough.

The question lurks: what political alternative offers the best chance in the face of unfathomable challenges ahead? How might the trajectory of ecological collapse be redirected toward some form of ecosocialism? Radical change calls for collective humanity to establish forms of control, fight the ruling elites, and eventually use the realm of politics – including modern state power – to mobilize resources for societal development, dismantling the entrenched interests in favor of a sustainable ecological politics. To embellish what Wolin calls "revolutionary transgression" points toward something unprecedented: overturning the structures of global power, a task well beyond anything contemplated by Marx, Weber, Gramsci, or Mills. Might such a Promethean task require an updated version of Jacobinism?

As mentioned, democratic objections to this kind of schema will be strong and compelling, similar to arguments made long ago by anarchists, Western Marxists, Frankfurt School critics, and of course liberals. Many have assumed that Jacobinism would automatically lead to Soviet-style Communist authoritarianism, but that historical trajectory was not likely to be repeated under the more advanced capitalist conditions. Here it is worth asking whether the Gramscian variant of Jacobinism could escape the worst political excesses of vanguardism and statism, but we know there can be no historical assurances. At the same time, most industrialized capitalist societies today are hardly beacons of democracy; on the contrary, they are most likely to be ruled by oligarchic power structures, none more so than the U.S. As Mann and Wainwright put it, "No nation-state today meets this [democratic] criterion." They add: "Democracy as we know it (especially its hegemonic liberal variety) seems profoundly inadequate to the problems that lie ahead, and to imagine that democracy in another form is going to fix things takes what many might justifiably see as an increasingly ludicrous leap of faith."[6]

The familiar trope that a modern Jacobinism might give rise to an even more monstrous authoritarian system – parallel to the earlier transition from Leninism to Stalinism – appears equally misplaced. To start, a more uniquely Gramscian strategy would presumably avoid the more rigidly authoritarian features of mostly pre-industrial societies like Russia, China, and Vietnam. It would be more closely aligned with the greater social and cultural complexities of advanced capitalism. Further, the very historical conditions associated with Stalinism, including a frenetic drive toward rapid industrialization (or "primitive accumulation") and agricultural collectivization, would obviously not have to be repeated in the world's leading nations. Stalinism nowadays is best considered a relic of the past.

Given twenty-first century realities, on the other hand, it might seem that any Jacobinism is destined to be negated by the spread of postmodern culture, where oppositional tendencies are increasingly fragmented and dispersed, broken into multiple interests, outlooks, and identities. Insofar as Jacobinism signifies a *global* aspiration, a grand narrative of the first order, it would be forced to move directly against the main historical currents. There are plenty of reverberations to this actuality, all the more so for many industrialized societies where contemporary identity politics around race, ethnicity, gender, and sexuality dominate the landscape. Indeed distinctly "global" issues such as imperialism, war, and ecology – not to mention class politics rooted in the Marxist tradition – now appear marginal, secondary at best. In the U.S., perhaps more than elsewhere, identity politics has for many years prevailed over agendas that might be congruent with Jacobinism or indeed any project of radical change.

The fatal deficit of identity politics, however, is a built-in failure to envision societal-wide change; its very logic is partial, fragmented, conservative. It is built around warring groups doing essentially horizontal battle while ruling elites continue business-as-usual. As such, identity politics can only impede oppositional movements. Its "strategy" (or lack thereof) is accompanied by a debilitating ethos of anti-politics. The modern crisis, on the other hand, demands full-scale political commitment along lines of a "climate Jacobinism," a mechanism serving two distinct purposes: to achieve a planetary or ecological set of objectives, while also creating a counter-force that could overturn the global power apparatus. If such a Jacobin force winds up the price of reversing a descent into uncharted horrors, could the bargain be worth securing?

Notes

1 See Peter Phillips, *Giants* (New York: Seven Stories Press, 2018), pp. 35–36.
2 Ibid., p. 29.
3 Ronald Aronson, *After Marxism* (New York: Guilford Press, 1995), p. 55.
4 Antonio Gramsci, "The Revolution against *Capital*", in *Selections from Political Writings 1910–20* (New York: International Publishers, 1977), p. 34.
5 Geoff Mann and Joel Wainwright, *Climate Leviathan* (London: Verso, 2018), pp. 126–127.
6 Ibid., pp. 176, 182.

1
MARXISM AND EARLY CAPITALISM

Any exploration of modern radical politics ought to inevitably begin with the work of Karl Marx and Friedrich Engels, though precursors (especially utopian socialists and anarchists) were in abundance. The ascendancy of classical Marxism during the era of early capitalism would, by the start of the twentieth century, eventually take several paths – the "orthodoxy" of Karl Kautsky, the reformism of Eduard Bernstein, the Bolshevism of V. I. Lenin, the mass spontaneism of Rosa Luxemburg along with the council communism of Anton Pannekoek and others. For classical Marxism, the historical expanse was essentially that of market-based capitalism, a focus that by the 1890s was also Kautsky's. That framework evolved as an alternative to not only liberal capitalism but to anarchism and Jacobinism, the latter referring to the leftist seizure of state power in the absence of well-developed popular mobilization.

Marxism in these diverse expressions would emerge as the most far-reaching project of social change in modern history, its powerful legacy still visible on the intellectual if not political terrain of Europe and elsewhere. For Marx at least, this theoretical breakthrough involved a unique synthesis of philosophy and politics, materialism and idealism, culminating in what could be defined as a "philosophy of praxis" (anticipating Antonio Gramsci's later elaboration). As such, early Marxism contributed not only a deep analysis of capitalism but a vision of historical transformation engaging different realms of human life: economics, politics, culture, even psychology. A systematic body of thought, classical Marxism would aspire toward scientific status, one reflection of an Enlightenment rationality that shaped the *Zeitgeist* of the period. These unifying characteristics would, however, never prevent the tradition from splintering into disparate paths – a motif central to arguments presented in the following pages (and chapters).

As the first coherent framework of revolutionary change, Marxism furnishes a point of departure for addressing the many challenges of capitalist modernity and,

DOI: 10.4324/9781003197461-2

by extension, the contemporary ecological crisis. How far that theory might take us along the path of actually *reversing* that crisis is a problem taken up throughout this book — a problem likely related to the very survival of planetary life. More than anything, Marxism in its early formulations did envision a unification of theory and practice, history and action. Whatever its flaws and limits, the Marxist tradition would deeply influence a wide range of movements, trade unions, political parties, even governments across more than a century. Later tendencies — Leninism, social democracy, anarchism, popular movements —would in some ways transcend classical Marxism while retaining some of its basic tenets and insights. Yet as Marxism expanded its reach during the twentieth century, its distance from actual political formations would in certain ways widen. Here the tense, uneasy, conflicted relationship between Marxism and ecology fits a common pattern: a theory grounded in early capitalist development loses its resonance within the modern world of global capitalism. Still, well more than a century after the deaths of Marx and Engels, the legacy persists as a source of critical analysis and political vision.

At the present juncture, the Marxism we have inherited faces two interwoven challenges: the world it initially theorized has been extensively transformed, while as a theory of revolutionary change it has bequeathed few political successes, especially within conditions of advanced capitalism. On this point Ron Aronson comments:

> [Marxism] is not simply a description of a given social reality or an idea of a better social reality, but a theoretical and practical guide of the transformation of the one [capitalism] into the other [socialism]. Its claims to validity are dependent on the realization of the entire process and project. Thus, if after a reasonable length of time, socialism has nowhere been achieved, if world-historical trends are moving away from, rather than toward, socialism, these claims can only undermine Marxism's claims to be true.[1]

Nonetheless, the continuing *intellectual* vitality of Marxism — along with its presumed relevance to ecological thought — remains fully worth engaging as a theoretical vantage point, though hardly as a scientific body of knowledge.

Even contemporary Marxists acknowledge the irreversible changes occurring not only within capitalism itself but within the world system more generally. Those changes have thoroughly altered class and power relations everywhere, not to mention the character of human-nature development. In fact very little has unfolded as anticipated by classical Marxism, in part owing to the enduring consequences of capitalist rationalization starting in the 1890s and, later, the ongoing process of globalization. Of course many nations have reached stupendous levels of growth, productivity, and affluence, at a time of capitalist stabilization and decline of working-class opposition. Nowhere has proletarian misery and alienation — much less class solidarity — been translated into broad political success, while nominally socialist groups and parties have become uniformly deradicalized across the world landscape.

Marxism and Ecology

There is nowadays a significant body of social theory that lays out coherent arguments for an ecological Marxism – more precisely, for an ecosocialist Marx. In many societies we have seen a convergence of theories around socialism and ecology, first visible in Western political discourse during the late 1970s and early 1980s, when leading figures if the West German Greens (Rudolf Bahro, Rainer Trampert, Thomas Ebermann) were laying the foundations of a "red-green" politics. That would be roughly one century after Marx completed his final work. Later ecological thinkers would further refine (and redefine) the outlook, among them Barry Commoner, James O'Connor, Murray Bookchin, Andre Gorz, and Joel Kovel. It would not be until the late 1990s and into the new century, however, that leftists around the journal *Monthly Review* (notably Paul Burkett, John Bellamy Foster, Fred Magdoff) would begin to formulate the compelling image of an "ecological Marx." The most recent, perhaps most ambitious, of these projects is Kohei Saito's *Karl Marx's Ecosocialism*, an effort to reconstruct Marx's thought from the vantage point of the modern ecological crisis.

Was the great Marx, who died in 1883, indeed something of an ecological radical – a theorist for whom, as Saito argues, natural relations were fundamental to understanding capitalist development? Saito's aim was to arrive at a new reading of Marx's writings based on previously unpublished "scientific notebooks" written toward the end of Marx's life. From this and related materials, Saito concludes that familiar views of Marx's productivism and Promethean attitude toward nature (meaning unrestrained economic growth) are misplaced. Accordingly, these myths should give way to a more enlightened view of Marx derived from broader appreciation of his writings. It follows, moreover, that classical Marxism as a whole deserves extensive re-reading, consistent with Marx's own supposed ecological turn beginning in the late 1860s.

Could Saito's rather careful exploration of Marx's writings signify a major step toward retrieving the long-obscured contributions of an ecological theorist – the first ecosocialist? Equally worth asking, did the theoretical paradigm fashioned by Marx and collaborator Engels manage to advance the kind of scientific materialism (said to be congruent with an ecological outlook) that would later be associated with the *Monthly Review* authors?

If Marx and Engels were indeed the first ecosocialists of record, that achievement – whatever its scientific imprimatur – would have been miraculous given the generally limited interest in matters environmental during the nineteenth century. Such intellectual pursuits would have encountered serious barriers, not least being a *Zeitgeist* of almost religious faith in Enlightenment values of maximum economic and technological growth, especially in the European context.

They would need to have been extraordinarily prescient. Ecosocialism even today is among the more peripheral tendencies, addressing deep origins of the modern crisis while seeking to avoid earlier (productivist, statist) traditions aligned with Communism and social democracy. As Michael Lowy writes, such politics "aims not only to transform the relations of production, the productive apparatus, and the dominant consumption patterns but to create a new way of life, breaking with the foundations of the modern Western capitalist/industrial civilization."[2] Lowy himself was rather skeptical that the Marxist classics were adequate to this task.

Failure to reverse the crisis will, in Lowy's view, leave the planet vulnerable to imminent descent into catastrophe. "In sum," he argues, "the capitalist world system is historically bankrupt. It has become an empire unable to adapt, whose very gigantism exposes its underlying weakness. It is, in the language of ecology, profoundly unsustainable, and must be changed fundamentally, nay replaced, if there is to be a future worth living."[3] This same point was more recently, and more vigorously, set forth by David Wallace-Wells, in *The Uninhabitable Earth*, where he suggests that managers of industrial society are presently on a "kamikaze mission" of endless material growth.[4]

Obsessive growth ensures not only worsening crisis but, in all probability, ultimate planetary collapse. Wallace-Wells, among more recent critics, has sounded the alarm:

> In that world … the oceans would eventually swell two hundred feet higher, flooding what are now two-thirds of the world's major cities; hardly any land on the planet would be capable of efficiently producing any of the food we now eat … probably about a third of the planet would be made unlivable by direct heat; and what are today literally unprecedented and unlivable droughts and heat waves would be the quotidian condition of whatever human life was able to endure.[5]

Writing in *Fossil Capital*, Andreas Malm comments: "The point of *too late* is coming closer by the day … The tradition of the dead is breathing down the necks of the living, leaving them with two choices: smash their way out of business-as-usual … or succumb to an accumulated, unbearable destiny."[6] A pressing issue we confront here is whether nineteenth-century Marxism, however theoretically refurbished, can be enlisted for purposes of overcoming the crisis – or can at least significantly contribute to such ends.

In Search of an Ecological Marx

Saito's book has been widely heralded as something of a theoretical breakthrough in the study of Marxist classics, having won the esteemed Isaac Deutscher Memorial Prize in 2017. Kevin Anderson describes *Karl Marx's Ecosocialism* (on the back cover) as "a new interpretation of Marx, one that is timely given the economic and ecological crises of contemporary capitalism." For his audacious efforts Saito relies heavily not only on Marx's early writings but on previously unpublished materials, including many entries of his "scientific notebooks" where, nearing the 1870s, Marx fixed increasing attention on the natural sciences.

After meticulous study of these materials, Saito concludes that ecology must now be seen as not merely important but *central* to Marx's theoretical interests as he navigated beyond the more important writings spanning the 1840s to 1860s. This interpretation clashes with the prevailing view of Marx based on the *Communist Manifesto* and other sources, where he assumed "unlimited economic and technological developments as a natural law of history and propagated the absolute mastery of nature, both of which run counter to any serious theoretical and practical consideration of ecological issues such as the scarcity of natural resources and the overloading of ecospheres."[7] The well-known emphasis in Marx and Engels on human domination of the natural world – familiar motif of the period – is now said to require rethinking that more fully takes into account Marx's later writings. Critics have been mistaken in the belief that Marx and Engels ignored the environmentally destructive force of modern industry, a system that was moving toward limitless material production and mass consumption. Lowy is one modern ecosocialist who argues that Marx did not adequately consider how industrialism as such would become so ceaselessly destructive of the natural habitat.[8]

Saito writes that since Marx's most important work, *Capital*, remained incomplete, the later notebook materials must be assigned special value. Roughly half of these entries dealt with several natural sciences – biology, chemistry, botany, geology – yet "the importance of this work remained neglected for more than a century."[9] Appreciation of these materials, along with such familiar earlier works as the 1844 *Economic and Philosophical Manuscripts*, now "allows scholars to see Marx's ecology as a fundamental part of his critique of political economy."[10] In other words, we have now reached a point where ecological contradictions must be understood as integral to the classical Marxist enterprise.

Saito's undertaking aims for no less than a systematic reconstruction of Marx's critique of capitalism, focused on a rupturing of the organic bond between humans and nature, between society and the natural environment. Thus: "... Marx consistently bestowed a central role in his critique of modern society to the problem of separation of humans from the earth"[11] – a problem already identified in the 1844 *Manuscripts*. During the 1870s, in particular, Marx came to see that "metabolic rifts [between society and nature] were the most serious problem of capitalism."[12] The notion of "metabolic rift" had been previously explored by such writers as Foster, but here Saito renders it a centerpiece of Marxian analysis. Alongside the degradation of labor, capitalism gave rise to an "historical deformation" of nature – the two processes convergent, part of the same dialectic.

As capitalism disturbs the "natural metabolism," according to Saito, "the capitalist tendency to degrade nature is derived from the law of commodity exchange" – though the precise ways that "law" winds up impacting the natural habitat is never fully explained.[13] Saito argues that Marx never abandoned his 1844 affirmation of the "absolute unity of humans and nature," which he proceeded to refine in his later work (including the notebooks), where he investigated such topics as soil depletion and climate change. While capitalism destroyed that (imputed) organic unity, it would presumably be the historic task of socialism to restore a dynamic, sustainable metabolic process. Human mastery of nature would come to an end, ultimately replaced by integration of the two realms. To fully comprehend this phenomenon, the theory would require a more rigorous materialist foundation: "An analysis of Marx's project needs to go beyond the earlier interpretation and include the analysis of the material world as a central object of the study."[14]

For Saito, as for Marx, labor within the capitalist economy is a purposeful, conscious activity where humans mediate, regulate, and control (or seek to control) the metabolism linking their own self-activity with the rhythms of nature – though here again the constituent elements of nature (addressed later) are never clearly elaborated. Where nature is fetishized, as is so often the case with Marx, it is left rather amorphous, undifferentiated. Under capitalism the developmental process is intercepted by an enduring "rift" associated with multifaceted environmental challenges. In Saito's reading, Marx was well ahead of his time, anticipating ecological crises that would eventually accompany the more familiar economic contradictions. If true, this would suggest an overturning of Marx's supposed Prometheanism according to which sustained industrial and technological expansion would continue into the new socialist order, endowing humans with even greater control over both history and nature. Saito writes: "Only a systematic analysis of Marx's theory of metabolism as an integral part of his critique of political economy can convincingly demonstrate, against the critics of his ecology, how the capitalist mode of production brings about various types of ecological problems due to its insatiable desire for capital accumulation."[15]

Beyond calling attention to the likelihood that Marx brought a discourse of environmental ethics into his work, Saito argues for its *centrality*: "In spite of its unfinished state, Marx's political economy allows us to understand the ecological crisis as a contradiction of capitalism."[16] Just how Marx and Engels – or any other theorists of the period – might have defined "ecological crisis" remains unclear. Saito insists that the problem of ecology was never of secondary or peripheral interest to Marx, that in fact "metabolic rifts were the most serious problem of capitalism."[17] Beyond that, modern theoretical approaches to ecology owe a great debt to Marx's deep insights into commodity production, labor, and the deep conflict between humans and nature.

If Marx's philosophy in his earliest writings transcended the antinomies of traditional materialism and German idealism – reaching a dialectical synthesis of the two – in Saito's view Marx turned increasingly toward scientific materialism from the late 1860s onward, consistent with his sharpening fixation on ecology. His notebooks during those years reveal keen attention to several natural-science disciplines, as noted. The very idea of "metabolic rift" affirms a profoundly scientific, if not ecological, preoccupation. Here we see glimpses of Marx's interest in further exploring the tensions between capital and nature, between economy and its surrounding landscape. After 1868, according to Saito, "Marx [in contrast to his earlier writings] came to clearly recognize natural limits as such, parting from a myth of unlimited technologically-driven increase in production."[18] Hardly Promethean, the Marx of Saito's reconstruction nearly comes across as a contemporary deep ecologist wedded to "limits of growth."

Despite his thorough probing of Marx's work, Saito is hardly the first interpreter of an "ecological Marx," or even the first to call attention to the idea of "metabolic rift." That distinction would be claimed by Foster, who in *Marx's Ecology* (2000) set forth arguments prefiguring those of Saito and approximating those of colleague Burkett in *Marx and Nature* (1999).[19] Later volumes – for example, *Creating an Ecological Society* (2017) by Magdoff and Chris Williams – have further sought to "ecologize" the Marxist tradition.[20] Saito's departure from earlier treatments of Marx thus appears considerably less radical than the boosters have wanted us to believe. His main contribution here lies in the greater emphasis he places on Marx's post-1868 work. All conclude that the long-accepted Marxist domination-of-nature motif has been finally and thoroughly debunked.

As for the concept of "metabolic rift," that already figured centrally in Foster's account, as did emphasis on a rigorous scientific materialism seen as indispensable to ecological thought. Foster likewise calls attention to a post-1860s shift toward Marx's heightened understanding of how capitalism degrades nature. In Foster's words: "In their later writings, significantly, Marx and Engels were to make the consideration of such ecological contradictions a central part of their critique of modern civilization (and particularly capitalist society)."[21] Renewed attention to the natural sciences was said to further solidify this far-reaching theoretical shift.

Foster stresses Marx's preoccupation with the "necessary unity of human and natural existence" that had appeared in the 1844 *Manuscripts*.[22] The same capitalist mechanisms that gave rise to alienated labor simultaneously produced the alienation of humans from nature. All of this, in Foster's view, could be analyzed though the lens of dialectical materialism or scientific naturalism, which was thought to have broadened the panorama of theory. Foster goes to great lengths to distinguish Marx's dialectical approach from earlier forms of crude, one-dimensional materialism – though, as we shall see, with at best only partial success. The crucial point here is that an "ecological Marx" would presumably have to rest on firm scientific mooring. That claim would be validated, in Foster as in Saito, with reference to the elevated focus of both Marx and Engels on natural sciences in their later years.

The seductive idea of an "ecological Marx" has been articulated, in rather different ways, across the literature explored here. Yet there remains the question of just how central an ecological outlook might have been to the overall work of Marx and Engels. Were identifiable ecological contradictions indeed basic to the process of capital accumulation – or could they have been simply incidental, peripheral? Despite several volumes of work on this topic, much of it centered around the journal *Monthly Review*, there is little certainty and indeed much disagreement.

Foster, for example, at one point adopted a rather extreme position: "I finally came to the conclusion that Marx's worldview was deeply and indeed systematically ecological ... and that this ecological perspective derived from his materialism."[23] Along similar lines, Saito contends that Marxist theory today cannot be grasped in the absence of its ecological dimension, that it was fundamental to his critique of capitalism.[24] Further: "In spite of its unfinished state, Marx's political economy allows us to understand the ecological crisis as a contradiction of capitalism."[25] In later work, however, Foster's approach evolved into a more elaborate, more nuanced view of the relationship between capitalism and ecology, while still adhering to a roughly materialist philosophy.[26]

Elsewhere in Saito, however, we encounter something of a minimalist view: "We see 'hints' in his unpublished writings that indicate his intention to explicate various tensions between capital and nature."[27] Hints? Intention? Tensions? Such language scarcely calls forth a powerful ecological dynamic in Marx, earlier or later. In fact this very discursive minimalism offers clues to theoretical problems ahead. Equally pressing questions arise as we scrutinize the *general* work of Marx and Engels. Marx's well-known emphasis on human-nature unity in the 1844 *Manuscripts* turns out to be countered by strongly productivist passages in such works as the *Manifesto, Grundrisse*, and *Capital* – revealing passages that should not be downplayed. Insofar as Marx and Engels are considered to have become more deeply ecological throughout the 1870s, their later writings (leaving aside the unpublished notebooks) could turn out to be even more revealing.

Capitalism and the Natural World

What possible meaning can we derive from the appearance of an "ecological Marx" that might be relevant to the twentieth century and beyond? Did the larger thrust of classical Marxist writings actually furnish the sort of ecological outlook so vigorously championed by Foster and Saito? Did the later, presumably more mature, contributions of Marx and Engels – writings with a decidedly natural-science preoccupation – alter the balance, finally driving the theory away from its earlier Promethean impulses? With all the attention some classical Marxist texts are said to have devoted to philosophical materialism, do we encounter signs in the later work of serious ecological analysis?

At the outset, Marx's own early attention to human-nature relations in the 1844 *Manuscripts* – a point of emphasis in Saito and others – while salient, scarcely rises above the level of abstract generalities. One finds relatively little substance on either side of this equation, less specificity yet when addressing the historical dimensions. Many passages reflect little more than truisms, starting with the premise that humans are part of the natural world, which they self-consciously transform by means of their labor. Thus in the *Manuscripts* Marx famously writes: "Man *lives* on nature – means that nature is his body, with which he must remain in continuous intercourse if he is not to die, that man's physical and spiritual life is linked to nature means simply that nature is linked to itself, for man is part of nature."[28] (All masculine references are retained throughout, consistent with Marx's own usage.) However profound Marx's statements here might appear, they are framed at such levels of generality as to be devoid of historical or political meaning; they could align with the most harshly instrumental approaches to nature. Marx goes on to say that "Conscious life-activity directly distinguishes man from animal life-activity,"[29] another truism that, in this case, actually feeds into Promethean assumptions. Throughout these pages, and later, Marx places overwhelming emphasis on *human* self-activity in the historical process of defeating external forces, that is, overcoming both personal and collective estrangement.

At many points in his most theoretically insightful texts, Marx stressed the liberating potential of productive forces – first within capitalism, then given fuller and more rational expression with the transition to socialism. Questions about harm from economic and technological (also urban) colonization of the natural world would be rare. One finds little analysis of how sustained material development might surpass natural limits or degrade the natural landscape. On the contrary, his prevailing attitude seemed consistent with that of an enlarged (presumably more enlightened) mastery of nature. In one familiar passage from the *Manifesto*, after praising the bourgeoisie for creating "colossal production forces," Marx and Engels write:

> Subjection of Nature's forces to man, machinery application of chemistry to industry and agriculture, steam-navigation, railways, electric telegraphs, clearing of whole continents for cultivation, canalization of rivers, whole populations conjured out of the ground – what earlier century had even a presentment that such productive forces slumbered in the lap of social labor?[30]

Elsewhere in the *Manifesto* they enthuse over how the proletariat, once having gained power, will wrest "all capital from the bourgeoisie, to centralize all instruments of production in the hands of the State ... and to increase the total productive forces as rapidly as possible."[31]

This more or less unfettered productivism found its parallels in both *The Grundrisse* and the first volume of *Capital*, not to mention later works (a point addressed in coming chapters). In *The Grundrisse* Marx writes:

> Nature builds no machines, no locomotives, railways, electric telegraphs, self-acting mules, etc. These are products of human industry; natural material

transformed into organs of the human will over nature, or of human participation in nature. They are *organs of the human brain, created by the human hand;* the power of knowledge, objectified.[32]

Such passages are repeated throughout the work of both Marx and Engels, virtually from beginning to end, reflecting an identifiable sentiment. Another example, from *Capital* (Volume one): "Animals and plants, which we are accustomed to consider as products of, say last year's labor, but the result of a gradual transformation, continued through many generations, *under man's superintendence, and by means of his labor.*"[33] Where might one locate a clearer statement of Promethean vision?

In *Capital* (Volume three), a work of detailed economic analysis, Marx writes:

> Freedom … can only consist in socialized man, the associated producers, rationally regulating their interchange with Nature, *bringing it under their common control* instead of being ruled by it as by the blind forces of Nature, and achieving this with the least expenditure of energy and under conditions most favorable to, and worthy of, their human nature.[34]

Here, as elsewhere, the "blind forces" of nature are to be tamed and mastered by the rational forces of modern production, built on the great achievements of modern science and technology. This same argument is carried forward in *Critique of the Gotha Program*, written at presumably the height of Marx's ecological turn (in 1875), where he writes: "And insofar as man from the beginning behaves toward nature, the primary source of all instruments and subjects of labor, as an owner, treats her as belonging to him, his labor becomes the source of use values, therefore also of wealth."[35]

Even more problematic for champions of an "ecological Marx" is a number of generalizations in Engels' classic *Anti-Duhring*, which appeared toward the end of Marx's ostensible ecological turn. This work of a rigidly materialist epistemology, first published in 1878, was read and approved by Marx, who also wrote an introduction to the section titled "Socialism: Utopian and Scientific." Engels had arranged three general chapters of *Anti-Duhring* as a pamphlet on the origins of Marxism, outlining its general approach to history. Originally published in French in 1880 (just three years before Marx's death), this section appeared in many languages and became – along with the *Manifesto* – the most influential presentation of Marxist theory for the late nineteenth century and beyond. An English translation appeared in 1892.

As with the *Manifesto*, this text celebrates the stupendous growth and concentration of capitalist economic power, allowing unprecedented dominion over society and nature – the trajectory of a new society. The great "expansive force of modern industry" was expected to open up wonderful new vistas of revolutionary change.[36] Overcoming the forces of anarchy, dispersion, and resistance, this behemoth was source of "an unbroken, constantly accelerated development of productive forces and therefore for a *practically unlimited* increase in production itself."[37] Humans now "for the first time, become the *real, conscious* lord of nature, because [they] have now become master of [their] own social organization."[38] For an essentially sanctified work of classical Marxism first circulating in the 1890s, it would be difficult to find a bolder affirmation of the human mission to control and exploit nature. With European intellectual attraction to Marxist ideas seemingly at its peak, could readers have been troubled by any confusion between early "philosophical" Marxism and later "scientific" Marxism?

Engels continues forcefully along these lines: "By this act – seizing power – the proletariat forces the means of production from the character of capital … and gives their socialized character complete *freedom to work itself out*."[39] And: "Man, at last the master of his own form of organization, becomes at the same time *the lord over nature, his own master – free*."[40] Here all ambiguity has been stripped from one of the most important classical Marxist texts. In the end, for both Marx and Engels, such human capacity to simultaneously remake society and the natural world would be *magnified* by the historic spread of "scientific socialism" – and would be clearly understood as such by inheritors of the orthodoxy, starting with Karl Kautsky, Georgi Plekhanov, and a circle of "legal Marxists" in Russia.

Beyond Marx, Engels had sought to build a general (materialist) philosophy on a foundation of natural sciences – a task he further pursued in *Dialectics of Nature*, which actually departed little from the more systematic work of *Anti-Duhring*. One problem is that *Dialectics* was both rudimentary and fragmentary, whatever the author's grand ambitions for it – a volume never completed and indeed never published until 1925. (Engels worked on the manuscript sporadically between 1872 and 1882, at a time of Marx's own stepped-up interest in the physical sciences.) In this work Engels construed science as a dialectical process of interconnections leading to qualitative change, though precisely in what ways *historical* change would replicate or be driven by *physical* change was suggested but never elaborated. This was surely the most "scientific" or "materialist" of classical Marxist writings. The point is not to judge this work in terms of its epistemology or even its political relevance, but rather to emphasize its congruence with the Promethean impulse. Hardly surprising, there is nothing in this widely read text to contradict above-cited passages from *Anti-Duhring* and other earlier Marxist sources.

Marx's own attention to the natural sciences toward the end of his life, along with what nowadays might be labeled "ecological" discourses, is not in doubt – yet neither is his agreement with those passages from *Anti-Duhring* cited above. Returning to Saito, the claims turn out to be substantially more, that indeed Marx had become a systematic ecological thinker, far ahead of his time and not to be confused with the rather commonplace Prometheanism, or Enlightenment rationality, of his time. Saito argues that "Marx developed his ecological thought as a critique of capitalism," adding: "A more complete investigation of new material published by MEGA showed that a stereotypical (and false) critique of his indifference to the scarcity of natural resources and the burdening of our ecospheres, and another critique of his Promethean superstition on limitless economic and technological development, are not tenable."[41]

Saito also points out that "Marx consistently bestowed a central role in his critique of modern society to the problem of the 'separation' of humans from the earth."[42] More precisely: "In contrast to a widespread critique that Marx is a blind supporter of absolute domination over nature, his vision of the future society demands a careful and sustainable interaction with nature, based on a distinct recognition of its limits."[43] In contrast to the destructive logic of capitalism, a more rational (socialist) form of material production would be congruent with an ecologically-sustainable mode of development.

Reading Saito – in alignment with both Marx and Engels – it is difficult to avoid some inescapable problems. First, while references to unified human-nature relations appear valid enough, they remain frustratingly abstract, even tautological. Much the same can be said regarding the "metabolic rift" between society and nature—a conflict simply rooted in the logic of advancing industrialization in any setting. Such generalizations lack both historical and ecological concreteness, suggesting little that might inspire critical analysis. The interaction between humans and nature, mediated by labor, was for Marx important to his overall theory, but was never given the specificity that shaped his deeper treatment of political economy. If we learn that humans, through continuous life-activity, transform the natural world, such truth is hardly illuminating.

More troublesome yet is how the very concept "nature" is framed in the writings of Marx and Engels. It is simultaneously vague, weakly defined, and incomplete – a criticism more fully discussed later. However often the reference is invoked across many pages of work, the concept ultimately reveals little and in fact obscures a great deal. Moreover, the passages (cited above) that affirm in clearest terms human mastery of nature, while revealing, actually embrace a standard ideological trope of the period, consistent with uncompromising faith in supreme industrial and technological growth. In this context, even the most extreme worship of nature – much like the common idealization of "human nature" – winds up signifying little.

Third, numerous passages cited in Engels' *Anti-Duhring* (again, fully endorsed by Marx) run directly and systematically counter to Saito's reading of the later Marx – even accepting some validity of Marx's "ecological turn" after 1868. We can observe here, with abundant clarity, how Marx and Engels shared an ethos of productivism right to the very end of their prolific careers. Given the stage of European capitalist development in the 1870s and 1880s, not to mention the well-known positivist ascendancy of the period, this reckoning is not very shocking. Saito's claim that Marx's Promethean impulse has been resolutely debunked is not very convincing when measured against these and kindred passages. It is worth noting, moreover, that the motif of limited growth (assuming finite resources) is never seriously taken up in the vast contributions of Marx and Engels, nor indeed in the work of their immediate successors (Kautsky, Plekhanov, and V. I. Lenin among them).[44]

At the same time, Marx's laudable interest in the natural sciences toward the end of his life does not *in itself* reflect an ecological sensibility – any more than we can automatically derive such views from the work of contemporary physicists or chemists, many of whom do military research. Obviously Marx's own ability to make contributions in these fields had to be severely limited, whatever his degree of interest. Further, attempts to extrapolate theoretical methods or political substance from the study of natural sciences for purposes of historical analysis were, then as now, not likely to be promising. Knowledge accumulated in those fields of study, moreover, has never been innately progressive, much less ecological.

More crucially, as we begin to examine the contemporary fortresses of wealth and power within global capitalism, the very actuality of human mastery of nature is difficult to avoid once we take into account the vast array of forces warring against every part of the planetary ecosystem. There is no avoiding the fact that advanced industrialism spells not merely control of nature but an *all-out assault* on nonhuman life and its support systems. In fact under *any form* of industrialization and urbanization, the very idea of an organic reunification of human-nature relations must be viewed as sheer delusion. The issue rather is precisely *what form* and *what scope* that domination will assume. It might be asked whether Marx and Engels ever arrived at a coherent ecological analysis of modernizing capitalism – that is, anything beyond their seminal work on (early) capitalist political economy. As Saito writes, there are surely hints here and there of Marx's interest in environmental concerns but, as noted, these never reached levels of systematic conceptualization. Why was so little of Marx's "scientific" work after 1868 published at the time? Why did so many heirs of classical Marxism adopt even more extreme forms of scientific materialism and systemic productivism than were present in Marx's own work?

In the end, Marx turned out to be rather consistent in his belief that humans had the need (and capacity) to define, shape, and exploit the natural world. Engels pushed this approach even further. To nowadays believe otherwise, in view of their larger theoretical enterprise, would seem far-fetched. Marx and Engels repeatedly insisted that the natural environment is subject to rational human intervention within a dynamic process of historical transformation, control of productive forces obviously being central to this process.

Notes

1 See Ronald Aronson, *After Marxism* (New York: Guilford Books, 1995), p. 43.
2 Michael Lowy, *Ecosocialism* (Chicago: Haymarket Books, 2015), p. ix.
3 Ibid., p. 79.
4 David Wallace-Wells, *The Uninhabitable Earth* (New York: Tom Duggan Books, 2019), p. 4.
5 Ibid., pp. 14–15.

6 Andreas Malm, *Fossil Capital* (London: Verso, 2016), p. 10.
7 Kohei Saito, *Karl Marx's Ecosocialism* (New York: Monthly Review, 2017), p. 9.
8 Lowy, *Ecosocialism*, p. 4.
9 Saito, *Karl Marx's Ecosocialism*, p. 17.
10 Ibid.
11 Ibid., p. 258.
12 Ibid., p. 263.
13 Ibid., p. 133.
14 Ibid., p. 119.
15 Ibid., p. 99.
16 Ibid., p. 20.
17 Ibid., p. 263.
18 Ibid., p. 217.
19 See John Bellamy Foster, *Marx's Ecology* (New York: Monthly Review Press, 2000). Also, Paul Burkett, *Marx and Nature: A Red and Green Perspective* (New York: Monthly Review Press, 1999).
20 Fred Magdoff and Chris Williams, *Creating an Ecological Society* (New York: Monthly Review Press, 2017).
21 Foster, *Marx's Ecology*, p. 139.
22 Ibid., p. 136.
23 Ibid., p. viii.
24 Saito, *Karl Marx's Ecosocialism*, p. 257.
25 Ibid., p. 20.
26 See John Bellamy Foster, *The Ecological Revolution* (New York: Monthly Review Press, 2009), and *The Return of Nature* (New York: Monthly Review Press, 2020).
27 Saito, *Karl Marx's Ecosocialism*, 217.
28 Karl Marx, "Economic and Philosophical Manuscripts of 1844," in Robert C. Tucker, ed., *The Marx-Engels Reader* (New York: W.W. Norton, 1972), p. 75.
29 Ibid., 76.
30 Karl Marx, "The Manifesto of the Communist Party," in Tucker, *The Marx-Engels Reader*, p. 477.
31 Ibid., p. 490.
32 Karl Marx, "The Grundrisse," in Tucker, *The Marx-Engels Reader*, p. 285.
33 Karl Marx, "Capital, Volume One," in Tucker, *The Marx-Engels Reader*, p. 347. Italics in original.
34 Karl Marx, "Capital, Volume Three," in Tucker, *The Marx-Engels Reader*, p. 441.
35 Karl Marx, "Critique of the Gotha Program," in Tucker, *The Marx-Engels Reader*, p. 526.
36 Friedrich Engels, "Socialism: Utopian and Scientific," in Tucker, *The Marx-Engels Reader*, p. 708.
37 Ibid., p. 715.
38 Ibid., p. 715.
39 Ibid., p. 717.
40 Ibid., p. 717. Italics in original.
41 Saito, *Karl Marx's Ecosocialism*, p. 257.
42 Ibid., p. 258.
43 Ibid., p. 259.
44 On the scientific materialism that shaped development of the Second International up to World War I, see Leszek Kolakowski, *Main Currents of Marxism – 2* (New York: Oxford University Press, 1981), chs. 1, 2.

2
CAPITALISM: FROM MARX TO WEBER

Our exploration of capitalist history begins with those modernizing forces, interests, and ideologies that were ascending during the late nineteenth century, before further expanding across the twentieth century into the present. As capitalist rationalization, this process has transformed all realms of human life: economic, political, cultural, global. Our exploration to the modern predicament – including the global ecological crisis – necessarily starts with this trajectory, from the era of liberal capitalism to present-day corporate-state capitalism that predominates in the West. That trajectory corresponds to the rise of classical Marxism and later theories shaped by Max Weber and others he influenced.

As feudalism and pre-industrial society waned, so too did its main ideological expressions, above all conservatism – though strong residues survived well into the modern era, often contributing to the growth of fascism in Europe and Asia. While classical liberalism served as the main hegemonic ideology of historical capitalism, its embrace of such ideals as free markets, individualism, and democratic politics would face severe challenges at a time of increasing concentration of state, corporate, bureaucratic, and (in many cases) military power. By World War I liberal capitalism was giving way to a more robust statism that would soon underpin competing systems of the period: social democracy, fascism, Communism. These variants of modernization would shape the mostly state-directed economies of the period and, for both fascism and Communism, a populist-style nationalism reinforced by military power. The first two were expressions of capitalist development, or corporate-state modernity, while the third (Leninism) would become the driving-force behind epic nationalist revolutions in lesser-industrialized nations: Russia, China, Yugoslavia, Vietnam, Cuba.

By the 1920s and 1930s, with both social democracy and fascism on the rise in Europe, the early liberal capitalism analyzed by Marx and Engels – its laissez-faire economics, limited government, and pluralism – was in sharp decline, eroding as

DOI: 10.4324/9781003197461-3

the ideological rationale of economic growth and political legitimacy. In fact the Great Depression effectively signaled the eclipse of neoclassical economics and its fantasy of free markets, a trend set in motion by World War I, if not earlier. Benito Mussolini's famous attack on liberal democracy and his exaltation of state power for Italy in the early 1920s was not the great aberration usually depicted; it reflected the *Zeitgeist*, at least in the European context. The U.S. appeared as something of a holdout against rising statism, its elites adhering stubbornly to the tenets of liberal capitalism – until Franklin Roosevelt's New Deal changed everything. By the early 1940s and World War II, American capitalism had come under broadened government controls through a mixture of social and military Keynesianism, a pattern that would continue through the postwar years. Over time, while retaining Keynesian features, the U.S. would begin to follow a *fourth* pattern – that of a militarized state-capitalism, built on an historic merger of corporate, government, and military power.

Taking into account all four paths to modernization, the ideals traditionally associated with liberal democracy would face mounting obstacles. Early liberalism had at least theoretically upheld the virtues of citizen participation, civic rights and freedoms, institutional access, and social autonomy. By the 1920s and 1930s, however, such virtues were superseded by the spread of state-organized economies, corporate-oligarchical power, and a strong nationalism that often fueled both warfare and fascism. Continuous expansion of such authoritarian power, whether in the form of Communism, fascism, or social democracy, was sure to hasten the eclipse of classical liberalism; it was just a matter of time.

The Logic of Economic Rationalization

While capitalism and liberalism endured an uneasy and conflicted marriage throughout the nineteenth century, that dynamic would follow new directions by the early twentieth century. Capitalism would increasingly flourish in its corporate-state and globalized modality, while liberalism would lose much of its dynamism as a vibrant belief-system underpinning freedom, democracy, and prosperity. A system that had long celebrated the blessings of laissez-faire economics – even if state power had been far more decisive than generally believed – liberal capitalism was destined to meet the limits of its own contradictions. As sprawling corporate interests and their oligopolistic markets took hold, the system grew ever more dependent on government supports, from subsidies to taxation, regulation, monetary policies, tariffs, public infrastructure, and law enforcement. Modernity required complex levels of public steering, organization, and planning, held together by integrated elite power: never again would classical liberalism furnish the basis of modern democratic politics, or indeed any politics. Under the weight of ceaseless economic and bureaucratic rationalization, the fragile link between capitalist accumulation and liberal politics would soon enough erode and then eventually dissolve.

Strong central governments would be indispensable, everywhere, to drive rapidly modernizing economies. For Europe and North America, that meant three broad alternatives: social democracy, fascism, or state-corporate liberalism – all departing, sooner or later, from the liberal tradition in their much fuller embrace of statism. The first and third alternatives would be attached to Keynesian economics introduced primarily to save capitalism from its own lethal dysfunctions. It was the third alternative that shaped American development, rooted in combined social and military Keynesianism, favoring a tight merger of corporations and government. Everywhere the state ended up a systemic *necessity*, hardly resembling an alien, external, or intrusive force. By the 1930s, if not earlier, foundational elements of classical liberalism had become more or less dormant: unfettered competition, "invisible hand," night-watchman state, free markets, citizen sovereignty – all this was now largely fiction.[1] The system was now driven mostly by the requirements of bureaucracy, science, technology, and public infrastructure (education, transportation, urban services, welfare, etc.). Institutional stability and economic growth – not to mention ideological legitimacy – came to depend overwhelmingly on state power.

The seminal theorist of capitalist rationalization was Max Weber, whose work happened to coincide with the beginnings of the historical period in question. A function of modernity – of the elite drive for maximum efficiency and control – capitalism in Weber's view could never expand without adopting large-scale organization rooted in a complex division of labor, routinization, and command functions. All this superseded the mythical free flow of resources, commodities, and markets. To survive, much less flourish, modern capitalism would depend on far-reaching networks of planning and coordination – the essence of state-corporate power advancing material and social progress within an Enlightenment framework.[2] That such concentrated state power would be integral to capitalist development was obvious even before World War I, first reflected in Bismarckian Germany and the rise of mass social-democratic parties, a phenomenon accelerated by several warfare systems emerging from the Great War.

For Weber, writing in *The Protestant Ethic and the Spirit of Capitalism*, the system in its modern incarnation had become "emancipated from its old supports" associated with early capitalism, yielding to economic rationalization and its contribution to state power.[3] Further, "this process of rationalization in the field of technique and economic organization undoubtedly determines an important part of the ideals of life of modern bourgeois society."[4] In the end, the very spirit of capitalism turns profoundly against the most "spontaneous aspects of life," favoring the incessant accumulation of capital.[5]

Weber's view of rationalized capitalism clashed in many ways with Marx's class-conflict model. For Marx, the system was so riddled with contradictions – between workers and bourgeoisie, universal ideals and private interests, social needs and capital accumulation – that prospects for stability, order, and control through bureaucratized state power were dismissed as illusory, at best ephemeral.

Commodity production gave rise to systemic alienation, social conflict, political instability, and economic crises that could only be resolved by overthrow of an exploitative capitalism.[6] While Marx never arrived at a comprehensive theory of the state, his work generally approached the political realm as secondary or "superstructural," subordinated to the mode of production. Thus statism (for him, Bonapartism) could be nothing more than episodic, a desperate but futile maneuver by ruling interests to overcome crisis-tendencies endemic to an otherwise anarchic and volatile capitalism. Class struggle leading to revolution was the historical tendency of modern bourgeois society, and no governmental power could in the long run stave off collapse – or advance the revolution. For both Marx and Engels, the state was little more than a constellation of dominant economic interests, the site of little if any autonomy.

Weber, for his part, was hardly unaware of systemic contradictions theorized by Marx, but writing decades later he could better conceptualize historical tendencies embedded in corporate, bureaucratic, and (especially) state power. Whatever its intractable problems, capitalism was destined to undergo rationalization aligned with some mode of state direction. History had already called into question central features of both classical Marxism and classical liberalism: the primacy of economics (markets, commodities, class relations) had yielded, in one way or another, to the privileged role of *politics* that would eventually define both Leninism and fascism.[7]

For early Marxism and liberalism alike, politics was always secondary to deeper, underlying conditions and forces. The complex Weberian inversion of this dynamic was compelling for early decades of the twentieth century, reflecting as it did newer historical trends first visible in Europe. As is well known, such affirmation of the political was vigorously set forth by Mussolini in the early 1920s. Attacking liberalism, Mussolini famously said, "The foundation of fascism is the conception of the state, its character, its duty, and its aim. Fascism conceives of the state as an absolute, in comparison which all individuals or groups are relative only to be conceived of in their relation to the state."[8] We know that Mussolini, crucially, was in some manner the main architect of the *corporate*-state.

While extreme, Mussolini's celebration of a dynamic and creative state apparatus generally fit the Weberian understanding of capitalist rationalization involving corporate efficiency, organizational hierarchy, and new modes of integration and control. As with fascism itself, the system would be run by elites atop the economy, government, military, and cultural life – hardly consistent with a liberal economy or democratic politics. This very organizational logic extended not only to fascism, to what remained of liberal capitalism, and of social democracy, but (in more exaggerated form) to Lenin's vanguard party in Russia, later central to the success of twentieth-century Communist revolutions. Reversing Marx, Lenin unapologetically turned to the primacy of politics in a context where the revolutionary party would morph into a new type of party-*state*. As for European social democracy, whose leaders sought to democratize both the social and political terrain of capitalism, it was Robert Michels (in his classic *Political Parties*) who argued that, beneath even the most democratic ideals large-scale organization was sure to create oligarchy, rule of the few – precisely the trajectory of early German Social Democracy. Wrote Michels: "It is indisputable that the oligarchical and bureaucratic tendency of party organization is a matter of technical and practical necessity."[9] Bureaucratic power meant that, under all conditions, popular sovereignty ends up as something of a political fiction. Michels, it turns out, was a keen student of Weber, pushing the theory of rationalization to new levels.

Writing as a keen observer of capitalist rationalization, Michels, an insightful observer of European politics, maintained a strong pessimism regarding socialist prospects, especially when facing deradicalizing tendencies endemic to large-scale organization and state power. Thus: "The social revolution would not effect any real modification of the internal structure of the mass. The socialists might conquer [state power], but not socialism, which would perish in the moment of its adherents' triumph."[10] In other words, the ideology was likely to be corrupted by the subversive workings of organized power in any setting. Michels went on to add: "History seems to teach us that no popular movement, however energetic and vigorous, is capable of producing profound and permanent changes in the social organism of the civilized [i.e., modernized] world."[11]

Michels has usually been situated among "elite theorists" of the period, along with Gaetano Mosca and Vilfredo Pareto, though the list could easily have extended to Weber, Lenin, and others, all rather pessimistic about the efficacy of mass participation. Such "elitism" in fact roughly coincided with the *Zeitgeist* of the period, bolstered by the growth of military systems during and after World War I. European liberal democracy was passing from the scene, under siege from both left and right. What Mosca observed had more than a little resonance with political reality: "In all societies ... two classes of people appear – a class that rules and a class that is ruled. The first class, always the less numerous, performs all political functions, monopolistic power, and enjoys the advantages that power brings ...."[12] Pareto, like Mosca and Michels, believed that democracy was a rather naïve idea easily corrupted by "demagogic plutocracy" that allowed a small elite stratum to easily dominate large-scale institutions.[13] While Michels considered his theory something of an "iron law," similar thinking could have applied to the others, all convinced that an authoritarian logic of rationalization was constitutive of capitalist development.

Capitalist rationalization was not simply a matter of bureaucratic and statist imperatives, but extended to the industrial workplace and other sites of everyday life. The modern corporation emerged in Europe and North America during the 1880s and 1890s, its economic and political power solidified by World War I. New rationalization techniques were already introduced in the U.S. by the Ford Motor Company, in the form of scientific management or "Taylorism," and these would rim against the stated principles of classical liberalism. Weber was not alone in theorizing that modern industry would need precision, routine, and speed, vital to both efficiency and control. In fact the capitalist workplace would be central to elite domination, though then and later subject to stiff resistance from labor unions, workers' councils, and leftist parties.[14] At the same time, corporate ability to stave off these challenges would ultimately depend on its tightening alliance with state power.

Taylorism was designed to ensure not only peak capitalist efficiency and control but as a means to short-circuit systemic crises. As giant enterprises like Ford (and Fiat in Italy) expanded, their rates of productivity and profit-making were expected to steadily increase. In the process, workers would be more fully subordinated, divided, and atomized. Italian fascism would in its time stress workplace rationalization for the purpose of attenuating conflict between capitalists (or management) and workers, rendering unions and councils marginal to the labor process.[15] A new era of labor-management collaboration was undertaken – a boldly authoritarian matrix broadly identified not only with Mussolini's "corporatism" but with Lenin's "revolutionary" adoption of "Fordism" based on strict party controls, one-man management, and the famous "transmission belt" approach where the party-state controlled both unions and councils.[16]

The rapid growth of corporate power in the West typically gave rise to some variant of Fordism at the workplace – a process meant to transform workers into interchangeable objects. This would at least partly supersede the impact of commodity fetishism or market-based reification, that was a centerpiece of Marxist theory. In "Americanism and Fordism," one of Gramsci's more overlooked works, the rationalization process was loosely equated with "Americanism," signifying a more coercive form of capitalism that transforms laborers into something akin to "trained gorillas."[17] Gramsci referred to "modernization of the worker," a phenomenon most fully achieved in the U.S. where the corporate form had been more developed than in Europe. Congruent with his general outlook, Gramsci viewed Fordism as both organizational and ideological in ways that anticipated Marcuse's work in *One-Dimensional Man* (1964).[18] Gramsci argued that for capitalism to create a "new type of worker" it meant that "coercion has therefore to be ingeniously combined with persuasion and consent," including higher wages.[19]

As capitalism entered new phases of economic development (and crisis) at the start of the twentieth century, rationalization would be expected to accelerate by means of innovation in science, technology, and bureaucracy – that is, modernity infused with an Enlightenment vision of material and social "progress." The major institutions fell into this framework, generating a new stratum of bureaucrats, managers, technicians, and professionals dedicated to order and stability. On this point Immanuel Wallerstein writes: "The process of rationalization central to capitalism has required the creation of an intermediate stratum comprising the specialists of this rationalization, as administrators, technicians, educators. The very complexity of not only the technology but the social systems has made it essential that this stratum be large and, overtime, expanding."[20] Consistent with Gramsci, Wallerstein adds that rationalization is not merely structural but a "form of socialization," an *ideology* – a "means of class cohesion for the upper stratum."[21]

The very scope and complexity of modern capitalism is nowadays unthinkable without high levels of bureaucratic integration and technological rationality – that is, a tightening of the legal-rational norms of routine and control. Administrative rules and procedures also facilitate the convergence of government and big business, not to mention bureaucratization of the military, churches, education, and other areas of social life. Bureaucratic structures, as Weber repeatedly stated, were likely to become an end in themselves, where instrumental rationality could adapt to virtually any political ideology. During the crucial period 1900 to 1930, rationalized forms of domination would come to define not only capitalism but, in different ways, fascism, social democracy, and Communism.

Needed for institutional stability and routine, bureaucracy reproduces obedience to rules and laws as well as technical expertise. As the system evolves into an organizational culture, those within it are often caught up in its intimidating machinery of control, the familiar "iron cage." Weber wrote: "This passion for bureaucracy is enough to drive one to despair. It is as if in politics … we were deliberately to become men who need "order" and nothing but order, who become nervous and cowardly if for one moment this order wavers."[22] The problem worsens when we consider the permanent character of bureaucracy, Weber adding, "Once it is established, bureaucracy is among those structures which are the hardest to destroy."[23]

Weber's projections turned out to be more prescient than even he probably imagined, although the other "elite theorists" likewise saw in large-scale organization a source of authoritarian politics. On the one hand, as Weber noted, bureaucratization was being carried out – in Europe and elsewhere – "in direct alliance with capitalist interests."[24] He also recognized (true to historical actuality) that rationalization was perfectly adaptable to most any political framework, noting that "The mere fact of bureaucratic organization does not unanimously tell us about the concrete direction of its economic effects."[25] In every case, however – whether corporate-state capitalism, fascism, Communism, or social democracy – that "direction" would involve concentrated power at the summits of both government and the economy. Given its innate authoritarianism, however, there was abundant reason to believe that bureaucratic controls might have a close affinity with not only state-capitalism but historical fascism.

Weber emphasized the superiority and permanence of bureaucracy for societies where the scope and complexity of public life was advanced. Just as technology and machine production marked a dramatic improvement over labor-intensive methods, so bureaucracy was superior to traditional patrimonial systems in its increased precision, speed, continuity, and division of labor,[26] thus allowing for the depersonalization and secularization of public functions. Yet another advantage was its concentration (and integration) of administrative tasks, which meant an expanded power structure. As rational public life reinforced power at the top, the system would become more resistant to disruptive change; institutionalization meant solidification of roles, commitments, and norms.

All this indicates that capitalist rationalization, with its varying degrees of "permanence," could operate rather smoothly within, or alongside, the practices and norms of liberal democracy. Referring to Weber, Reinhard Bendix writes that "The population ruled by a bureaucracy cannot … dispense with it or replace it with something else." Public affairs in modern industrial society depend on the expert training, functional specialization and integration of bureaucratic structures "allowing for uninterrupted performance of tasks" regularly assigned to the state.[27] It is here, moreover, that capitalist rationalization and statism become tightly interwoven. As for liberalism itself, authoritarian pressures mounted historically as modern party systems experienced their own bureaucratization and loss of democratic politics. From this standpoint, Weber and Michels ended up more or less theoretically (if not politically) aligned: the scope, complexity, and cost of party activities (including elections) would centralize decision-making, a sphere eventually taken over by corporate elites in partnership with a rising professional-managerial stratum – both equally detached from organizational membership and the larger population.

Modernity and State-Capitalism

Weber's prescient analysis of bureaucratic organization, rational-legal culture, and capitalist rationalization – the thrust of what he called "higher capitalism" – pointed toward expanding spheres of domination and rise of a new power structure: state-capitalism. That system would be, as Weber anticipated, increasingly coordinated, bringing together politics and economics, government and business, state and capital. Though Weber himself never outlined a coherent theory of state-capitalism – that would be a task for later theorists – his seminal work laid the conceptual foundations of a more dynamic, streamlined capitalism transcending the conceptual antinomies of classical liberalism and classical Marxism. Beyond that, Weberian theory would uphold the primacy of politics, resonant with prevailing historical forces at work in Europe and beyond.

The neoclassical tenets of liberal capitalism had become problematic even before Weber and the elite theorists appeared on the scene. That doctrine naively viewed the capitalist economy as self-perpetuating, a system in equilibrium and infused with rational choice, individual sovereignty, and open competition – that is, a beautiful and perfectly self-reproducing social order. It was a society in which free markets, limited government, and citizen participation flourished within a natural, more or less organic historical process. State power was roughly understood as an *external* phenomenon, alien to natural relations basic to entrepreneurial activity of the sort envisioned by Adam Smith and a parade of utopian nineteenth-century neoclassical economists.

Such a romanticized world, devoid of hierarchy, authoritarian rule, and social conflict, was always a fantasy, as government had long been indispensable to capitalist development in the U.S. and elsewhere, if for nothing more than infrastructural, police, and military supports. The Marxist tradition had revealed the emptiness of bourgeois pretenses regarding democratic politics and free markets in a system rife with exploitation, coercion, and dysfunctions. Contrary to neoclassical mythology, capitalist growth brought sharpening class divisions along with new levels of concentrated power. The reality was that any social order based on founding capitalist principles was sooner or later destined to collapse of its own heavy weight, its own severe contradictions. The requirements of systemic organization, integration, and coordination best satisfied by bureaucratic power had been obvious from the onset, emphatically so by the end of the nineteenth century. Weber (along with Michels and the other "elite theorists") was in some measure merely theorizing what history had already bequeathed.

Capitalist modernity generated a complex division of labor that, as Weber argued, was drastically transforming all realms of public life. One result, as mentioned, was the merger of state and corporate power, however conflicted and tenuous, that formed the matrix of state-capitalism that, in its diverse forms, would eventually define most industrialized societies. Here neoclassical ideology took on features of a religious outlook, a belief-system increasingly detached from the world of giant corporations, oligopolistic economies, bureaucratic structures, and authoritarian state power. Government had become less an intrusive "external element" than an historically organic, indispensable presence within a functioning capitalism. In contrast to Marx's well-known views, however, the transition from early capitalism to later statist variants would be rather smooth, peaceful, and evolutionary, hardly associated with economic breakdown and revolutionary upheaval.

As for Weber, his views of capitalist rationalization actually outstripped his own rather conventional liberal politics, which he retained until the end. The bureaucratization of public life, expansion of corporate and state power, coercion in the workplace – all this meant broadening controls within an enlarged power apparatus, yet Weber somehow believed that his preferred liberal capitalism might survive, even flourish, at least in Europe. Or perhaps it was nothing more than sheer *hope*. Randall Collins, among others, concludes that Weber retained an idealistic view attached to the broad parameters of neoclassical economics.[28] It is hard to imagine that Weber could reconcile such entirely disparate paths of development. In any event, it would be left to later theorists – many within the orbits of Austro-Marxism and the Frankfurt School – to explore the fuller implications of a thoroughly rationalized capitalism.

By the 1920s and 1930s, overtly statist views of industrialism were coming into vogue, reflected in the work of Rudolf Hilferding, Joseph Schumpeter, and Friedrich Pollack, the latter's writings coming under the aegis of the Frankfurt School. The 1930s, of course, signified introduction of Keynesian economics in the U.S., an epic shift under FDR that was already defining European social democracy that was looking to "socialize" (and thus stabilize) a crisis-ridden capitalism. In fact, as noted, state-driven economies had appeared earlier – in Germany under Bismarck, Russia with the advent of Leninism, and in Italy in the form of Mussolini's corporate-state, or fascism.

Hilferding, Schumpeter, and Pollack understood, in different ways, that "organized capitalism" was becoming integral to modern European development. Hilferding anticipated a new stage of capitalist evolution rooted in corporate domination, growth of state power, and large-scale planning, all potentially helpful to progressive socialization of the economy. Capitalism, innately anarchic and unstable, would require elaborate forms of organization, integration, and regulation in order to avoid escalating crises and possible collapse. Hilferding, for his part, combined important motifs from both Marx and Weber, central to the work of Austro-Marxism. Neither Marx nor Weber, of course, had fully theorized the more advanced stages of capitalist development – nor could they have. In the tracks of Weber, Hilferding jettisoned the familiar assumption that class struggle would be the crucial mechanism of modern capitalist development.[29]

In *Capitalism, Socialism, and Democracy*, Schumpeter took his analysis beyond that of either Weber or Hilferding: capitalist rationalization unleashed tendencies toward both systemic expansion and its transcendence, potentially giving birth to a new order consistent with "state socialism."[30] The modern economy was innately corporate, bureaucratic, and statist, a far remove from the proliferation of private, small-scale entrepreneurial firms considered basic to earlier capitalism. Small and even medium-sized firms were likely to disappear or become marginalized, yielding to heightened industrial concentration and state power relative to *both* capital and labor. Further, the Enlightenment flourishing of bureaucracy, science, and technology would ultimately create a new stratum (*not* class) with more progressive ideas for a (post-capitalist) order along lines of socialism, moving toward egalitarian class and power relations. Put differently, advanced capitalism would sooner or later destroy its own underpinnings, not by means of class struggle or revolution but through a somewhat peaceful, evolutionary process. This scenario in fact veered close to earlier schemas, around 1900, laid out by Eduard Bernstein and kindred "evolutionary socialists" within European social democracy. Whatever its specific definition, the very logic of modernizing capitalism (or industrialism, as in the USSR) would be emphatically *statist*.[31]

For Pollack and a few other Critical Theorists, however, expanded state power could only mean formation of a dynamic state-capitalism. The liberal, market-oriented phase of capitalism had exhausted its limits, as shown by the global economic crisis of the 1920s and 1930s, and by the Great Depression – a catalyst for Keynesianism in the U.S. The era of unplanned, unregulated capitalism had come resoundingly to a close, the system no longer capable of standing on its own. To merely survive, much less flourish, capitalism would need a state-centered process of rationalization with enlarged public ownership, strong regulations, tax-generated revenues, economic planning, and elevated social priorities.[32] Pollack believed that irreversible corporatist and statist trends in the U.S. and Europe demonstrated that some type of state-capitalism was the wave of the future, development now shaped by a combination of "market" and public agendas. The apparent success of Leninism in Russia, rapid spread of European social democracy, and astonishing rise of Italian fascism seemed to reinforce this historical *Zeitgeist*.

As for the Frankfurt School, the appearance of state-capitalism (including a "Keynesian Revolution" in the U.S.) was understood as a mechanism for regulating class conflict and containing systemic crisis-tendencies – the very *raison d'être* of early fascism. A fusion of corporate and governmental power would be the very essence of state-capitalism, where the state took over a widening range of public activities, from economic planning to banking, social infrastructure, business subsidies, and social welfare. The expectations of Hilferding and Schumpeter, along with those of Pollack, had in fact already been confirmed by the time they were theorized.

For some Marxists and Frankfurt School critics, the historic shift toward state-capitalism (or "monopoly state-capitalism") pointed toward an administered society that might be seen as veering toward fascism or "totalitarianism."[33] The space between a highly-rationalized capitalism and an emergent corporatist fascism had by the late 1920s become somewhat narrowed. Indeed the Italian fascists had already begun to move in this direction, hoping to restrain class conflict and other sources of "chaos" endemic to liberal capitalism. The logic of capitalist rationalization, as Weber had indicated, would give rise to state-bureaucratic system at odds with personal freedoms and social autonomy. One key difference between state-capitalism and fascism during the 1920s and 1930s was that the latter involved a single party-state ruled by a dictatorial leader presumably able to "stand above" mundane bureaucratic pressures.

For other Frankfurt School theorists – notably Max Horkheimer, Theodor Adorno, and Herbert Marcuse – the new capitalist power apparatus pointed to an ever-widening system of domination already verging on fascism: the Enlightenment schema of social, technological, and economic progress was in crucial ways being turned upside down, just as it was being "realized." The classical Marxist belief that advancing capitalism would generate heightened class conflict and social crises, leading to socialism, had been undercut by the all-encompassing force of economic and bureaucratic rationalization. Systemic dysfunctions remained, however, but in most cases they were driving politics *rightward*, as in Italy, Germany, Spain, and Eastern Europe. Meanwhile, Schumpeter's expectation of a novel form of socialist transition was being undercut by those institutional and ideological changes consistent with authoritarian politics.

In their classic *Dialectic of Enlightenment* (1944), Horkheimer and Adorno advanced a dystopic scenario of rationalizing capitalism, having reluctantly concluded that modern industrial society was "sinking into a new kind of barbarism."[34] Enlightenment ideology celebrated "progress," yet in reality it produced a culture of anxiety and despair as the tentacles of domination expand, leading to a world in which "heaven and hell hang together."[35] Influenced by Marx and

Weber, Horkheimer and Adorno took the problem of capitalist rationalization to new levels, to a more deeply critical view of Enlightenment ideology – a legacy infused with dark elements of coercion and violence behind surface ideals of freedom, democracy, and diversity. Thus: "The paradoxical nature of faith with humility degenerates into a swindle and becomes the myth of the twentieth century and its irrationality turns it into an instrument of rational administration by the wholly enlightened as they steer society toward barbarism."[36] Regarding "barbarism," the authors had in mind not only wars and genocide, but the fruits of everyday domination that had come to define modernity and industrialism.

Within these historical conditions it mattered little what ideological agendas prevail, for the "enlightened few" are entitled to dominate through the mechanisms of rational administration. For Adorno and Horkheimer, the modern system objectifies and dehumanizes where "domination lends increased consistency and force to the social whole in which it establishes itself."[37] Two decades later, in *One-Dimensional Man*, Marcuse would arrive at nearly identical conclusions, though more focused on the process of *technological* rationalization. The historical rise of state-capitalism would have enduring consequences for the economy, politics, and society: free enterprise or "free markets" within a system of competitive capitalism had lost all relevance for the new system of power.

The period following World War I saw the appearance of three modes of statism: Leninism, fascism, social democracy, followed later by a militarized corporate-state that would shape postwar American society. Only the social-democratic variant would be compatible with socialization of the economy and democratization of governance – most visible in Scandinavia, Holland, Germany and a few other European countries. Even social democracy, however, would encounter new limits as authoritarian trends began to shape the expanding corporate and state sectors. As for the U.S. – the main concern of this book – a pressing question is whether the fourth variant might evolve into a modern-day fascism, or "fascist equivalent." For that to happen, of course, factors well beyond those related to capitalist rationalization would have to come into play.

The Rise of Corporate Globalization

The onset of capitalist globalization goes back two centuries or more, when the great leaders of industry and banking set out to marketize the world in their endless pursuit of wealth and power. In the *Communist Manifesto*, Marx wrote: "The need of a constantly expanding market for its products chases the bourgeoisie over the whole surface of the globe. It must nestle everywhere, settle everywhere, establish connections, everywhere."[38] Capitalism had done precisely that, no doubt succeeding far beyond Marx's firmest expectations. That system has more recently achieved such heights as to thoroughly reshape the planet – first economically, then in the realms of politics, the military, culture, technology, social life, and the environment. The most far-reaching change can be seen in the awesome power of transnational corporations, which have steadily built their control over markets, trade, finance, the media, and most governments – far surpassing anything imagined by Marx, later Marxists, or even Weber. Vast planetary destruction has been an inescapable outcome of these epochal changes.

That predicament has only worsened, in part because there exists no effective Keynesian "solution" at the global level, no effective counterweights against transnational corporate power. Popular forces in favor of labor rights, consumer protection, and environmental sustainability are at an overwhelming disadvantage. "Free trade," like "free markets," has given broadened leverage to commercial interests in manufacturing, banking, agriculture, technology, and communications to exploit and dominate with impunity. Even formal centers of decision-making at the United Nations have become mostly impotent in the face of corporate globalization, or neoliberalism, insofar as the system operates well outside any concrete democratic processes. There is, at the same time, a profound weakening of nation-states that, however, does *not* fully extend to the wealthiest and most powerful countries, the actual beneficiaries of a more open flow of capital, technology, and communications.[39]

An integrated global economy nowadays develops along lines of the neoclassical model – increased capital mobility, weak regulations, a shackled working class, limited public programs, fiscal austerity, and banking as a casino operation. Yet that system itself is hardly "neoclassical" in any meaningful sense. For one thing, corporate markets (as in technology, autos, agriculture, media, chemicals, drugs, retail) are highly oligopolistic: typically a few, perhaps several, business giants dominate a particular market, where competition is restrained. Second, while the vast majority of nation-states are subordinated to global imperatives, the world system depends heavily not only on transnational corporations but on the World Bank and International Monetary Fund (IMF), institutions firmly controlled by leading nations such as the U.S. and those of the Eurozone. Third, bureaucratic and technological rationalization typical of advanced capitalism simultaneously pervade the global scene, with profoundly anti-democratic consequences. Finally, perhaps most crucially, globalization relies on military force to protect and ensure a smooth flow of resources and money that, by the early twenty-first century, amounts to many trillions of dollars. The world is no free-market capitalist paradise.[40]

Hardly a paradise: international capital has penetrated and reshaped every corner of the globe, creating growth and prosperity for roughly 10 percent of the world population while bringing considerable misery to large sectors of the other 90 percent – destroying communities, weakening labor, lowering wages, undermining working conditions, wreaking havoc on the global ecology. Globalization has undoubtedly improved the quality of life at the core of major world cities, where massive business and government investment is concentrated, but social existence for those in retail industries, the McDonaldized service sector, agriculture, mining, and of course the industrial sweatshops continues to deteriorate.

The victims of this system must endure poverty, crime, dislocation, environmental deterioration, and abject powerlessness. Meanwhile, as the global economy is threatened with endemic chaos and possible collapse, an emboldened power structure – now centered in the U.S., Europe and, Japan – strives relentlessly to perpetuate its enormous leverage, wealth, and social privilege.

As in the case of domestic capitalism, those who own and control the means of production, distribution, exchange, and communication on the global terrain constitute a relatively narrow and insular elite, typically removed from popular decision-making bodies.[41] The elites make key decisions on capital investment, allocation of resources, and government policy, looking for the freest circulation of capital, goods, and resources across the planet. It is not yet the case, however, that globalization has generated an independent ruling class existing apart from the wealthiest and most privileged networks of power in the U.S. and other leading nations. A nucleus of power exists at the apex of this system based on its industrial, banking, technological, and military supremacy, yet predictions about the death of nation-states seem rather premature: weaker nations are fully subordinate to the world system, but the stronger ones maintain varying degrees of superior leverage.[42]

What global corporations have achieved during recent decades, however, is a massive concentration of power and wealth in the hands of a few industrial, banking, agricultural, and media elites. A neoliberal order has been consolidated, though not without contestation, on the fiction of free markets, open trade, wide prosperity, and democratic promises. Opposition naturally appears, but it has been largely fragmented and neutralized thanks in no small measure to the workings of U.S. economic, political, and military supremacy. Despite what cheerleaders of this system argue, popular leverage against transnational capital has never gained serious momentum, in the U.S. or elsewhere.

The War on Nature

The fate of the earth in an era of deepening ecological crisis might well depend, in the final judgment, on philosophical approaches to nature – a concept often romanticized to insignificance. Theorists of diverse outlooks have long extended (seemingly obligatory) references to it. The first problem is that references have easily been given to vague and formless usage, subject to myriad interpretations. Many thinkers have been inclined to endow the natural world with wondrous ethical content – that is, a uniquely noble state vulnerable to endless threats: industrialization, urban colonization, technology, military violence, consumerism. Nature has been ritually wrapped in mystical, romantic, even primitive virtues menaced by an always-debilitating modernity, above all *capitalist* modernity.

With advancing levels of industrialization, the search for a social order in which humans do *not* exert dominion over nature would seem to be futile. Going back to the era of classical Marxism, radicals and other progressives have envisioned some kind of reunification of humans and nature, society and the natural habitat as part of a new, more ecological phase of development – an order based on human rationality, environmental sanity, and sustainable growth. The notion is that ecosystems develop and mature within constantly-evolving, thriving, interactive communities of human and nonhuman life, a viewpoint first developed by such theorists as Rousseau and Kropotkin. Paul Taylor has referred to this approach simply as "the ethics of respect for nature."[43] This approach contends that humans should not exert dominion over other forms of biological life, a maxim of course harshly at odds with the daily imprint of modern industrial society.

Whatever its philosophical merits, the problem here is the highly implausible rejection of modernity itself, not to mention absence of any political strategy for getting there – a virtual celebration of anti-politics. It can also be argued that Foster, Saito, and other proponents of an "ecological Marx" often veer toward utopianism, identifying the approach with Marx and Engels in order to dismiss implications of a Promethean Marx. As shown by passages from the *1844 Manuscripts*, Marx himself seemed vaguely dedicated to historical unification of humans with nature – a prospect conceivable, however, not only with final transcendence of capitalist power and class relations but with a full exit from modern industrial society.

The complex interplay of humans and nature, mediated by production and labor, did inform a good deal of Marx's work – though, as mentioned, it was eventually compromised by an instrumentalism notable in the *Manifesto* and elsewhere. As humans transform the external world, they simultaneously transform themselves within the larger ensemble of relations. With any future transition to socialism, it follows, longstanding divisions separating city and countryside would presumably shrink, though this process too is never elaborated. In any case, based on the logic of historical development, humans would dialectically interact with nature, re-appropriating it within a process of revolutionary change.

Beyond these and other similarly general propositions, however, Marx never developed a philosophy of nature that could anticipate the work of later ecologists; his categories of analysis were much too grand, too imprecise, too malleable. As Saito points out, Marx did lay out a theory of "metabolic rift" possibly integral to the critique of political economy, yet it appears this too was never fully elaborated or effectively combined with the broader critique.[44] Saito adds that Marx's "vision of the future society demands a careful and sustainable interaction with nature, based on a distinct recognition of its limits."[45] Yet this claim is muddied by the aforementioned productivism and instrumentalism that, despite suggestions to the contrary, pervades Marx's overall body of work.

Aside from a rather diffuse view of nature, Marx's theoretical limits just as critically extended to what was left out, diminished: the entire universe of nonhuman life, including other species that have long inhabited the earth, nowadays threatened as never before. In his dialectical treatment of (human) "species-being," integral to the transition from (human) necessity to freedom, Marx reveals a void never addressed by Saito, Foster, and other "Marx-as-ecologist" boosters. This problem becomes all the more illuminating once we consider that humans – long embedded in anthropocentrism and speciesism – continue to wage nonstop war against nonhuman nature, a savagery intensified under advanced capitalism. At this point the concept of "metabolic rift" so central to Saito's reading of Marx falls pathetically short of capturing a barbaric reality; the distance between "war" and "rift" could not be wider.

For Marx, nonhuman beings simply never figured in his concept of "nature," never mattered within the ecological calculus. He refers to a "humanized nature" that reflects the "essential powers of *man*" – another tribute, it turns out, to the ethos of instrumental rationality.[46] He writes: "Man makes his life-activity itself of his will and his consciousness He has conscious life-activity ... Conscious life-activity directly distinguishes man from animal life-activity. It is just because of this that he is a species-being."[47] Passages like this recur throughout Marx's work, not surprising given prevailing ideological norms of the period. It is commonplace nowadays to acknowledge the sentience, or life-purpose, of members of other species, increasingly so within ecological circles. Still, while Marx and Engels might be excused for this sparse understanding of nature, that merely reaffirms the severe limits of classical Marxism as cornerstone of modern ecological thought. The problem resides less in the classical theory as such than in the unpardonable failure of more recent interpreters to question and transcend those limits.

The widening critique of speciesism actually goes back several decades, well before recent efforts to promote an "ecological Marx." Of course Marx's own work could never have benefited from the contributions of present-day ecologists – of an entire generation of animal-rights research and theorizing. As early as the 1940s Adorno and Horkheimer in *Dialectic of Enlightenment* questioned how "mankind, instead of entering into a truly human condition, [was] sinking into a new kind of barbarism." Crucial to this dystopic view was a critique of ruling interests for their ruthless pursuit of superiority over the rest of society, over nature, over all nonhuman life within it.[48] For modern capitalism, animal populations were routinely subjected to unspeakable horrors – a savagery viewed as reflecting the absolute powers of human dignity and supremacy.[49] In such a gruesome world, "the whole earth bears witness to the glory of man."[50] This war against nature had all the features of a planned, routinized, celebrated destruction of "animal existence."[51] Written several decades ago, these passages would offer glimpses into a future carnage of factory farms, slaughterhouses, medical experimentation, hunting as sport, and myriad other contemporary horrors.

No longer a submerged issue, the systematic torture and murder of billions of animals yearly is better understood as intrinsic to the entire matrix of industrial and technological society, integral to both capitalism *and* post-capitalism. The practices are fully normalized, embedded in the basic rhythms of daily life: corporations, government, the military, churches, health care, the food system. While critical social theory might be expected to deconstruct *all* institutions and practices of domination, here we have an instance of intellectual work indulging an inexplicable political exemption. The unfathomable scale of this violence against nature, endemic to industrial modernity, far exceeds anything encompassed by the notion of "metabolic rift." Does such a "rift" ever apply to other species? On this point John Sanbonmatsu is prompted to ask: "When atrocity becomes the very basis of society, does society not forfeit its right call itself moral?"[52] Unfortunately, Marxism in its different variants has lent its credibility to this particularly savage "domination of nature." Here the all-too-familiar fetishism of nature turns into the ugliest of fictions.

Sanbonmatsu argues that this global system of institutionalized brutality is simultaneously a "mode of production itself," profiting scandalously from animal goods, services, and resources – a sector of the political economy ignored only by dint of fierce determination.[53] Over past decades it has indeed become an expanding mode of production (and consumption) without equal. Speciesism thus amounts to far more than an ideology: it fits squarely within an ensemble of relations, fundamental to the self-activity of humans in pursuit of their privileged "species-being." All the cherished signifiers of "progress" – science, technology, industry, medicine, education – are employed to advance this ubiquitous, intensifying war against nature. We know that a global meat complex that "processes" billions of animals yearly is widely regarded as a sign of affluence, development, good health, modernity. It is, at the same time, among the worst contributors to global warming and assorted environmental dangers such as deforestation, ocean pollution, and biodiversity loss.[54]

Conventional political discourse that romanticizes "unification of humans and nature," whether Marxist, liberal, or some other, is meant to sound enlightening but points toward exactly the opposite – a cruel fraud. Could such a fraud be ethically tolerable within a viable socialist politics? Sanbonmatsu's answer: "… to affirm a socialism without animal liberation is to affirm a civilization based on a continual antagonism with the rest of nature."[55] Idealization of Nature (caps intentional) turns despotic under the most progressive of ideological covers. As for Marxism, even "ecological Marxism" in the name of "science" and "materialism," what ought to affirm deep moral, ecological, and political concerns ends up obscured in the fog of productivism. It is no secret that neither Marx nor Engels (said to be a fox hunter) ever questioned the prejudice of anthropocentrism or speciesism in their own time, in effect laying the intellectual underpinnings of ideological debility for later generations of Marxists and socialists. As more refined technological methods of mass killing are employed by huge corporate meat and dairy interests, as nonhumans wind up more (not less) central to the power of agribusiness and sources of capital accumulation, political opposition winds up silent and ultimately complicit. Meanwhile, the globalized power structure proceeds along its routine, ever deadly, course.

What kind of ecosocialism might flourish within such a yawning theoretical and political void? What kind of radical politics could effectively support this aggravated warfare against the natural habitat? What could justify a structure of power so willfully responsible for the worsening ecological crisis – contributing not only to climate change but to exhaustion of natural resources, biodiversity destruction, and shrinking arable land, not to mention depletion of oceans and forests? As the planet further descends into calamity, those few critical thinkers with the audacity to raise such urgent concerns are sadly derided by leftists as "extremists," "food fascists," and worse, often reminded that, after all, "Hitler was a vegetarian" (he was not, though it is irrelevant). Even the very limited opposition to speciesism is trivialized, the worst types of animal exploitation conveniently ignored while more enlightened critics tend to the "bigger issues," working to "save the planet."

One aspect of speciesism – what humans eat on a daily basis – is perhaps the most impactful of all problems, yet also the most concealed and least understood. Richard Oppenlander, in his unsettling book *Comfortably Unaware*, argues that meat consumption is doing more to destroy the earth than anything else. "Global depletion in some form will occur," he writes, "simply because the earth can only support so many people doing so many things over so long a period of time." He adds: "We have developed a complex system of producing more and more animals that use more and more of our resources, while leaving a massive amount of waste and climate change in their wake ... This system has become complicated in that it is now heavily intertwined with our culture, politics, economic, and the suppression of the reality of its effect on our planet." Ecological sanity demands a public accounting of this dreadful reality, yet another product of capitalist rationalization, but concerted ignorance prevails instead. Oppenlander laments: "To make matters worse, individuals and institutions that are in a position to expose myths, enlighten the public, and change the direction of public opinion clearly are not doing so."[56] The reference here is to *American* public opinion, but it is just as applicable to most other countries.

Issues related to agriculture and food consumption deserve far more attention than they have gotten, above all in the case of progressives and Marxists. As for Marx himself, his views on the topic did not extend very far. The authors of *Food, Politics, and Society* point out that he "overlooked the role of what we have called the 'food system' as itself a driver of social, economic, and political transformations."[57] That system, probably more than any other, lies at the core of historic changes in the relationship between agriculture and industry, agrarian and urban life, development and ecology – clearly vital to any in-depth understanding of the modern crisis, any move toward reversing the crisis. Within this matrix problems of everyday consumption, environmental deterioration, corporate power, and vast health challenges of our time are thoroughly interwoven.

Lester Brown, writing in *Full Planet, Empty Plates*, argues that food politics nowadays engages – or should engage – what is most central to facing the challenge of ecological sustainability. He writes: "We are entering a time of chronic food insecurity, one that is leading to intense competition for control of land and water resources – in short, a new geopolitics of food."[58] Rising global meat consumption poses one of the gravest challenges – again, scarcely acknowledged, even among ecologists. More than at any time in history, the animal-based food system veers out of sync with land availability, natural resources, climate stabilization, human health, and survival of other species. One is prompted to ask: could such immeasurable human assault on "nature" be adequately captured through the notion of "metabolic rift"?

Returning to Marx, the very notion of harmony in natural relations had long been torn asunder, fractured under the modern onslaught of industrialization, urbanization, and perpetual wars. The dialectical synthesis humanism–naturalism was never historically grounded, whether before or during the rise of capitalism; it was soon enough obliterated by the process of economic rationalization. The concept of nature in Marx, as Ted Benton argues, was always flawed by a sharp dualism visible, for example, in those frequent passages separating humans from animals.[59] Humans arrogantly retain the capacity to treat (especially this part of) nature through crudely instrumental practices – a legacy forwarded by later generations of Marxists and socialists. Those who celebrate an "ecological Marx" usually fall silent on the painful question of human-animal relations as if "nature" did not extend to many billions of nonhuman beings, other species with their own subject of life, their own capacity to suffer pain and loss, their close interaction with (often dependency on) human populations. One can only conclude that such ethical neglect mirrors an incomplete, callous, utilitarian conception of nature.

Subject to a tormented logic, contemporary progressives and Marxists predictably wind up tolerating or just ignoring corporate giants like Tyson Foods, Monsanto, Cargill, and McDonald's –all deriving their criminal profits from all-out war against nature. Formally progressive ideas coexist with tightening systems of domination that have become so pervasive, so normalized, as to be nearly invisible. The cruelest violations of nonhuman life are taken for granted, as humans psychologically detach themselves from daily mechanisms of destruction.[60] All the accumulated references to "species-being," human-nature unity, and liberation from necessity can never conceal this systematic and deliberate transgression of the natural world – a topic entirely ignored by Saito and other proponents of an "ecological Marx."

Despite its undeniable achievements in the realms of industrial development, scientific advances, and technological innovations, capitalist rationalization – supposed pinnacle of the Enlightenment – bequeathed a sharply-divided legacy for Europe and, later, across the world. By the 1920s and 1930s, the dark side of modern "progress" could scarcely be ignored: corporate-state domination, oligarchical rule, deterioration of public life, workplace exploitation, destruction of the natural habitat. One by-product of this historic process was, for Marxism especially, the steady decline of the industrial proletariat as revolutionary agency in a setting where class conflict was being (unevenly) institutionalized and domesticated. Yet another by-product was, for a Weberian standpoint, a certain historical irony: the great theorist of liberal politics would lay the theoretical basis of an *authoritarian* politics reinforced by the spread of large-scale organization. Viewed thusly, capitalist rationalization would ultimately coincide with the decline of community, democracy, individual freedoms, and natural relations. It would therefore set in motion conditions hostile to all the great promises contained in Enlightenment ideals, while at the same time impeding the growth of oppositional politics.

Notes

1 On the narrowing of the American power structure, see Carl Boggs, *Phantom Democracy: Corporate Interests and Political Power* (New York: MacMillan, 2011), ch. 3. See also Chris Hedges, *Death of the Liberal Class* (New York: Nation Books, 2010), ch. 3.
2 See H. H. Gerth and C. Wright Mills, *From Max Weber* (New York: Oxford University Press, 1946), pp. 232–235.
3 Max Weber, *The Protestant Ethic and the Spirit of Capitalism* (New York: Charles Scribners, 1958), p. 72.
4 Weber, *The Protestant Ethic*, p. 76.
5 Ibid., p. 166.
6 See Karl Marx, "Manifesto of the Communist Party", in Robert C. Tucker, ed., *The Marx-Engels Reader* (New York: W. W. Norton, 1978), pp. 473–491.
7 For an excellent discussion of the primacy of politics in Lenin, see Sheldon Wolin, *Politics and Vision* (Boston, MA: Little, Brown, and Co., 1960), pp. 424–427.
8 See Benito Mussolini, "What is Fascism" (www.thirdworldtraveler.com/fascism), first published in 1932.
9 Robert Michels, *Political Parties* (New Brunswick, NJ: Transaction Publishers, 1999), p. 72.
10 Ibid., p. 344.
11 Ibid.
12 Gaetano Mosca, *The Ruling Class* (New York: McGraw Hill, 1939), p. 50.
13 Joseph V. Femia, *Pareto and Political Theory* (New York: Routledge, 2006), ch. 4.
14 On capitalist rationalization of the workplace, see Richard Edwards, *Contested Terrain* (New York: Basic Books, 1979), chs. 7, 8. See also George Ritzer, *The McDonaldization of Society* (Thousand Oaks, CA: Pine Forge Press, 2000), ch. 6.
15 Ritzer, *The McDonaldization of Society*, pp. 97, 104.
16 See Fred and Lou Jean Fleron, "Administrative Theory as Repressive Politics: The Communist Experience," *Telos* (summer 1972).
17 Antonio Gramsci, "Americanism and Fordism," in Quintin Hoare and Geoffrey Nowell Smith, eds., *Selection from the Prison Notebooks* (New York: International Publishers, 1971), pp. 309–310.
18 Herbert Marcuse, *One-Dimensional Man* (Boston, MA: Beacon Press, 1964), ch. 6.
19 Gramsci, "Americanism and Fordism", p. 310.
20 Immanuel Wallerstein, *Historical Capitalism* (London: Verso, 1983), pp. 83–84.
21 Ibid., p. 84.
22 Reinhard Bendix, *Max Weber: An Intellectual Portrait* (New York: Anchor Books, 1962), p. 464.
23 Gerth and Mills, *From Max Weber*, p. 228.
24 Ibid., p. 230.
25 Ibid., p. 231.
26 Bendix, *Max Weber*, p. 426.
27 Ibid., p. 430.

28 Randall Collins, *Max Weber* (Beverly Hills, CA: Sage Publications, 1986), pp. 84–85.
29 See Rudolf Hilferding, *Finance Capital: A Study in the Latest Phase of Capitalist Development* (London: Routledge and Keegan Paul, 1981).
30 J.A. Schumpeter, *Capitalism, Socialism, and Democracy* (London: Allen & Unwin, 1976).
31 Ibid., pp. 46–49.
32 Frederick Pollack, "State Capitalism: Its Possibilities and Limitations", in Stephen Eric Bronner and Douglas Kellner, eds., *Critical Theory and Society* (New York: Routledge, 1989), pp. 58–74.
33 Herbert Marcuse, *Negations* (Boston, MA: Beacon Press, 1968), p. 9.
34 Max Horkheimer and Theodor W. Adorno, *Dialectic of Enlightenment* (New York: Continuum, 1995), p. xi. Originally published in 1944.
35 Ibid., p. 14.
36 Ibid., p. 20.
37 Ibid., p. 21.
38 Marx, "Manifesto of the Communist Party", in Tucker, *The Marx-Engels Reader*, p. 476.
39 Jerry Harris, *Global Capitalism and the Crisis of Democracy* (Atlanta, GA: Clarity Press, 2016), ch. 5.
40 Robinson, *Global Capitalism*, pp. 43–48.
41 Sklar, *Transnational Capitalist Class*, p. 38.
42 Ibid., pp. 5–6.
43 See Paul W. Taylor, "The Ethics of Respect for Nature", in Michael E. Zimmerman et al., eds., *Environmental Philosophy* (New York: Prentice-Hall, 1993).
44 Saito, *Karl Marx*, p. 99.
45 Ibid., p. 259.
46 Karl Marx, "Economic and Philosophical Manuscripts of 1844", p. 89.
47 Ibid., p. 76.
48 Horkheimer and Adorno, *Dialectic of Enlightenment*, pp. xii–xiv.
49 Ibid., p. 245.
50 Ibid.
51 Ibid., p. 249.
52 See John Sanbonmatsu, "Introduction", in Sanbonmatsu, ed., *Critical Theory and Animal Liberation* (Lanham, MD: Rowman & Littlefield, 2011), p. 12.
53 Ibid., p. 21.
54 On the contribution of meat consumption to the ecological crisis, see Lester R. Brown, *Full Planet, Empty Plates* (New York: W.W. Norton, 2012), chs. 3–8.
55 Sanbonmatsu, *Critical Theory*, p. 31.
56 Richard Oppenlander, *Comfortably Unaware* (New York: Beaufort Books, 2012), pp. 11, 81.
57 Alejandro Colas et al., *Food, Politics, and Society* (Berkeley: University of California Press, 2018), p. 83.
58 Brown, *Full Planet*, p. 141.
59 See Ted Benton, *Natural Relations* (London: Verso, 1993), p. 45.
60 Victoria Johnson, "Everyday Rituals of the Master Race", in Sanbonmatsu, *Critical Theory*, pp. 205–207.

3
FROM LENIN TO GRAMSCI

Was the revolutionary theory developed by Marx across three or more decades actually a form of *scientific* analysis, as many later interpreters have claimed, or something entirely different – more akin to a *critical* theory, a "philosophy of praxis" affirming the unity of theory and politics? The question as to whether Marx's work on the whole was scientific no doubt matters, as its status determines how we view its numerous historical claims, its political efficacy, and surely its ecological relevance. (While Marx and Engels worked in tandem on some major writings, epistemological differences appeared to surface toward the end of their careers.) Debates over to what extent classical Marxism could lay claim to scientific validity – or could be viewed in such terms – would pervade the tradition up to the present, always imbued with political meaning. Champions of an "ecological Marx," including Saito and Foster, have generally arrived at a scientific reading of both Marx and Engels, endowing their work with firm grounding in some variant of "dialectical materialism." Both Saito and Foster, at least, do make a point to distance their approach from cruder forms of positivism.

Breaking the Theoretical Impasse

While Marx's outlook has been widely understood as "materialistic" (thus also presumably scientific), roughly the same theoretical edifice that would by the 1930s morph into official Soviet Marxism, it is worth noting that Marx himself scarcely employed the term in any philosophically consistent way. Engels was more inclined to embrace materialism in his theoretical writings, most often in texts like *Dialectics of Nature*, completed after Marx's death. Marx's philosophy, going back to his early years, actually differed from that of Engels – and the later scientific pretensions of Kautsky, Plekhanov, and other leading figures in

DOI: 10.4324/9781003197461-4

European social democracy. Engels had argued in *Dialectics* that matter fundamentally precedes ideas and consciousness; the subjective realm was little more than reflection of the external world, worthy at best of secondary importance. Marx himself never fully shared this outlook. In fact the stricter version of materialism later adopted by Engels and his disciples was identical to the very mechanistic theories Marx had earlier criticized in *Theses on Feuerbach*.

Marx's own philosophy was never strictly materialist or scientific in ways his writings have so often been interpreted. He remained much too indebted to his strong Hegelian origins to adopt such an outlook, yet critical enough of Hegel and other German idealists to avoid being trapped in their legacy. For Marx, historical development was much too complex to be regarded as simple unfolding of objective forces independent of human thought and action; social change always depended vitally on some type of subjective intervention. It might be argued that Marx's epistemology was formed sui generis, a dialectical synthesis of earlier materialism and traditional idealism – prelude to what Gramsci would later refer to as a "philosophy of praxis," the approach he believed most consistent with the logic of revolutionary politics. As such, it avoided the rigid dichotomy subject/object of historical transformation.

For Marx, conscious human activity (including politics) was fundamental to revolutionary change. From this standpoint, it seems probable that Marx's heightened attention to the natural sciences after 1868 did not necessarily coincide with efforts to adopt a scientific methodology for purposes of explaining human behavior or, by extension, the dynamics of historical change. Moreover, it can hardly be assumed that Marx shared all facets of the later Engels' more rigorous materialism though, as mentioned, he was at least partially involved in some thought-processes that behind *Anti-Duhring*. There is scant evidence to indicate Marx viewed historical development in rigidly scientific terms consistent with Engels' later work – much less with Nicholai Bukharin's even stricter materialist sociology of the 1920s. In this realm as in others, what later became known as "scientific" theory, within and outside Marxism, turned out to be no more than rigorous pursuit of knowledge through well-grounded historical analysis, even where positivism served as something of a veneer. The much-celebrated "science of society" in effect amounted to meticulous efforts to identify and analyze broad tendencies of historical development – a mode of critical social theory.

One problem with stricter versions of materialist philosophy is that overwhelming focus on the objective (material) side of history must inevitably devalue the subjective side, viewed by Marx himself (and many later Marxists) as indispensable to revolutionary change. Without decisive political intervention – a realm of creative vision and action – it would be hard to imagine a process of far-reaching historical transformation. Longstanding debates over whether and to what degree a strict materialist approach can be attributed to Engels alone has served to obscure the main epistemological properties of classical Marxism. European social democracy, for its part, was for years divided between Kautsky's uncompromising materialism and Bernstein's "pragmatic" reformism, while Rosa

Luxemburg was usually identified with the "spontaneist," masses-make-history approach. Lenin, influenced by Plekhanov, initially embraced a scientific approach laid out in *Materialism and Empirio-Criticism*, then turned toward a praxis-oriented philosophy in the 1914–16 *Philosophical Notebooks* where he is said to have "rediscovered" Hegel. Leading architect of the Bolshevik Party and October Revolution, Lenin would naturally be inclined to valorize subjective intervention (later referred to as the "external element") as vital to transformative politics. Toward the end of his life, Lenin (and most other Bolsheviks) came to regard "dialectical materialism" as recipe for intellectual contemplation and political passivity – a distinctly conservative outlook. It would be Stalin, of course, who managed to bring "Diamat" into the realm of official Soviet ideology during the 1930s.[1]

The limits of scientific materialism become all the more evident once classical Marxism is situated in its historical period – the early decades of capitalist development. While the theory might have been endowed with elements of universality, even the brilliant Marx and Engels could never fully escape the limits of their era; they too were in definite ways products of the *Zeitgeist*. It is thus hardly coincidental that Saito's treatment of Marx revolves around categories of classical political economy – capital formation, commodity production, reification, exchange relations, and so forth. This makes sense as part of a meticulous effort to capture the central dynamics of Marx's thought, meaning Saito's treatment is appropriately historicized. Of course the world has changed beyond recognition since the mid-nineteenth century, a market-centered capitalism superseded long ago by a globalized system of corporate-state domination that would be unrecognizable to Marx and Engels. We have available no widely agreed-upon scientific methods – no rigorous "laws" – that could thoroughly analyze this historical change, much less the epochal political events of the twentieth century.

The contemporary world system, associated with advancing capitalist rationalization not to mention imperialism, wars, and revolutions, bursts the old categories of early capitalism that serve to delimit the scope of Marx's (and Saito's) work. These newer factors scarcely enter that classical panorama of concerns, understandable given the focus. Viewed thusly, scientific materialism obscures more than it illuminates, especially given the contours of historical disorder and lawlessness. Insofar as this is true, prospects for renewed ecological theorizing based on traditional categories would appear futile. The problem, once again, can hardly be laid at the doorstep of Marx and Engels, or even Kautsky and Plekhanov. Rather, the difficulty lies in strained efforts by "ecological Marx" proponents to scientifically legitimate claims of a new theoretical breakthrough. Viewed historically, therefore, theory (Marxist or otherwise) is bound to reflect the contours of its own time. In his dialectical synthesis of materialism and idealism, Marx himself formulated a philosophy of praxis sufficiently historicized to avoid certain pitfalls. Not so, unfortunately, for so many "heirs" of Marx. By late twentieth century the system of corporate globalization had already grown so concentrated, so expansive, so riddled with newer conflicts that more resonant categories of analysis would be obligatory.

Whatever its scientific claims, one can see how theory evolving within large-scale organizational settings can become ritualized, rendered more or less lifeless. Marxism itself has not been spared such pressures, a tendency long ago explored by Frankfurt School theorists, especially by Herbert Marcuse in his classic *Soviet Marxism*. Marcuse writes that the theory

> has undergone a significant change: it has been transformed from a mode of critical thought into a universal 'world outlook' and universal method with rigidly fixed rules and regulations, and this transformation destroys the dialectic more thoroughly than any revision. The change corresponds to that of Marxism itself from theory to ideology; dialectic is vested with the magical qualities of official thought and communication.

At this point Marxism "ceases to be the organon of revolutionary consciousness and practice and enters the superstructure of an established system of domination."[2]

In the West, the fate of twentieth-century Marxism has more or less mirrored the very trajectory of capitalist rationalization, shaped and re-reshaped by what is essential to it: science, technology, and bureaucracy. Any supposed "laws of development" here have little in common with capitalist tendencies emphasized within classical Marxist texts. This is not to suggest that Marx's theorization of capitalist political economy for his time – whatever its flaws – is to be judged as anything but superlative. By the late twentieth century, however, the steady expansion of corporate-state power, transnational institutions, and technological rationality would require altered categories of historical analysis.

Among newer concerns (leaving aside the ecological crisis) is the stupendous growth of military force, which dominates the global landscape at a time when resource wars are sure to intensify – a crisis and response pattern that in itself explodes the conceptual parameters of nineteenth-century Marxism. Capitalist rationalization in the U.S. has unleashed the destructive power of militarism and war, culminating more recently in sophisticated modes of technowar. Postwar U.S. military interventions have brought unspeakable carnage to the world, driven and legitimated by science and technology. Referring to the Vietnam debacle, James William Gibson writes: "War managers are at the top of the stratification system. They think in instrumental categories taken from technology and production systems, and the business accounting rationales of the debit and credit ... and had a virtual monopoly on socially-accepted 'scientific' knowledge."[3] As with the architects of Hiroshima and Nagasaki – and urban terror bombings in several countries – that "knowledge" would be fully detached from its unspeakable consequences.

Several decades ago, Horkheimer's seminal distinction between "traditional" and "critical" theory situated classical Marxism within the former, its passion for regularity, rigor, and lawlike tendencies resonant with the "given order of things." Such mechanistic thinking, in his view, could never grasp the chaotic, irregular, indeterminate elements of historical change – precisely what characterized so much of twentieth-century politics. The complex dynamics of social psychology, the point at which individuals engage society and history, was met by "traditional" theorists with some indifference, probably deemed beyond theoretical coherence owing to the often irrational, unpredictable character of that history. The more scientific (or *scientistic*) the framework, the more burdensome will be efforts to analyze historical events – one of several reasons the transfer of investigative methods from physical to social sciences was destined to fail.[4] The fact that Marx himself never succumbed to such pretenses did not, unfortunately, deter later disciples.

The Retrieval of Politics

For scientific materialists, the space for collective subjectivity (politics foremost) was something of an after-thought, largely peripheral. Their search for ironclad regularities in social behavior would have definite anti-political consequences, one reason Lenin chose to abandon his earlier materialist philosophy when what Georg Lukacs called the "actuality of revolution" gained momentum in Russia. Here Sheldon Wolin has more recently called attention to the innately "fugitive" character of politics – a realm given to the unsettled and unpredictable, resistant to established patterns.[5] Experience suggests that political action has rarely been theorized with precision, for that would clash with the typically multifaceted, unstable features of historical change. No one has yet discovered a "political science" reliable enough to determine what truths might be valid across widely-diverse historical periods or ideological viewpoints, and Marxism is no exception. The standpoint of objectivity or neutrality cannot be sustained in a context where knowledge is accrued through selective criteria of focus and interpretation. In Wolin's words: "Perforce, a political theory is among many other things a sum of judgments shaped by the theorist's notion of what matters, and embodying a series of discriminations about where one province begins and another leaves off."[6] There is no convincing reason why Marxism should be exempt from such propositions.

   Kindred arguments were put forward decades ago within Marxism itself, most systematically by Gramsci. In re-framing Marx's original philosophy of praxis, Gramsci turned his attention to the nexus history-philosophy-politics that he contrasted with the more fashionable materialism of his day, identified first with the Russian Plekhanov and the Italian Marxist Amadeo Bordiga and later with Soviet theorist Bukharin, greatly praised by Foster. In the *Prison Notebooks* Gramsci attacked such materialism as both philosophically and politically constricted, a source of intellectual detachment. His work turned to an emphasis on historicism, since "The philosophy of an historical epoch is nothing other than the 'history' of that epoch itself ...," here revealing the influence of Benedetto Croce and Italy's first Marxist, Antonio Labriola.[7] To properly engage Marxism, it too would have to be historicized to avoid schematic or ritualized formulations.

In Gramsci's case, the philosophy of praxis captured a revolutionary impulse he regarded as fundamental to Marxist politics. Trans-historical generalizations, abstract regularities, and rigorous "laws," he argued, have validity only under conditions of mass disempowerment and political stasis. Thus: "It should be observed that political action tends precisely to rouse the masses from passivity, in other words to destroy the laws of large numbers."[8] Elsewhere Gramsci frames Marxism as a theoretical structure with special temporal relevance, in the form of "absolute historicism."[9] Put differently: "Separated from the theory of history and politics philosophy cannot be other than metaphysics ...."[10] Here Gramsci in effect proceeded to turn the scientific materialism of Engels, Plekhanov, and Bukharin on its head, dismissing it as a newer form of "metaphysics."

Proponents of a "scientific" Marx grounded in dialectical materialism are usually dismissive of "Western Marxists" like Gramsci and Lukacs, owing to their ostensible distance from the real world of political activity – a criticism likewise directed at theorists of the Frankfurt School. In the case of Gramsci, however, the charge is entirely misplaced: in his early years Gramsci was a leading activist in the Italian Socialist party, then was an influential theorist of the factory-council movement before co-founding the Italian Communist Party (PCI), serving as parliamentary deputy, and spending the last decade of his life in fascist prisons. This biographical reference is meaningful insofar as it contradicts the longstanding fiction that a critique of strict materialism implies a form of religious or spiritual resignation.

Marxism in History

Traversing the modern historical terrain, it seems worth revisiting the question as to whether Marxist theory can be a source of oppositional politics for the twenty-first century. Such questions, we know, were posed long ago for the *twentieth* century. Does the more recent case for an "ecological Marx," for example, have resonance for an era of deepening global crisis? Earlier Marxism in its multiple variants did, of course, help shape the rise of movements, unions, parties, and governments in Europe and beyond, though increasingly with limited anti-system potential. That rich intellectual heritage continues to this day, within artistic circles, universities, and media culture especially in the West. In deradicalized form, it continues to provide ideological legitimacy for such regimes as China, Vietnam, Cuba, and North Korea.

A Marxism of sorts first emerged in the period spanning the 1840s to 1870s, then reached its heyday between the 1880s and 1920s, crucial to the rise of both Second (Socialist) and Third (Communist) Internationals. In some ways a mirror reflection of early capitalism, Marxism was widely understood in terms of its imputed universality and scientificity. Yet the main analytical focus of traditional Marxism – competitive markets, commodity production, proletarian expansion, intensifying class conflict – would eventually lose political relevance in an age of merging corporate and state interests, oligarchic rule, militarization, technological rationality, and more pervasive forms of ideological hegemony. The modern behemoth would be reinforced by sweeping globalization – not only in the economy, but in politics, culture, technology, and communications. Meanwhile, the post-World War II era witnessed unimpeded growth of the U.S. superpower, an imperial Leviathan with hundreds of military bases scattered across the globe, launching pad for perpetual wars, and armed with enough nuclear weapons to destroy the planet many times over.

In the years after World War I anti-system politics already began to experience crisis and decline – whether for labor movements, local councils, social movements, political parties, or international organizations. Revolutionary optimism that had infused the first decades of the twentieth century started to wane, thanks in part to the rise of fascism and social democracy, not to mention Stalinism. By the end of the century, it could be said that Marxism no longer presented a threat to capitalism anywhere on the planet. Despite a range of endemic dysfunctions, contradictions, and crises, modern state-capitalism is today probably stronger than ever, seemingly immune to direct overthrow. Hardly anyone in the twenty-first century believes the famous economic crisis-tendencies of capitalism will pave the way toward socialism – though crisis-tendencies, of a different sort, do indeed persist.

Given such reality, obvious questions arise – among them, whether a deterioration of Marxist *politics* might stem from the kind of scientific claims we have come to associate with the portrait of classical Marxism. What might be the efficacy of a materialist philosophy like that embraced by ecological Marxism at a time when distinctly *political* hopes appear so remote? Facing the specter of obsolescence, where does a conceptual paradigm rooted in the very distant past achieve certitude in the face of an unprecedented, complex, rapidly moving global crisis? My conclusion, evident from arguments presented so far, is that Marxism has become so theoretically marginal that hopes for its revival in the face of ecological crisis are now best regarded as illusory.

The Marxist tradition – notably that tendency nearest the classics, to scientific materialism – has been a poor guide to the most consequential developments and events of twentieth-century politics, and beyond. As noted, it has long been commonplace that the Bolshevik Revolution violated central precepts of Marxist theory that preceded it, despite later adoption of the "Marxist-Leninist" label by the Soviet and other Communist regimes. The Russian success was not widely anticipated, much less predicted, by Marxists at the time. Following the Bolshevik conquest of power, Gramsci wrote his seminal "Revolution against *Capital*," referring to an historical moment made possible more by imperialism and war rather than the "lifeless facts" of political economy. The work of Marx and

Engels, it turned out, had in reality less to offer Lenin and the Bolsheviks than is commonly believed. For Gramsci, a real living revolution in Russia collided with old theoretical schemas, however elaborate and rigorous. Those schemas allowed no room for socialist insurrection in countries that had not yet experienced capitalist industrialization, and Russia was still largely a peasant society, with no liberal-democratic politics until World War I. But historical events ultimately proved more decisive, more powerful than even the most sophisticated conceptual paradigms.[11]

Drawn to Lenin despite involvement in the Turin factory-council movement, Gramsci already by 1918 saw advantages in a vanguard party that could orchestrate epic historical change. No doubt Lenin's Jacobinism brought to Gramsci' mind the rich Italian legacy of Machiavelli and *The Prince*.[12] The party functioned not only as mechanism for seizing state power, but as vehicle of mass mobilization – neither concern rigorously addressed within classical Marxism. In Russia, of course, capitalism was both poorly developed and mostly foreign, meaning that revolutionary change would have to proceed against the main contours of *Capital* and the world it reflected, against what Gramsci called a "book of the bourgeoisie." He wrote: "Why should they [Russians] wait for the history of England to be repeated in Russia?, adding: "History is not a math calculation; it does not possess a decimal system, a progressive enumeration of equal quantities ...."[13] In the end, despite all the inflated claims of Engels, Kautsky, Plekhanov, and (in Italy) Bordiga, actual historical forces ended up sweeping aside "every pre-established schema."[14]

By virtue of his searing critique of the nexus economism/spontaneism, Lenin was able to "solve" the problem of revolutionary consciousness left open by the Marxist classics. The focus, as noted, was on what Lukacs would later refer to as the "actuality of the revolution" – that is, a sharp turn toward the subjective element of historical change. Strict theoretical formulas were disdained as a path toward ideological passivity and political inertia.[15] Since there were few compelling insights from Marx and Engels as to how oppositional class solidarity was expected to develop, Lenin's stark response was that spontaneous mass behavior, under conditions of bourgeois rule, could never escape its own social immediacy. Socialism would in fact be the repository of revolutionary intellectuals who, taking the initiative against a suffocating power structure, would furnish the badly-needed "external element" as political vanguard. Wrote Lukacs after the Bolshevik Revolution: "The Leninist party concept represents the most radical break with the mechanistic and fatalistic vulgarization of Marxism."[16] (The great Hungarian theorist of class consciousness would himself come around to Leninism in the years following the Bolshevik Revolution.)

It turned out that classical Marxism would have little to say about the most dramatic events of the twentieth century: several Communist revolutions, rise of fascism, the growth of imperialism and militarism, two world wars, the phenomenon of corporate globalization. As for the Bolshevik Revolution, it opened up a new revolutionary phase at the juncture of imperialism, wars, Jacobin politics, the ascendancy of state power – a juncture well beyond the scope of Marx and Engels. The October events were a product of richly complex variables, not least being decisive intervention of a vanguard party. Contrary to any widely accepted "laws" of historical transformation, Lenin and the Bolsheviks set about reordering society on their own terms, relying heavily on instruments of political organization and state power.

Contrary to facile generalizations about capitalism (e.g., the "falling rate of profit"), the variables here were multiple, rapidly changing, global, somewhat unpredictable. Commenting on the Russian events, E. H. Carr wrote: "It would have been an astonishing anomaly if that revolution, far removed in time and space from anything Marx knew, had conformed in detail to the prescriptions of classical Marxism."[17] Bolshevik exploits conformed more closely to Lenin's *What is to be Done?* and other writings than to anything Marx wrote in *Capital* or indeed any other text. Lenin himself eventually had no problem with such an assessment. Writing in *Left-Wing Communism*, after the revolution, he reflected: "History as a whole, and the history of revolutions in particular, is always richer in content, more varied, more multi-form, more lively and ingenious than is imagined by even the best parties, the most class-conscious vanguards of the most advanced classes."[18]

One can go further: revolutionary change by definition invites chaos, disruption, and uncertainty under circumstances where the lives of millions of people overturned – their habits, routines, and expectations altered, probably forever. That was emphatically the case in Russia, a pattern roughly duplicated by later twentieth-century Communist upheavals. Writing in *The Proletarian Revolution and the Renegade Kautsky*, Lenin asked: "Are there historical laws governing revolution which know of no exceptions? No, no such law exist. These laws only apply to what is typical, to what Marx once termed the ideal, in the sense of an average, normal, typical capitalism."[19] (There has never been anything resembling a "typical capitalism.") Most of all, Lenin was a great believer in creative, even Promethean intervention – a dreamer, romantic, utopian, adventurer – in the service of revolution.

The Problem of Revolution

In reality Leninism marked not so much a "vulgarization" of Marx as a process of *overturning*, or negating, crucial tenets of the theory, as Gramsci had forcefully argued. What earlier theorists had not seen, according to Lukacs, was the dramatic historical (and political) impact of imperialism and war, not only for Russia but across the world. This pivotal insight would have its validity repeated across later decades, transforming geopolitics forever. Leninism was decisive for insurrectionary politics across the twentieth century, a mechanism of party-state governance strong enough leverage to destroy the old centers of power. They were all to some degree "revolutions against *Capital*": Russia, China, Yugoslavia, Vietnam, Cuba. All succeeded in an historical context of imperialism, war, and popular struggles against foreign occupation.[20] Mass energies were galvanized by an intense nationalism that politicized not only workers but peasants, the middle strata, and other groups, forming a social bloc. Once state power was won, Leninist elites were able to pursue twin interwoven objectives: national independence and economic modernization, first visible in the Soviet path charted during the 1920s. Those objectives made sense in countries that were not yet industrialized, a *reversal* of classical Marxism under conditions where the primacy of economics gave way to the primacy of politics.

If Marxism oddly never served as much of a guide to revolutionary politics, the theory would lose even more relevance to those (post-capitalist) societies over time. The broad trajectory was either bureaucratic centralism (the USSR, North Korea) or some variant of state-capitalism (Yugoslavia, China, Vietnam). While elites adopted "Marxism-Leninism" as legitimating doctrine for maturing Communist regimes, that ideology bore little resemblance to actual development much less basic categories of Marxist theory. The process of ideological ritualization went so far in the Soviet Union – became so detached from historical reality – as to eventually contribute to regime collapse in 1991. Since the Cuban events of 1959–60, when agrarian revolt rapidly turned Communist, there has been no revolution akin to those mentioned above, an expanse of fully six decades. More telling, there have been no victorious proletarian revolutions in any advanced capitalist society – indeed nothing close.

As for working-class upsurges in any setting, only *four* have achieved what might be considered revolutionary potential: Italy in 1919–20, Spain in 1936–39, Italy during World War II, Poland in the early 1980s (directed against *Communist* rule). In fact only the first Italian case – the great postwar *Biennio Rosso* uprisings – would broadly fit the conventional Marxist idea of proletarian revolt against capitalist power, which failed exactly one century ago owing to its geographical (and political) isolation. That failure would be followed by the world's first fascist conquest of power, which had revealed the very uneven level of class consciousness among northern Italian workers.[21] Across Europe since World War II, labor movements have generally supported unions, parties, and (both local and national) governments that have uniformly experienced deradicalization.

If years of warfare gave rise to mass insurgency in Italy during 1919–20, similar conditions materialized toward the end of World War II, cradle of the anti-Nazi Resistance movement. As in the case of Leninist revolutions, this was a multiclass "historical bloc" (Gramsci's term) mobilized around strong nationalist appeals, usually led by Socialists and Communists. Between 1942 and 1945 the Italian Communists grew from a pre-war nucleus of perhaps five thousand militants to a major political force with over 2 million members and control of several large cities and provinces. Partisan forces across the country were incited by very conditions that had prevailed in Russia, China, and these other cases. None could be explained within a Marxist framework.

For the history of proletarian upheavals as such, the record since the *Biennio Rosso* has been dismal, while even that episode is frequently lamented as "the revolution that failed." The overall trajectory of decline can be situated partly within the relentless process of capitalist rationalization, less a function of leadership betrayal, working-class "immaturity," or "labor aristocracy." The momentous growth (and convergence) of corporate and state power, the bureaucratization of society, and enlarged forms of ideological hegemony have bolstered elite power, institutionalized class conflict, and reinforced political legitimation throughout Europe and beyond. Further, with heightened rationalization and globalization has come political decline of the working class in both numbers and leverage, above all within advanced capitalism.

While Marxism in scholastic form retains appeal to intellectual groups in the West and elsewhere, in both theory and practice it no longer represents even a slight threat to capitalist power. The capitalism described by Marx – and faithfully reconstructed by Saito – featured commodity production, market relations, expanding proletariat, limited state power, and relatively feeble ideological controls. Weber's emphasis on state-corporate domination, technological rationality, and bureaucratization of public life far better captured the twentieth-century developmental pattern. Attention to a newer ruling-elite capacity to build a durable apparatus of domination was foundational to the work not only of Weber but (in different ways) of Gramsci, the Austro-Marxists, and so-called "elite theorists" (Michels, Pareto, Mosca), all to varying degrees influenced by Weber. That influence would extend to the later work of Mills in *The Power Elite*, where he brilliantly combined Weberian and Marxist approaches. None of these theorists, however, dealt systematically with the problem of globalization and the ways it served to expand capitalist power and weaken political opposition. To the extent this was the case, one cannot but wonder how the problem of globalization would profoundly alter a body of theory so thoroughly shaped by nineteenth-century capitalism.

It bears repeating that sources and dynamics of revolutionary consciousness were never adequately explored by Marx or Engels. It could be that for the Marxist classics this problem would somehow get "solved" through the very dialectics of historical transformation – a premise that, as we have seen, could not be sustained. What then? Lenin (Jacobinism) and Bernstein (reformism) would develop their own competing solutions at the dawn of the twentieth century, others joining the strategic debate later. None, however, would ultimately find much theoretical solace in earlier Marxist writings. Where crucial political questions were left unattended, there could be no meaningful revolutionary theory. That would turn out to be yet another implication of Gramsci's "Revolution against *Capital*": the texts as such contained nothing very helpful about the social psychology of consciousness formation, much less the organizational and strategic requirements for winning state power.

It might seem puzzling that neither Marx nor Engels, dedicated socialists, ever arrived at a theory of revolutionary politics, but that is indeed the case. One difficulty was the very fragmented character of their work on topics related to politics and the state, which in any case the theorists had devalued as "superstructure" relative to the economic "base." That could at least partly account for their meager interest in processes whereby those most exploited might arrive at psychological rejection of the status quo – meaning a traumatic break with long-established patterns of social and individual life. We have seen that Lenin believed workers could never develop class consciousness when left to their own resources, needing a particularly robust "external element" to lift them out of bourgeois ideology. Confined to everyday economic demands, the proletariat would never get beyond a path of limited reforms. Revolutionary politics, on the other hand, would depend on the organizational and ideological coherence of a fighting party. In this Lenin discovered a vital historical truth: class consciousness would never arise from organic, local, spontaneous activity, nor would it result from the unfolding of "objective" historical forces. Lenin's epic departure from classical Marxism would be taken up (and further elaborated) by Gramsci and a few other Marxists of the Third International – a point of departure, as noted, for twentieth-century Communist revolutions.

For both Lenin and Gramsci, the episodic and unpredictable ("fugitive") moments of historical change, marked by a cycle of response and counter-response, was more decisive than any conceivable "laws" of development. Class consciousness would be formed within an ensemble of psychological attitudes, feelings, and beliefs, most keenly aroused at times of social turmoil and political breakdown, Gramsci famously writing that "history sweeps aside every pre-established schema."[22]

If Marx had been able to critically analyze the broad patterns of nineteenth-century capitalism, his theory paid little attention to subjective elements of change, whatever his critical insights here and there. On the one hand, Marx looked to the steady expansion of an oppressed, alienated proletariat whose very life-conditions would generate anti-capitalist consciousness, a step toward the transition to socialism. Widening contradictions of an economic system that could never satisfy general material needs, one that perpetuates alienation and opposition, would sooner or later give rise to (both objective *and* subjective) revolutionary forces. Mass consciousness itself never seemed much of a priority insofar as it was thought to be a natural outgrowth of intensifying class conflict. Here Marx's *political* outlook suffered from the hindrance of a simple rationalist psychology, where material self-interest would be seamlessly translated into anti-capitalist attitudes and beliefs. We know from abundant historical evidence, however, that mass politics rarely follows such rationalist premises.

Marx thus never arrived at an understanding of how workers might become active (collective) subjects or agents of history – how alienation might be overcome. References to a future socialist society do not suffice. This very question was faced head on by Lenin and Gramsci, as they addressed the imperatives of revolutionary action. That void in classical Marxism as it evolved following

Marx's death was partly a function of scientific materialism that, for Europe at least, would become the burdensome legacy of Engels and Kautsky, the same legacy that would be resurrected decades later by advocates of a new scientific Marxism. The political outlook shared by Lenin and Gramsci addressed the issue of ideological domination that Gramsci would later define in the *Prison Notebooks* as "hegemony": the role of religion, education, and culture in sustaining ruling-class legitimacy.[23] That legitimacy, as historical experience shows, allows even shaky power structures to survive grave economic crises and even wars. Over the past century, of course, mechanisms of ideological control available to capitalist elites (notably in media and communications) have expanded beyond anything imagined by Lenin or Gramsci. For that same period, Weber foresaw that capitalist rationalization would likely contain insurgent consciousness and subvert radical politics. Gramsci too understood this process fully, laid out in his oft-overlooked essay "Americanism and Fordism" in the *Notebooks*.[24] Concentrated power would enlarge organizational and ideological controls across public life, most emphatically in the expanding Fordist (Taylorized) workplace. As workers and others come under the influence of hegemonic norms, beliefs, and laws, their social individuality yields to relentless conformist pressures.

Gramsci's Jacobinism

The problem of revolutionary politics within Marxist theory deserves far more attention than it has generally received. Here it is worth considering how twentieth-century thinkers (Marxists and others) managed to fill a void in the Marxist classics regarding consciousness formation and, by extension, *political* conditions of an expected transition from capitalism to socialism. From Lenin to Gramsci, from Lukacs to Marcuse, the verdict concerning a potential class-conscious proletariat in the West has been typically bleak: capitalist development, in whatever setting, meant subordination of workers to class domination – a conclusion at odds with Marx's well-known optimism. Many decades after Marx and Engels passed from the scene, that problem for Marxists would remain and even deepen.

Lenin's argument, mostly taken for granted by later generations of Communists, stressed that the power elite would always have the upper hand "for the simple reason that bourgeois ideology is far older in origin than socialist ideology, that it is more fully developed, and that it has at its disposal *immeasurably* more means of dissemination."[25] While classical Marxism had emphasized the organic (or spontaneous) element of workplace struggles, Lenin (against prevailing Social-Democratic opinion) assigned Promethean importance to a radical intelligentsia, drawing on its unique tradition in Russia.

Given his lack of faith in proletarian self-activity, Lenin turned to an organization of professional cadres – a decidedly non-Marxist repository of socialist consciousness. Leninism would soon enough have its well-known authoritarian consequences – and of course its critics, starting with prominent Mensheviks such as Peter Struve and the eminent Plekhanov, later including the radicals Rosa Luxemburg and Anton Pannekoek, both dedicated to mass spontaneity. Among Lenin's harsher critics of the period was Jan Waclaw Machajski, convinced the Bolsheviks constituted the origins of a "new class" of intellectuals aiming to channel popular energies toward industrialization under a contrived (socialist) banner. As for the workers, still bereft of self-activity, they would go on being exploited and controlled by another ruling elite.[26]

What favored a revolutionary outcome for Lenin was large-scale organization, built on command principles, creative leadership, coherent ideology, a strategy for winning state power. Machajski's thesis, on the other hand, happened to finally converge with Weber's thesis of capitalist rationalization, which fixated on the expanding role of government, bureaucracy, and technology integral to modern European economies. Ironically, at the very moment Lenin and the Bolsheviks were drawn to organizational politics, American capitalism (driven by auto assembly-line production) was introducing tighter structural controls in the form of Taylorized scientific management.

Weberian theory would have considerable influence across succeeding decades – first among the "elite theorists" and Austro-Marxists, then among Frankfurt School intellectuals (notably Marcuse) and the later work of Mills. Even Gramsci, as noted, bore the imprint of Weber. Michels, as we have seen, called attention to the innately conservative pressures of large-scale organization, visible during his own time for its anti-democratic impact on unions, parties, and governments. The German Social-Democratic Party (SPD) that Michels studied was just as vulnerable as any other – its entrenched leadership able to take advantage of the psychological "incompetence of the masses," a motif that in the end differed little from Lenin's "ideological enslavement" argument. Wrote Michels in 1911: "Political organization leads to power. But power is always conservative."[27] And: "Thus the majority of human beings, in a condition of eternal tutelage, are predestined by tragic necessity to submit to domination by a small minority, and must be content to constitute the pedestal of an oligarchy."[28] Even the most determined oppositional forces, it turned out, would likely wind up assimilated into the process of capitalist rationalization.

While Gramsci's view of ideological hegemony called attention to the *general* capacity of ruling elites to legitimate their rule through a mix of cultural traditions and ideological discourses, less well known was his more Weberian focus on Fordist control of the capitalist workplace. "Hegemony," Gramsci argued, "is born in the factory," noting that Fordism develops to the point where it "succeeds in making the whole life of the nation revolve around production," leaving the masses in a state of alienation and disempowerment – the focus here on "production" over "commodities," worth noting. He wrote: "In America rationalization has determined the need to elaborate a new type of man suited to the new type of work and productive process." That "new type of work" was typically suited to the "trained gorilla" of Fordist lore.[29] In another twist of irony,

Lenin had (in the years after the revolution) grown fascinated with Taylorism and its Soviet equivalent known as "*edinonachalia*," or one-man management.

During this same period Lukacs, in *History and Class Consciousness*, sought a different line of argumentation, looking to resuscitate Marx's fetishism of commodities through the concept of reification. Marx, it will be recalled, wrote in *Capital* that the commodity process intrinsic to capitalism had become fetishized as it transforms relations between humans, between humans and nature, into relations between objects. Capitalism degrades humans into the status of objects while objects as such acquire human attributes. Insofar as bourgeois society matures into a system fully dependent on objects (and also objective laws), those engaged in the labor process lose any sense of self, their collective subjectivity and autonomy – and finally, their psychological capacity for revolutionary action. Capitalist development would forever be shrouded in ideological mystification. For Marx, as noted, no concept of transcendence is forthcoming – thus no identifiable (subjective) exit from the existing order of things.

Lukacs provocatively took up this motif at a time when Gramsci and others were departing from the classic texts. It seems the Hungarian theorist wanted to deepen Marx's fixation on commodities – notably their mystifying consequences for the proletariat – while simultaneously looking for a way out, ultimately arriving at Leninism. At a time when capitalism was entering its rationalized (or state-capitalist) phase across Europe, Lukacs opted for the motif of "universally-dominant commodities," where the "fate of the worker becomes the fate of capitalism as a whole."[30] (Here Lukacs anticipates Karl Polanyi's 1944 classic *The Great Transformation*, where marketization permeates and defines capitalist society.) This familiar over-emphasis on markets, sometimes mythologized into "free markets" or "market fundamentalism," had been effectively countered by Weberian theory.[31] Writing in 1923, Lukacs argued that, "for the first time in history the whole of society is subjected ... to a unified economic process, and the fate of every member of society is determined by unified laws."[32] In other words, the proletariat was subjected to such crushing (apparently lawlike) ideological domination, that no exit seemed possible – that is, until the heroic Leninist party comes to the rescue.

Against a background of class strife and political turbulence, Gramsci saw ideological contestation – and overcoming spontaneism – a cornerstone of revolutionary change, Chantal Mouffe writing: "Antonio Gramsci must be the first theorist to have undertaken a complete and radical critique of economism, and it is here that the main contribution to the Marxist theory of ideology lies."[33] Gramsci, as we have seen, followed Lenin's devastating critique of economism, Lenin having argued that a theory so crippled (as in the case of Bernstein along with the Russian Mensheviks) would severely narrow the range of political action. Both Lenin and Gramsci nurtured their revolutionary outlooks in the tracks of earlier anti-system intellectuals – Herzen, Chernyshevsky, and Nechaev in Russia, Labriola in Italy.[34] Those outlooks retained a sharp distinction between revolution and reform, socialism and liberalism.

One lesson to be retrieved from the legacy of Lenin and Gramsci – indeed from history itself – is that revolutionary change usually occurs in defiance of rigorous schemas. Their work signaled a sharp turn from the theoretical primacy of economics, a shift generally associated with the Comintern that both Lenin and Gramsci helped establish in 1919. They believed, credibly enough at the time, that without a vanguard party socialism would forever remain a utopian ideal. (Contrary to received wisdom, the autocratic Tsarist system that Lenin and the Bolsheviks faced offered considerably *less* political challenge than would be the case for later corporate-state power structures.) Distinctly national groups, movements, and parties would likely remain isolated or confined to reformist initiatives, where in fact they were not crushed and defeated, as in Italy. Reformism could secure better wages and social conditions, but on the larger political terrain would be easily neutralized. It was also likely that workers and their allies would be less willing to pursue risky, disruptive anti-system change – a chasm the Bolshevik leadership was perfectly ready to fill. Many decades after Lenin and Gramsci passed from the scene, at a time of worsening ecological crisis, it seems worth asking whether such a political strategy – in effect a revolution from above – could make sense when life and death for billions of people might hang in the balance.

At this juncture the old Marxist notion of imputed revolutionary consciousness falls well short of the urgent political challenges faced by humanity. In their provocative book *Climate Leviathan*, Geoff Mann and Joel Wainwright call for radical departure from political normalcy, even where few viable counter-forces are present. They write: "On political and existential grounds … the left needs a strategy – a political theory, one might say – for how to think about the future."[35] One crucial factor is that ideological legacies inherited from the past appear exhausted: Communism, social democracy, liberalism, anarchism. As for liberalism, it now serves mainly to legitimate capitalist power, while social democracy has never systematically (or radically) taken up ecological politics. Communism, such as it is, remains far too closely identified with extreme authoritarian power grown increasingly bureaucratic and conservative to be taken seriously as an alternative.

In the seemingly forgotten lexicon of Lenin and Gramsci, an answer might be found in political mechanisms strong enough to dispatch ruling elites and launch an ecological path forward – that is, a return to some kind of "external element," or vanguard force, with a strategic eye on state power. That could be a future wellspring of radicalized *mass* opposition, not its substitute. Jacobinism suggests, now as before, an historic revitalization of politics. Mann and Wainwright argue that their version of "sovereign" is congruent with an already hyper-globalized order, the ecological crisis itself being of course planetary in scope.

The discussion of Jacobinism has a long – sometimes confusing – history within (and outside) the Marxist tradition. For Marx himself, the reference invoked fearsome images of dictatorship, conspiratorial activity, even terrorism – more than anything, abject failure. By imposing a "political solution" on civil society, it subverted the organic flow of historical forces and recalled the disaster of Bonapartism during the French Revolution. Jacobinism came to signify an authoritarian politics that was either dangerous or illusory, a trap ensnaring Marx's contemporary Louis Blanqui (and the League of Communists). Blanqui, like Bonaparte, was ready to force a political revolution before its time, side-stepping the need for sustained mass radicalization. Here the supposed futility of Jacobinism turned on its addiction to state power, which soon enough would become a tyrannical end in itself.

Viewed differently, Jacobinism can be located within an epic expression of social (and ecological) transformation centrally reliant on state power – that is, revolution both from above and below. Historically, this type of revolution required definite conditions for success: wartime chaos, struggle against foreign enemies, collapse of elite legitimacy, a tightly organized revolutionary opposition, coherent ideological direction, multi-class social mobilization. In its Leninist expression, overthrow of the established order took place only in countries that had not yet undergone advanced levels of industrialization, starting with Russia. Contrary to Marx, however, Jacobinism in these settings generally won state power not through a Bonapartist coup but required popular mobilization – witness Yugoslavia, China, Vietnam. There is reason to believe that any modern-day "Climate Jacobin" could advance only through such a "national-popular" force, to use Gramsci's reference, given the more complex structure of advanced capitalism.

Marx's view, as we have seen, affirmed the primacy of economics – the approach later stood on its head by Lenin and Gramsci. Their Jacobinism self-consciously avoided that label but embraced its central meaning: the primacy of politics, revolutionary mobilization, an eye toward state power. Across the twentieth century, it turns out, historical development would in crucial ways work against Marx and for the equivalent of Jacobinism – for better or worse. Among changing realities, it is no longer true that the political apparatus of capitalist society is a simple manifestation of the economy, if indeed that was ever the case. For most societies, state power has its own historical logic, its own center of gravity – reinforced by the stupendous growth of military power, intelligence networks, and surveillance operations. This is no mere "superstructure." At the same time, if the state constitutes its own expanded nucleus of power, for industrialized societies we have also seen a tightening merger of corporate, state, and military interests along lines theorized by Mills in *The Power Elite*.

Nothing within twentieth-century conditions would call forth emphasis on a proletarian revolution, scientific materialism, sustained economic growth, or theoretical focus on primacy of economics factors. The biggest unresolved question today, as before, is one of *political strategy* – and here, as we have seen, too the classical Marxist texts offer little inspiration or guidance. Gramsci, in the final reckoning, did adopt his own particular variant of Jacobinism (despite his frequent attacks on "Bonapartism" or "Ceasarism") – a strategy influenced by his local council experience and his later emphasis on counter-hegemonic, or "national-popular," revolution.[36] By virtue of the Italian setting, moreover, his Jacobinism was more strategically oriented to the structural and ideological complexities of advanced capitalism, in ways intended to avoid the authoritarian pitfalls of Soviet politics – pitfalls that, by the 1930s, Gramsci had come to recognize within the *Prison Notebooks*.

Gramsci's well-known Jacobinism in the *Notebooks* derived much of its inspiration from the classic writings of Machiavelli, dubbed the "first Jacobin" as Gramsci transformed "The Prince" into "The Modern Prince." For Gramsci, the idea of creative political leadership associated with Machiavelli was to "arouse and organize a collective will of shattered, dispersed people" – a mythical leadership that could be the "protagonist of a real and effective historical drama."[37] One function of such a political force, resonant theme across Italian history, would be to create broad ideological consensus against a backdrop of social fragmentation and conflict. Thus: "An effective Jacobin force was always missing [in Italy] and it was precisely such a Jacobin force which in other nations awakened and organized the national-popular collective will, and founded modern states."[38] In his final reading, Gramsci saw in Machiavelli's "precocious Jacobinism a germ of national revolution" – in the modern context, meaning transition to socialism.[39]

It would be foolish here to expect an ironclad guarantee against the kind of statism that deformed Communist regimes after the 1920s, but that risk must in the final calculus be weighed against the specter of ecological calamity. We know that the Marxist tradition has greatly enhanced critical understanding of early capitalism. The theoretical debt to Marx and Engels cannot be overstated, but for the contemporary setting it remains sharply limited. As we enter the third decade of the twenty-first century, the theory – whatever its scientific claims – falls rather short in terms of both historical analysis and political vision. A thriving ecosocialism, whether in a Jacobin or some other framework, will have to confront a wide panorama of urgent challenges, including the ever-present dangers of imperialism and militarism, if anything resembling a worldwide "green agenda" is to be achieved. Whatever the strategy, a vigorous revitalization of politics will be the *sine qua non* of planetary survival in an era when the ecological crisis has so far eluded decisive human intervention, above all in the U.S. and other modern capitalist societies.

Notes

1 For an excellent discussion of Stalin's theoretical shifts and turns, see T. H. Rigby, ed., *Stalin* (New York: Prentice Hall, 1966).
2 Herbert Marcuse, *Soviet Marxism* (New York: Vintage Books, 1956), p. 122.
3 James William Gibson, *The Perfect War* (New York: Atlantic Monthly, 1986), p. 462.
4 Max Horkheimer, "Critical and Traditional Theory," in *Critical Theory: Selected Essays* (New York: Continuum, 1972), p. 216.

5 Sheldon Wolin, "The Epic Tradition of Political Theory," in Nicholas Xenos, ed., *Sheldon S. Wolin: Fugitive Democracy and Other Essays* (Princeton, NJ: Princeton University Press, 2016), p. 108.
6 Wolin, "Political Theory as a Vocation," in Xenos, *Fugitive Democracy*, p. 23.
7 Antonio Gramsci, "The Study of Philosophy," in Quintin Hoare and Geoffrey Nowell Smith, eds., *Selections from the Prison Notebooks of Antonio Gramsci* [hereafter *SPN*] (New York: International Publishers, 1971), p. 345.
8 Antonio Gramsci, "Problems of Marxism," in *SPN*, p. 430.
9 Ibid., p. 465.
10 Ibid., p. 436.
11 Antonio Gramsci, "The Revolution against *Capital*," in Quintin Hoare, ed., *Antonio Gramsci: Selections from Political Writings* (New York: International Publishers, 1977), p. 34.
12 Antonio Gramsci, "The Modern Prince," in *SPN*, pp. 125–136.
13 Antonio Gramsci, "The Russian Utopia," in *Selections*, p. 48.
14 Antonio Gramsci, "The Conquest of the State," in *Selections*, p. 76.
15 Georg Lukacs, *Lenin* (Cambridge, MA: MIT Press, 1971), p. 70.
16 Lukacs, *Lenin*, p. 31.
17 E. H. Carr, *The October Revolution* (New York: Vintage Books, 1969), p. 164.
18 V. I. Lenin, "Left Wing Communism: An Infantile Disorder," in Robert C. Tucker, ed., *The Lenin Anthology* (New York: W. W. Norton, 1975), p. 611.
19 V. I. Lenin, *The Proletarian Revolution and the Renegade Kautsky* (New York: International Publishers, 1934), 21.
20 See Eric Wolf, *Peasant Wars of the Twentieth Century* (New York: Harper and Row, 1968).
21 See Paolo Spriano, *The Occupation of the Factories* (London: Pluto Press, 1964), ch. 10.
22 Gramsci, "The Revolution against *Capital*," in *Selections*, p. 36.
23 Antonio Gramsci, "State and Civil Society," in *SPN*, pp. 324–342.
24 Antonio Gramsci, "Americanism and Fordism," in *SPN*, pp. 277–319.
25 V. I. Lenin, "What is to be Done?," in *Lenin Anthology*, pp. 29–30.
26 Very little of Machajski's work, mostly completed the first decade of the twentieth century, has been translated into English. It did, however, lay the groundwork for later "new-class" theories. See the discussion in Richard Gombin, *The Radical Tradition* (London: Methuen and Co., 1978), pp. 65–69.
27 See Robert Michels, *Political Parties* (New Brunswick, NJ: Transaction Publishers, 1999), p. 333.
28 Ibid., p. 354.
29 Gramsci, "Americanism and Fordism," pp. 285–287.
30 Georg Lukacs, *History and Class Consciousness* (Cambridge, MA: MIT Press, 1968), pp. 90–91.
31 Karl Polanyi, *The Great Transformation* (Boston: Beacon Press, 1944).
32 Lukacs, *History*, p. 92.
33 See Chantal Mouffe, "Hegemony and Ideology in Gramsci," in Mouffe, ed., *Gramsci and Marxist Theory* (London: Routledge & Kegan Paul, 1979), p. 170.
34 On the great influence of nineteenth-century radical intellectuals on the development of Bolshevism, see Adam B. Ulam, *The Bolsheviks* (New York: Collier Books, 1965), chs. 2, 3.
35 Geoff Mann and Joel Wainwright, *Climate Leviathan* (London: Verso, 2018), p. 130.
36 See Antonio Gramsci, "The Modern Prince," in *SPN*, p. 130–133.
37 Ibid., p. 130.
38 Ibid., p. 131.
39 Ibid., p. 132.

4
AUTHORITARIAN STATE, MASS SOCIETY

In the decade or so following World War I, the Marxist emphasis shifted toward a confluence of two interconnected trends: authoritarian state and mass society. That motif would persist, in one form or another, well into the post-World War II era. The relentless growth of statism would reach its extremes in the rise of both fascism and Stalinism, one sign that liberal capitalism was under siege across Europe and beyond. Even social democracy, on the ascendancy in northern Europe, would embrace strong elements of authoritarian state power, reinforced by the integration of corporate and government sectors. While these trends were at odds with the expectations (or hopes) of classical Marxism, they would profoundly influence the work of both Western Marxists and Frankfurt School theorists from the late 1920s onward. Their contributions – and the very capitalist trajectory they mirrored – would point toward a steadily broadening system of domination far beyond what Marx and Engels could have theorized.

Sources of Domination

For Western Marxists, beginning with Lukacs and Gramsci, the system of domination characteristic of capitalist modernity relied increasingly on *ideological* forces – cultural traditions, nationalism, religion, mass media – visible in the European setting. In the case of fascism, domination rested on a confluence of corporatism, ultra-nationalism, and disparate cultural influences. As elite legitimation solidified, oppositional politics could be more easily neutralized or repressed, often without need for much direct institutional force. During the 1920s and 1930s, as fascism initially emerged in Italy, Germany, Spain, and parts of eastern Europe, capitalism strengthened its legitimacy through a complex network of social and ideological controls that concealed the real mechanisms of authoritarian power.

DOI: 10.4324/9781003197461-5

That conceptual shift within Marxism would be exemplified by Gramsci's theory of ideological hegemony, inspired not only by Leninism but by the philosophical legacy Antonio Labriola and Benedetto Croce in Italy. That emphasis would incorporate the sphere of the culture industry explored by Frankfurt School critics, then technological rationality in the work of Herbert Marcuse, both reflective of Weber's dark view of capitalist rationalization and, more generally, the Enlightenment. In the case of Gramsci's version of Western Marxism, the Italian theorist retained a certain (mostly long-range) optimism about socialist transformation in the West. Others – Karl Korsch, Lukacs, Wilhelm Reich, Marcuse – adopted what turned out to be a more pessimistic outlook. Much of this pessimism turned on a deep skepticism about the capacity of workers to develop revolutionary consciousness against the pressures of capitalist rationalization.

In the early 1920s Lukacs, starting with *History and Class Consciousness*, looked to refurbish Marx's fetishism of commodities through the concept of reification. Marx, it will be recalled, wrote in *Capital* that the commodity process embedded in capitalism had become fetishized, transforming relations between humans, as well as between humans and nature, into relations between objects. Capitalism turns human beings into objects while the objects as such acquire essential human attributes. Insofar as bourgeois society matures into a system fully dependent on objects (and objective laws), those engaged in the labor process lose any sense of self, deprived as they are of collective subjectivity and autonomy – and, finally, their psychological capacity for oppositional politics. Capitalist development would be forever shrouded in processes of ideological mystification. For Marx, as noted, no workable concept of transcendence was forthcoming – thus no identifiable (subjective) exit from the prevailing social order.

Lukacs provocatively took up this same motif at a time when Gramsci and other Marxists were questioning the classic texts. It seems the Hungarian theorist wanted to deepen the Marxist fixation on commodities – notably their stultifying consequences for the proletariat – while simultaneously looking for a way out, ultimately arriving at Leninism. At a time when capitalism was entering its more rationalized (state-capitalist) phase across Europe, Lukacs opted for a discourse of "universally-dominant commodities," where the "fate of the worker becomes the fate of capitalism as a whole."[1] (Here Lukacs anticipated Karl Polanyi's 1944 classic *The Great Transformation*, where marketization permeates and defines capitalist society.) This familiar over-emphasis on markets, later mythologized into "free markets" or "market fundamentalism," had in fact been effectively countered by Weberian theory.[2] Writing in 1923, Lukacs argued that "for the first time in history the whole of society is subjected ... to a unified economic process, and the fate of very member of society is determined by unified laws."[3] In other words, the proletariat was subjected to such crushing (apparently lawlike) ideological domination that no exit seemed possible – that is, until the heroic Leninist party came to the rescue.

The Lukacsian view of class consciousness was in fact consistent with the pessimistic strain of Western Marxism based on failed revolutionary opposition in Europe, the eclipse of "permanent revolution," and apparent capitalist stabilization – or was it the reverse? Frankfurt School theorists would soon enough explore the hegemonic power of capitalist rationalization, which some (Friedrich Pollack most notably) believed was leading toward a new order, state-capitalism. Others, including Marcuse, saw incipient "totalitarian" tendencies in liberal capitalism as early as the late 1920s. Assessing the (earlier) legacy of liberal capitalism, Marcuse could write: "This rough sketch of liberalist social theory has shown how many elements of the totalitarian view of the state are already present in it."[4] Were conditions associated with the rise of fascism in Italy, Germany, and Spain already being theorized?

By the 1930s, others (Gramsci, Horkheimer, Adorno) had begun to detect the growing influence of the "culture industry" on mass populations in the U.S. where the corporate media, along with its advertising sector, was on the ascendancy. None of these theorists apparently saw the need to emphasize commodity fetishism, being more likely drawn to Weberian themes of capitalist rationalization, cultural hegemony, and authoritarian state power. None, more significantly, were convinced that proletarian revolution in the West was on the immediate agenda. With the onset of fascism, moreover, anti-system movements and parties across Europe were mostly crushed, many simply vanishing from the scene.

The first casualty of new, more effective agencies of domination was the Western proletariat – more accurately, the efficacy of worker self-activity, now increasingly subordinated to the logic of large-scale organization and ideological hegemony. If prospects for class consciousness had been previously undermined by the enormous weight of bourgeois values and attitudes – as Lenin had been the first to realize –what could be expectations in the 1920s and 1930s when Fordism, statism, and deepening forms of ideological hegemony shaped the public landscape? How might the proletariat constitute a class agency by itself, for itself? By disgorging an amorphous mass society, modern capitalism had by means of its natural evolution managed to pulverize sources of political opposition. That very reckoning would infuse the work of both Western Marxism and Critical Theory for decades. The void in the classical Marxist approach to class consciousness had, by the start of World War II, laid bare its social and political consequences. Across this expanse, Leninism remained the only viable Marxist *political* modality in the face of expanding corporate-state power – and that would be mainly in lesser-developed countries.

From this standpoint, Marxism had by the 1930s ceased to be a viable revolutionary project, at least for Europe – a development no doubt assisted by the emergence of Stalinism in the USSR. Leninism, such as it was, remained the official guide for parties of the Third International, but they were ultimately either marginalized or destroyed. Communist parties would be rejuvenated during the 1940s in Italy, France, Greece, and elsewhere, but now more as agencies of "structural reformism" than of revolutionary change. The very social (and ideological) foundations of anti-system politics appeared to have been corroded. Meanwhile, the newer forms of ideological hegemony were leaving an ever-stronger imprint. Widespread proletarian upheavals in Italy at the end of World War II, driven by partisan mobilization to expel the Germans, would turn out to be the final such drama of modern European history. Under Palmiro Togliatti's leadership, postwar Italian Communism turned emphatically toward parliamentary activity – in fact a uniform trajectory of such multi-class parties in advanced capitalism. Proletarian solidarity would never escape the confines of a modest dual-strategy: electoral politics and trade-union reformism.[5]

How could the masses, in Italy or elsewhere, have ever achieved revolutionary consciousness under the circumstances? How could the extensive power of ideological hegemony have been broken? The failure to engage the all-important realm of social psychology had always been a problem, and this would deepen across the 1920s and 1930s as new conditions took hold. Expanded corporate-state power, now on somewhat firmer ideological foundations, would prove nearly impenetrable for even the most vigorous counter-forces. The exalted Jacobinism embraced by Lenin and Gramsci seemed to be a passing illusion, at least for Europe.

The situation in Germany was especially revealing – a point systematically reflected at the time in the work of Reich and his associates in Germany. Throughout the Weimar period both social-democratic and Communist parties commanded large popular followings, but given the feeble attention of their leaders to subjective concerns (not to mention the hostility between these parties) the German masses were never effectively mobilized, allowing the initially weaker forces of reaction (mainly Nazis) to triumph. As statism advanced, oppositional mass activity receded. In his classic "What is Class Consciousness?," Reich spoke of how German Marxist leaders and theorists utterly "failed to speak the language of the broad masses … who in the end assured the triumph of reaction."[6] Echoing Gramsci, Reich identified a fatal defect in Marxist political discourse – the masses were presented superb economic treatises and historical analyses while the subjective, ideological dimension of politics was forgotten.[7]

For Reich, as for both Lenin and Gramsci, a difficult problem for Marxism was its *economism*: when compared with the always complex subjectivity of people struggling to improve their lives, the "lofty principles" of material needs stressed by theorists and leaders will never be enough. Those principles will not awaken the masses from their ordinary routines, much less inspire them to break with the "old ways of life." Change eventually depends on the power of collective subjective engagement.[8] Reich believed, like Gramsci, that ordinary people were most likely to be politically activated within the sphere of popular culture, which for him included the German Sex-Pol movement aligned with youth and leftist organizations.

What Reich observed in Germany was actually all too common for Marxist parties of the period: leaders were detached, cut off from the rhythms of everyday working people, who responded with disinterest to the lectures of party intellectuals steeped in dry abstract theory. That ethos had been overturned by the Bolsheviks, precisely the reason they were able to carry out a successful revolution. Thus: "Lenin taught, rightly, that the revolutionary must be able to feel at home in every sphere of life."[9] Unfortunately, Marxism as a general phenomenon had reproduced a social (therefore ideological) gulf between leaders and masses, theorists and workers, leading in the end to political futility. Reich added: "If we look for the effect of high politics on the broad masses, we shall see that, at the very most, it is aped in the form of beerhall politics by a few individuals. The vast majority tend always to react passively, without interest, playing the role of mere extras in the fairground show of 'high politics'."[10]

Reich's insightful commentary, on the eve of the Nazi conquest of power, prompts a revisit of Lenin and Michels a few decades earlier, both having been exasperated over the futility of mass politics (although they differed radically on the role of organization). Michels' famous "iron law of oligarchy" focused precisely on the German context – specifically the widening gulf between elites and followers. Such pessimism, as noted, would permeate both "Western Marxism" and the Frankfurt School in coming decades, testimony to the decline (and eventual deradicalization) of established Socialist and Communist parties. While critical Marxists beginning with Korsch, Lukacs, and Gramsci lamented the failure of European workers to achieve revolutionary consciousness on a large scale, the Frankfurt theorists (while conceding that outcome) turned their attention to rising sources of control within liberal capitalism – the family, technology, culture industry, authoritarian state. Since classical Marxism understandably had little to say about those phenomena, the newer, more eclectic theorists were far better positioned to fill the theoretical void. Their work would reveal more than anything the many imposing obstacles that would serve to domesticate anti-system politics.

Rise of the Authoritarian State

There is no need (or space) here to develop a full discussion of the Frankfurt School – that has been done superbly by many others.[11] The central point in this chapter is to identify broad trends associated with the eclipse of oppositional politics in the West. The Frankfurt critics were generally exploratory and diverse, influenced by a wide variety of predecessors: Hegel, Marx, Hilferding, Lukacs, certain strains of continental philosophy. Their work never amounted to a coherent theoretical system along lines of classical Marxism, nor in fact was that intended. They were forever skeptical of philosophical certitudes and historical laws, averse to any system resembling scientific materialism. What fueled their passionate anti-authoritarianism was opposition to both fascism and Stalinism, and then ultimately to the "administered society" of advanced capitalism. It will be recalled that already by the late 1920s Marcuse was able to identify "totalitarian" features at work in European capitalist societies.

Critical Theory embellished no "science of society," no reductionist crisis scenarios, no faith in the proletariat, indeed no revolutionary pretenses; all that was discarded with their farewell to classical Marxism. Their investigations went far beyond the realm of production and class forces to social relations, culture, psychology, and of course politics. The capitalism they set out to analyze was no longer a strictly market-based economy but rather an organized, planned, increasingly state-centered system where old distinctions between economy and politics had become blurred. Everywhere the 1930s witnessed onset of an entirely new phase of capitalist development – more corporatist and statist – a reality perhaps better understood through the lens of Weber than of Marx and Engels. These were societies morphing into expanded forms of domination rooted not only in large-scale business enterprises but in the growth of bureaucracy and technology as well as state power. This system would be constitutive of two phenomena nowadays still visible: authoritarian state and mass society. Against the enormous power of an authoritarian state, the dispersed and fragmented character of mass society would generate strong tendencies toward alienation, passivity, and (in some cases) depoliticization – at odds with the requirements of collective subjectivity and class agency, without which anti-system politics is unthinkable.

For theorists such as Friedrich Pollack, the historical appearance of an authoritarian state within liberal capitalism would be described as a form of "state capitalism," first visible in the social democracies of northern Europe. In Pollack's rendering, the rise of state-capitalism after World War I extended in some fashion to both "totalitarian" (fascist) and "democratic" (modern state-corporate) variants – in both instances transcendence of the liberal model that preoccupied classical Marxism. "In stressing the politicization of the economy," writes Martin Jay, "Pollack was very much in the mainstream of Critical Theory."[12] Here, as elsewhere, we can recognize a jettisoning of some basic concepts associated with Marx and Engels.

From the standpoint of classical Marxism, capitalism was a system rooted in market relations, commodity production, private property, minimal state apparatus, and appropriation of surplus value – the supposed essence of a competitive economy. (Those features had been idealized well beyond their historical actuality.) Such an economy, as Marx theorized, was innately anarchic, dysfunctional, and destructive, effectively doomed to crisis and breakdown. The system was plagued by lack of planning, falling rates of profit, a tendency toward overproduction, and generally uneven development over which ruling elites had at best sporadic control. Given these contradictions, capitalist economies would sooner or later face the tide of change, one possibility being in the direction of state-capitalism that, for some Institute theorists, meant either social democracy or fascism. By the early 1930s, with the world economy in a state of collapse, Pollack could argue that the liberal phase of capitalism was perforce coming to an end. An enlarged role for the state in planning, regulation, ownership, and public infrastructure could serve to block or at least ameliorate crises that classical Marxism had assumed would pave the way toward socialism.

For Pollack, the ascendancy of state-capitalism within the most advanced economies would enable elites to at least temporarily derail opposition while stabilizing class and power relations. By the 1930s Europe had already seen the rise of fascism in Italy, social democracy in several European nations, and the beginnings of Keynesian economics (Roosevelt's New Deal) in the U.S. State power would be the means by which the system managed to head off socialist challenges. That naturally meant a convergence of economic and governmental functions leading, most likely, to a greatly expanded role for politics. Wrote Pollack:

> Performance of the plan is enforced by state power so that nothing essential is left to the functioning of laws of the market or other economic "laws". This may be interpreted as a supplementary rule which states the principle of treating all economic problems as in the last analysis political ones.[13]

Under these circumstances, power "is free from the tyranny of an uncontrolled market."[14] Put differently, "It signifies the transition from a predominantly economic to an essentially political era."[15]

With the emergence of state-capitalism (non-fascist variant), a "general plan" is adopted to give overall direction to key economic functions – investment, regulations, trade, monetary policy, etc. – allowing for administrative control of the system. The profit motive would be subordinated to the plan, governed by criteria set by technical expertise and professional management. In the end, nothing essential is left to markets. With all this, presumably, the economic sources of crisis would be contained, if not checkmated altogether, thus upsetting time-honored Marxist assumptions predicting capitalist failure. In fact Pollack's analysis threw into question the taken-for-granted primacy of economics, replacing it with a (non-Leninist) primacy of politics more resonant with twentieth-century reality.

It appears that Pollack anticipated both the growth of corporate power and merger of economic and governmental power within advanced capitalism – a process that seamlessly gravitated toward social democracy. Yet Pollack clearly overstated the relevance of a "general plan" for most capitalist economies, insofar as the ruling interests managed to exert vast "private" leverage over development. On this crucial issue there would be extensive debates among Institut theorists, including Franz Neumann (author of the classic *Behemoth*), Marcuse, and Horkheimer.[16] Whatever these conceptual differences, Pollack was still able to analyze deep statist trends at work in modern economies that would continue across the decades – the same trajectory later explored by Mills.

In describing modern capitalist development through the lens of integrated power at the summits, Pollack was advancing the Weberian concept of rationalization, which turned out to be vital to fascism as well as social democracy.[17] Thus:

> once this principle of rationalization has become mandatory for all public activities, it will be applied in spheres which previously were the sanctuary of guesswork, routine, and meddling through: military preparedness, the conduct of war, behavior towards public opinion, application of the coercive power of the state, foreign trade, and foreign policy, etc.[18]

Pollack later referred to the "rationalization of all technical and administrative processes"[19] consistent with the even fuller integration of corporate and state power.

In the final analysis, however, Pollack makes clear that statism reigned supreme, that centralized governing functions had become decisive for social democracies just as much as for "totalitarian" regimes. He wrote:

> Every decision is at bottom oriented to the goal of maintaining and expanding the power of the group as a whole and of each of its members. New industrial empires are being built and old ones expanded with this goal in mind ... This principle in turn contributes decisively to strengthening governmental control, since only a strong government can integrate conflicting interests while serving the power interests of the whole group.[20]

If such passages did not anticipate Mills, writing two decades later, we might consider the following: "We have defined this new class as an amalgamation of the key bureaucrats in business, state, and party, allied with the remaining vested interests." Pollack goes on: "The new ruling class, by its grip on the state, controls everything if it wants to, the general economic plan, foreign policy, rights and duties, life and death of the individual. Its decisions are not restrained by any constitutional guarantees but by a set of rules only designed for maingaining and expanding its own power."[21] Given such integrated power, the new reinvigorated capitalism would not only escape deadly crisis but emerge more productive and efficient, just as Weber would no doubt have expected. That is precisely why the trend toward state-capitalism was intensifying – and was seemingly irreversible. While Pollack believed the main variant of state-capitalism was "democratic," the seeds of an authoritarian power structure had clearly been sown in Europe and North American during the 1930s.

What this historic shift meant for the fate of classical Marxism was, in effect, a profound diminution if not domestication of class conflict within the process of economic change. This developmental model was widely accepted among Frankfurt theorists of the period, including both Adorno and Horkheimer. On this point Martin Jay comments:

> The capitalist mode of exploitation was now seen in a larger context as the specific, historical form of domination characteristic of the bourgeois era of Western history. State capitalism and the authoritarian state spelled the end,

or at least the radical transformation of that epoch. Domination, they argued, was now more direct and virulent without the mediations of bourgeois society.[22]

This approach would, from different angles, leave an enduring legacy for the Institut – obviously a major source of their mounting pessimism after World War II. Pollack's theory turned out to be far more Weberian than Marxist, with its ultimate intellectual and political consequences. Here Kellner writes that "in Pollack's theory there are no analyses of the contradictions, tendencies, and struggles that might lead to a society beyond capitalism – as one finds in classical Marxism."[23] That much is clearly true, but whether that represented a real *problem* for the Frankfurt theorists – as opposed to a theoretical advance – seems unlikely.

The Problem of Mass Culture

By the 1940s, if not earlier, the emergence of mass culture (or "culture industry") within advanced capitalism had become a theoretical centerpiece for both "Western Marxism" and the Frankfurt School. Indeed the very idea of "massness" – of mass society associated with the growth of mass production and mass consumption – would be connected, in different ways, to the larger problem of authoritarianism and rise of a corporate-state power structure prevalent in the West.

For classical Marxism, as is well known, economic crisis was expected to lead to epic change, proletarian upheavals, and socialism – a world free of domination that later Marxists (from Kautsky to Lenin, Luxemburg, and Gramsci) had more or less taken for granted. Instead of worker uprisings, factory occupations, and liberation, however, came two world wars, the Bolshevik Revolution, Stalinism, and fascism, all far removed from anything theorized by Marx and Engels; history had confounded all earlier optimistic expectations. Class conflict never unfolded in accordance with the Marxist classics, never conformed with visions of Enlightenment progress. Along with steadily expanding production and consumption, capitalist rationalization bequeathed a new system of domination closer to what Weber, the "elite theorists," and early Critical Theorists had anticipated. Faith in science, technology, and industrialism had turned illusory.

Writing several decades later, Sheldon Wolin would ask: "How was it that in enlightened times unenlightened despotism was possible?"[24] How could the masses within modern capitalist society be condemned to ever more alienation and powerlessness? It turned out that the trajectory of mass society would steadily work against, not for, proletarian solidarity and oppositional politics in general. The failed labor upheavals of post-World War I Italy actually marked the final revolutionary outburst of industrial workers anywhere. The modes of structural and ideological control available to the bourgeoisie would eventually endow ruling elites with virtually unassailable power. Reflecting on this development, Wolin writes: "Critical theory has culminated in a theory of the non-revolutionary subject," adding:

"Where Nazism had exploited technology in the interests of propaganda, capitalism was using it to fashion a popular culture that would reinforce the psychology of domination without the rough hand of terror."[25] With the expansion of mass culture, first explored by Gramsci, a more integrated power structure would be formed on the edifice of mass society.

The very phenomenon of a culture industry had never been foreseen by classical Marxists. Here Adorno wrote that "the power of the culture-industry ideology is such that conformity has replaced consciousness."[26] Movies, newspapers, radio, television would carry out the heavy tasks of bourgeois propaganda in the guises of furnishing entertainment and information, with devastating political consequences. In Adorno's words: "The concoctions of the culture industry are neither guides for a blissful life, nor a new art of moral responsibility, but rather exhortations to toe the line, behind which stand the most powerful interests."[27] In the end, according to Adorno, this "impedes the development of autonomous, independent individuals who judge and decide consciously for themselves."[28]

In *Dialectic of Enlightenment*, Adorno and Horkheimer set forth a nightmarish vision of capitalist modernity, where culture wedded to technology was giving rise to a bland, stultifying, conformist mass culture that standardizes virtually everything it touches. Indeed "the whole world is made to pass through the filter of the culture industry."[29] Popular and media culture had not only generated sameness and conformism, but also obedience to social hierarchy. An ideology of domination was built into the very logic of the culture industry, at that time (in the 1930s and 1940s) surely most visible in American society. Within advanced capitalism culture had become thoroughly interwoven with both corporate power and technology, leading to an especially potent form of ideological hegemony. The very belief in individual (or collective) self-activity had turned into a sad delusion, Adorno and Horkheimer commenting: "A technological rationale is the rationale of domination itself. It is the coercive nature of a society alienated from itself."[30] *Dialectic of Enlightenment* resonated with the conviction that mass culture and the authoritarian state were dialectically interconnected – similar to the argument later advanced by Mills.

While this claim was surely overstated for the time, its theorists clearly foresaw a culture-politics dynamic that would assume far greater relevance in coming decades. Above all, this dynamic explained the decline of a revolutionary proletariat and the related solidification of capitalist power in the West. Mass culture, for all its routinization and conformity, had served to erode the historic impact of locale: family, neighborhood, community, workplace, town. Cultural (and social) norms were becoming ever more uniform, one dimensional. The central mechanism of socialization was rapidly becoming media culture – reinforced by television starting in the late 1940s. Politics was fast becoming subordinated to capitalist rationalization, to the rhythms and flows of bureaucracy, technology, and the culture industry.

As Frankfurt theorists departed further from the Marxist classics, also losing hope for any transition to socialism, they came to view mass culture as integral to capitalist domination – to sustaining elite power. The hegemonic potential of corporate media and mass consumption, driven by the new practices of advertising and public relations, turned out to be especially crucial to mechanisms of social control. As those sectors expanded through the 1950s, they worked against individuality and critical thinking – even as the nonstop propaganda celebrated those supposed attributes of pluralist democracy. As everyday life was being colonized by the culture industry, as larger areas of human activity became homogenized, Leo Lowenthal could refer to the "idols of consumption," a reference akin to Fromm's "alienated consumption." However defined, this was a form of modernity where social progress would be measured in terms of material affluence.[31]

Such transformation was in many ways politically numbing, harmful to the fortunes of Marxism in particular and anti-system politics in general across the industrialized world. The 1950s would be accurately described as a period of political quietism. On the one hand, the very amorphousness of mass society served to undercut democratic participation, ceding new power to the ruling elites. A diluted variant of liberal pluralism forced economic sectors into the orbit of state power, which itself had grown more concentrated and integrated. Wolin would later characterize this phenomenon as follows: "The society of Leviathan is the antihero's utopia: a society of formal equality, where all subjects have been humbled and made dependent upon the sovereign for the security of their lives, goods, rights, and status."[32]

This very social-psychological dynamic explored by Fromm in *Escape from Freedom*, attentive to the rise of fascism in Germany but just as applicable to the trajectory of capitalist modernity noted above. Fromm argued that as mass society gave rise to heightened personal alienation and political impotence, individuals looked to empowerment through identification with powerful external forces – a surrender of the self to an ideology, leader, party, or state. This mechanism could also extend to media or cultural entities where the individual is fully subordinated to a "higher power," allowing for a (false) transcendence of loneliness and isolation.[33]

In Fromm's view, within capitalist modernity individuals want to "become a part of a bigger and more powerful world outside of oneself, to submerge and participate in it."[34] Instead of actual empowerment, however, the result is "annihilation of the individual self," which in the end means loss of political agency. Surrender of individuality coincides with formation of strong authoritarian character traits consistent with what Adorno and associates later found in their classic *The Authoritarian Personality*. The likely outcome in both cases would be the kind of submission to external authority typical of fascism. Fromm asks: "Is there not also, perhaps, besides an innate desire for freedom, an instinctive wish for submission?"[35] At this juncture mass society is dialectically connected to authoritarian politics, or at least some form of loyalty to a higher power, which could include some mode of authoritarian state power. As Adorno concluded: "People are continuously molded from above because they must be molded if the overall economic pattern is to be maintained ..."[36] That naturally means reproduction of established class and power relations.

Across the post-World War II landscape, the accumulated effects of media and popular culture – much of it designed to manipulate "public opinion" – would constitute a form of ideological hegemony far more intrusive than anything foreseen by Gramsci. Among newer factors was the historic marriage of technology and culture, a trend explored by Marcuse in *One-Dimensional Man*, where growth of technological rationality signaled both the eclipse of critical thought and decline of political opposition. Here, it appears, capitalist rationalization was rapidly, and devastatingly, reaching its zenith, to the great benefit of ruling elites.

For Marcuse, a central problem of modern capitalism was the *ideological* consequences of modern technology. Technological rationality had begun to pervade all zones of social existence, deflecting popular efforts to achieve self-activity. Technology now served as a medium of reification, beyond the power of the commodity.[37] By the time *One Dimensional Man* appeared, in 1964, mass consumption was just beginning to assume new significance in the West. Thus: "At its most advanced stage, domination functions as administration, and in the overdeveloped areas of mass consumption the administered life becomes the good life of the whole, in the defense of which opposites are united."[38] In Marcuse's view, this unification of opposites meant that embedded in mass culture would be powerful illusions of individual if not collective subjectivity. The dominant values were being replicated by and through the complex linkage of technology, culture, and politics.[39]

From this standpoint, one-dimensionality corresponded to the rise of mass society theorized by Mills and mass culture theorized by the Frankfurt School. These motifs, both reflected in the process of capitalist rationalization, would increasingly shape postwar American society and other industrialized systems. Could this mark what seemed to be the requiem for a Marxist theory wedded to belief in class conflict leading to proletarian revolution? Could the historical search for an agency of revolutionary change have turned futile? For Marcuse, the very social-psychological impulse toward anti-system thought and action now seemed to have been extinguished, nowhere more so than in the U.S. Marcuse writes: "The distinguishing feature of advanced industrial society is its effective suffocation of those needs which demand liberation – liberation also from that which is tolerable and rewarding and comfortable – while it sustains and absolves the destructive power and repressive function of the affluent society."[40]

With the advent of mass society, finally, we encounter a range of plural identities coexisting with states of amorphousness and conformity, while those identities routinely wind up assimilated into the larger apparatus of domination, their critical and oppositional potential muted and nullified. Massification thus points toward the logical decline of political agency that, in cultural terms, finds little material or social grounding. As for the proletariat itself, its still sizable presence (in the 1960s) was unlikely to be transformed into an effective *political* force, that is, beyond the scope of liberal reformism. In the U.S. especially, industrial workers were now for their part fully integrated into capitalist modernity – the outgrowth of consumerism, the culture industry, and perhaps most centrally, technological rationality. All modes of identity and subjectivity would henceforth be shaped, and reshaped, by increasingly powerful instruments of technological and cultural domination.

Notes

1 See Georg Lukacs, *History and Class Consciousness* (Cambridge, MA: MIT Press, 1068), pp. 90–91.
2 Karl Polanyi, *The Great Transformation* (Boston: Beacon Press, 1944).
3 Lukacs, *History*, p. 92.
4 Herbert Marcuse, *Negations* (Boston: Beacon Press, 1968), p. 8.
5 On the postwar deradicalization of the Italian Communist Party, see Carl Boggs, *The Impasse of European Communism* (Boulder, CO: Westview Press, 1982), chs. 3, 4.
6 Wilhelm Reich, "What is Class Consciousness?," in *Sex-Pol Essays* (New York: Vintage Books, 1972), p. 283.
7 Ibid., p. 284.
8 Ibid., pp. 291–295.
9 Ibid., p. 340.
10 Ibid., p. 322.
11 The best general treatment of the Frankfurt School is Martin Jay, *Dialectical Imagination* (Berkeley: University of California Press, 1973).
12 Ibid., p. 155.
13 Frederick Pollack, "State Capitalism: Its Possibilities and Limitations," in Stephen Bronner and Douglas Kellner, eds., *Critical Theory and Society* (New York: Routledge, 1989), p. 100.
14 Ibid., p. 101.
15 Ibid.
16 See the discussion in Douglas Kellner, *Critical Theory, Marxism, and Modernity* (Baltimore: Johns Hopkins University Press, 1989), p. 61.
17 Pollack, p. 100.
18 Ibid.
19 Ibid., p. 102.
20 Ibid., p. 104.
21 Ibid., p. 113.
22 Jay, *Dialectical Imagination*, p. 256.
23 Kellner, *Critical Theory*, p. 62.
24 Sheldon Wolin, "Reason in Exile," in *Fugitive Democracy and Other Essays* (Princeton, NJ: Princeton University Press, 2016), p. 230.
25 Ibid., pp. 231–232.
26 Theodor W. Adorno, "The Culture Industry Reconsidered," in Stephen Bronner and Douglas Kellner, eds., *Critical Theory and Society*, p. 133.
27 Ibid., p. 134.
28 Ibid., p. 135.
29 See Max Horkheimer and Theodor W. Adorno, *Dialectic of Enlightenment* (New York: Continuum, 1995), p. 135.
30 Ibid., p. 121.

31 Kellner, *Critical Theory*, p. 164.
32 Wolin, "Hobbes and the Epic Tradition of Political Theory," in *Fugitive Democracy*, p. 148.
33 See Erich Fromm, *Escape from Freedom* (New York: Avon Books, 1965), p. 163.
34 Ibid., p. 177.
35 Ibid., p. 21.
36 Theodor W. Adorno et al., *The Authoritarian Personality* (New York: W.W. Norton, 1969), p. 480.
37 Herbert Marcuse, *One Dimensional Man* (Boston: Beacon Press, 1964), pp. 168–169.
38 Ibid., p. 255.
39 Ibid., p. 257.
40 Ibid., p. 7.

5
MILLS: BEYOND MARX AND WEBER

To fully understand the enduring historical influence of C. Wright Mills it is useful to address capitalist history as theorized by Karl Marx and Max Weber, both of whom helped shaped Mills' seminal work in the period after World War II. One cannot grasp the meaning of *The Power Elite*, for example, without taking into account these conflicting (yet overlapping) legacies, which perpetually struggled for attention in Mills' voluminous work.

In a theoretical outlook also shaped by Western Marxism and the Frankfurt School, Mills brought to his analysis of advanced capitalism a healthy distrust of traditional scientism and materialism, which he (correctly) understood as sources of conservative thinking. Thus in *The Sociological Imagination*, he wrote: "In bureaucratic social science ... the whole social science endeavor has been pinned own to the services of prevailing authorities."[1] As such, theory inevitably falls short of addressing crucial public issues. Further: "No problem can be adequately formulated unless the values involved and the apparent threat to them are stated."[2] Like Gramsci, Mills adhered to an historicist approach to the study of politics, lamenting:

> Early socialist theorists tried to formulate invariant laws of society – laws that would hold for all societies just as the abstracted procedures of physical science had led to laws that cut beneath the qualitative richness of "nature." There is, I believe, no "law" stated by any social scientist that is trans-historical, that must not be understood as having to do with the specific nature of some period. Other laws turn out to be empty abstractions or quite confused tautologies.[3]

As Mills set out to theorize the dynamics of American society for the postwar era, he cautioned: "We do not know any universal principles of historical change ... just as there is a variety of principles of historical change."[4] Without a combined historical and comparative framework, the theorist loses all-important *context*. Here Mills was clearly distancing his rich empirical and structural focus from the stricter materialist elements of Marxism. Indeed by the mid-1950s he had lost faith in what seemed to be the guiding ideologies of the period: "I also mean that our major orientations – liberalism and socialism – have virtually collapsed as adequate explanations of the world and of ourselves."[5] This departure from conventional wisdom helped impart to Mills' work so much of its freshness and originality.

A starting point is Weber's well-known analysis of capitalist rationalization –a process leading toward what he called "higher capitalism." That development pointed toward expanding forms of domination and a new power structure that would approximate state-capitalism. That system would be, as Weber anticipated several decades earlier, increasingly centralized and integrated, merging politics and economics, government and business, state and capital. Though Weber himself never formulated a coherent theory of state-capitalism – that would be left to Friedrich Pollack – his pathbreaking work laid the conceptual foundations of a dynamic, streamlined capitalism beyond the ideological scope of both classical liberalism and classical Marxism. Weberian theory, closer to Marxism than commonly assumed, did ultimately affirm the primacy of politics, in ways that engaged prevailing historical forces at work across the twentieth century in Europe and North America.

The neoclassical tenets of liberal capitalism were rather problematic well before Weber and other "elite theorists" (Michels, Pareto, and Mosca) appeared on the scene. That doctrine naively viewed the capitalist economy as self-perpetuating, a system in equilibrium shaped by rational free choice, individual sovereignty, and open competition – that is, a beautiful and perfectly harmonizing social order.

This was a society where free markets, limited government, and citizen participation flourished as part of a relatively natural, organic historical process. State power had been understood as an *external* phenomenon, alien to natural relations seen as basic to entrepreneurial self-activity consistent with that envisioned by a parade of utopian nineteenth-century neoclassical economists.

Turning to twentieth-century American politics – Mills' overriding focus – what appears most striking is the widening gulf between the old ideals and pretenses of liberal capitalism and the dysfunctional actualities of a globalized state-corporate system that, for the U.S., also involved the military dimension of a global superpower. While contemporary mainstream thought celebrates the virtues of constitutional democracy, free markets, open exchange of ideas, and individual choice, the system nowadays marches headlong in another direction: greater concentration of economic and political power, neoliberal globalization, expanded warfare state, a mass society subject to an elaborate opinion-making machine. World War II had transformed public life extensively and forever, giving rise to a dominant superpower ruled by an elite stratum in relentless pursuit of wealth, power, and geopolitical advantage. The result was a militarized form of state-capitalism, oligarchical and authoritarian in its power relations, coexisting with a fragmented, atomized, and largely disempowered mass population, just as Mills had theorized in the 1950s. Fully seven decades after World War II reached its barbaric conclusion, this historical trajectory continues apace with only slight impediments.

The Authoritarian State Revisited

One point of departure here for conceptualizing the postwar American power structure is Mills' seminal *The Power Elite*. Appearing barely a decade after the end of World War II, Mills' book was the first truly systematic effort to conceptualize power relations in the U.S. during that crucial period. Despite its flaws, the work retains its central meaning several decades later. A product of diverse traditions – Marxism, Critical Theory, Weberian sociology, homegrown American radicalism – Mills' work, in tracing the complex evolution and convergence of economic, political, military, and cultural forces, arrived at probably the most sophisticated understanding of American politics that had been set forth. Avoiding the pitfalls of reductionist and positivist thinking, he was able to move beyond familiar labels of the time: pluralism, totalitarianism, state-monopoly capitalism, bureaucratic collectivism, simple dictatorship, New Class – to formulate the concept of a "tripartite elite" comprised of shifting government, corporate, and military interests, none simply reducible to the others. Mills was one of the few theorists who saw in the rise of military Keynesianism and warfare state the crucial ascendancy of the Pentagon in American politics. He also expertly unmasked some of the great deceptions and illusions of public discourse, bringing to light deeply problematic features of modern liberal capitalism.

In contrast to then-prevailing opinion in American society, Mills argued that postwar America was experiencing new augmentations of power at the summit – a trend sharply accelerated by World War II. Coinciding with this development, the general population was growing more alienated and disempowered. He began with the view that "The hierarchies of state and corporate and army constitute the means of power ... [and] are now of a consequence not before equaled in human history ..."[6] Everything else is deeply impacted by these interwoven forms of domination, each characterized by its own oligarchical and bureaucratic tendencies, Mills writing: "As each of these domains becomes enlarged and centralized, the consequences of its activities become greater and its traffic with the others increases."[7] As this new "triangle of power" expands, American society winds up increasingly defined by a "political economy linked, in a thousand ways, with military institutions and decisions."[8]

These strands of power have more thoroughly converged structurally and ideologically over time, narrowing the supposed distinctiveness of social and personal relations. Thus: "As each of these domains has coincided with the others, as decisions tend to become total in their consequence, the leading men in each of these domains of power – the warlords, the corporate chieftains, the political directorate – tend to come together, to form the power elite of America."[9] Mills was quick to insist on the uniqueness of this power structure, which clashed with the taken-for-granted American understanding of a smoothly functioning pluralist democracy, writing: "As the institutional means of power and the means of communication tying them together have become steadily more efficient, those now in command of them together have come into command of instruments of rule quite unsurpassed in the history of mankind."[10] This had produced a scope of elite power unrivalled in world history – no doubt a shocking contention only decade after the Allies had defeated arguably the most brutal dictatorial regime ever (the Nazis), and just when the U.S. was facing off against yet another form of authoritarian rule in the Soviet Union.

While the ruling interests were tightly interwoven, Mills also stressed that major corporations – the Fortune 500 – had come to dominate the landscape, using their obvious resources, wealth, and communications leverage to manage public life, commodifying and rationalizing virtually everything at the same time. Here the Constitution and other legal pressures would be unable to block the corporate accumulation of wealth and power.[11] An expanding warfare state had given the "warlords" partnership at the summits, Mills noting: "Alongside the corporate executives and the politicians, the generals and admirals – those uneasy cousins within he American elite – have gained and have been given increased power to make and to influence decisions of the greatest importance."[12] If a weaker armed forces edifice had in earlier years been subordinate to civilian governance, its postwar institutionalization and centrality to public life brought the Pentagon and its surrounding agencies (intelligence, law enforcement, etc.) into far greater prominence.

For Mills, World War II had been an historic turning-point for the military, as for much of American life: by the 1950s the Pentagon would have a stronger role in both domestic and international politics, elites having adopted a "military definition of reality."[13] U.S. superpower status, visible through armed forces bases scattered across the world, brought the military to ascending heights, evident with new levels of military spending, a broadening global presence, and general transformation of American society in the direction of "military values."[14] What Mills observed in the 1950s, always prescient, hinted at a future trajectory of militarism and war, underpinned by a permanent war economy. Education, science, technology, and the media would be in different ways be exposed to military ideology. Few writers of the period – Seymour Melman and Fred Cook being notable exceptions – would call attention to the outsized military role in American public life.[15] President Dwight Eisenhower, famously warning about the perils of a "military-industrial-complex" in 1961, would belatedly add his voice to this list.

As for Mills' "political directorate," it was easy enough to see during the 1950s that state power in the U.S. was growing at a rapid rate, sparked by the earlier full-scale war mobilization. The social Keynesian edifice that President Franklin Roosevelt created during the 1930s would be joined by military Keynesianism, another indication of how obsolete classical liberalism and its fantasy of a laissez-faire market economy had become. Federal spending had quadrupled during the war and, despite a brief postwar "demobilization," statist expansion would continue across future decades, whatever party happened to occupy the White House. Despite a number of surface differences, Democrats and Republicans would be equally dedicated Keynesians, each fully attuned to the stimulus function of massive government programs: corporate subsidies, R & D investment, social welfare, infrastructure funding, law enforcement, the military. Without fiscal stimulus the capitalist economy would most likely have collapsed, quickly and painfully.

Mills' criticism of the American power structure was unsparing – a system largely devoid of human values, dedicated mainly to the pursuit of wealth and power, a degradation of politics such that "… political rhetoric seems to slide lower and lower down the scale of cultivation and civility."[16] Elites, accustomed to prattling on about "pragmatism" and "realism," were in the final analysis little more than a club of "crackpot realists." Mills concluded: "America – a conservative country – appears now before the world a naked and arbitrary power as, in the name of realism, its men of decision enforce their crackpot definitions upon world reality."[17] These elites were "commanders of power unequaled in human history [having] succeeded within the American system of organized irresponsibility."[18]

Taking into account the reality of a "tripartite of power," American society in Mills' time (he died in 1963) had evolved into an oligarchical system ruled by a small, relatively stratum of white men – roughly a few thousand of the most wealthy and powerful.[19] It would appear that Michels' bleak pre-World War I prognostications had come true. Those at the top might have differed in their opinions and lifestyle, but regarding central decisions on the economy and foreign policy their outlook had effectively narrowed or converged. Thus: "American capitalism is now in considerable part a military capitalism, and the most important relations of the big corporations to the state rests on the coincidence of interests between military and corporate needs, as defined by the warlords and corporate rich."[20] This historic confluence of interests would soon bolster each sector in turn, as Mills was the first to emphasize.

The ascent of a cohesive power elite reflected the historic eclipse of liberal capitalism, as decision-making at the summits became detached from popular interests and demands. Oligarchy developed at odds with even the more restrictive "pluralist-elitist" model of liberalism identified by C. B. Macpherson.[21] Mills himself concluded that "America is now in considerable part more a formal political democracy than a democratic social structure, and even the formal mechanisms are weak."[22] This would confirm the most pessimistic views of Michels and other "elite theorists," now several decades later. Important decisions were now being made by the ruling interests while Congress and state legislatures were becoming largely disenfranchised, elections reduced to a process of rituals and spectacles geared more to legitimation rather than to democratic participation. Mills stressed that ascendancy of a power elite was not the result of any secret conspiracy – there were no elaborate plots or shadow organizations wielding power behind the scene. Nor was there was nothing particularly mysterious or irrational about such developments. The system came into being as part of an intelligible historical process rooted in concrete economic and political interests.

The "Higher Immorality"

While the ruling elites of Mills' discourse can surely fall prey to individual greed, corruption, and criminality, a more useful rendering is that their *modus operandi* is shaped by the larger structures and interests they represent. As with any political system, elites were the product of historical forces, however varied their personal characteristics; their roles were entirely *systemic*. At the same time, this new system of militarized state-capitalism was largely bereft of public values and ethics, driven instead by an obsession with wealth, power, and geopolitical competition. It was being governed, Mills wrote, by a "higher immorality" where everything (workers, consumers, communities, the environment) had lost all intrinsic worth. Mills noted that "the higher immorality is a systemic feature of the American elite; its general acceptance is an essential feature of the mass society," adding: "Within the corporate worlds of business, war making, and politics, the private consciousness is attenuated – and the higher immorality is institutionalized."[23]

As a comprehensive and detailed analysis of American politics in the 1950s, Mills' work was remarkable enough – yet just as noteworthy was its identification of historical trends that would become even more visible in subsequent decades. His infamous "power tripartite" would in fact expand dramatically in each sector, fueled by a swollen military state committed to perpetual warfare. At the time Mills wrote *The Power Elite*, U.S. military spending (in 2020 dollars) was barely $100 million; today, after lengthy wars in Afghanistan, Iraq, Libya, and elsewhere, that figure has risen to nearly one trillion dollars (nearly matching all other world military expenditures combined). That would be a tenfold increase, well exceeding the growth of federal spending in general. Corporate power? By 2020 it had become larger, more oligopolistic, more globalized – and in general less regulated – than at any time in the postwar years. The American power elite today has far more leverage over the course of events than anyone (including Mills) could have imagined during the reputedly placid Eisenhower years.

Meanwhile, debates over existence of a "power elite" had never gained much traction in American political or media culture, still attached to longstanding fictions of an exemplary liberal democracy and market economy. It is only *other* nations that are beset with such "power structures," elites, oligarchy, and militarism. Of course Mills' work, then as later, would be pilloried by mainstream social scientists wedded to the myths of a smoothly functioning constitutional, or pluralist democracy. Theirs continues to be a world of equilibrium, ideological consensus, and multiculturalism aligned with the tenets of classical liberalism. Mills' deeply critical ideas also clashed with the biases of orthodox Marxism and its outmoded "base-superstructure" construct according to which politics is a simple reflex of the production apparatus and class domination. Mills, as we have seen, was strongly indebted to Marxism but adopted a more complex view of power relations allowing for the autonomy (or semi-autonomy) of government and the military. Many have concluded that Mills' concept of a power elite, while suggestive for its period, would lose its relevance many decades later – a rather puzzling conclusion insofar as what Mills was describing, far from vanishing, has only taken on added historical importance.

A few contemporary writers have carried forward Mills' seminal contributions, revising some conclusions to meet new conditions: G. William Domhoff, Sheldon Wolin, Chris Hedges, Henry Giroux, Chalmers Johnson, Michael Parenti. Among these, Domhoff has been most closely associated with the Mills legacy in sociology, and his body of work reflects a continuity in American power studies from 1950s to the present. In his classic *Who Rules America?* (sixth edition, 2010), Domhoff writes that the U.S. today remains dominated by a "corporate community" of interests – e.g., big business, banks, agribusiness – that operates almost entirely beyond popular reach.[24] Both major parties are instruments of capital, having some differences on social issues but agreeing generally on economics and foreign policy. A power elite remains, even more solidified and institutionalized than when Mills was writing, barely opposed in its efforts toward new accumulations of wealth and power. Following Mills, Domhoff has recognized that class conflict has never been extinguished, concluding instead that it has been more effectively regulated and domesticated.

For Domhoff, the power elite today is comprised of a few thousand leading figures in big business, government, the military, and media (the latter now having a prominence it clearly did not have in Mills' time). While corporations are obviously the most powerful of these interests, they do not control everything nor do they constitute a "base" upon which everything else forms. Thus: "This combination of economic power, political expertise, and continuing political success makes the corporate owners and executives a *dominant class*, not in the sense of complete and absolute power, but in the sense that they have the power to shape the economic and political frameworks within which other groups and classes must operate."[25] Here Domhoff and Mills are in alignment on the ascent of corporate power, yet Mills would endow "other groups" (government, military) with more institutional autonomy, or relative autonomy, as we have seen. Both would agree that elites tend to converge on the "big issues," especially at moments of crisis, and both agree the general population is marginalized and increasingly disenfranchised, though Mills probably had a more jaundiced view of liberal democracy. In the end, notes Domhoff, " … it is the combination of insights from class and organization theories that explains the strength of the American power elite."[26]

Where Domhoff inexplicitly departs from Mills is in the realm of military power. While that power – historically a function of U.S. imperialism, the warfare state, and militarized economy – has dramatically expanded in recent decades, Domhoff believes the Pentagon today is somehow *more* subordinate to the corporate community and *less* relevant in terms of larger influence. Oddly, the first five editions of *Who Rules America?* contained *nothing* about the role of military power in American society – though, of course, the book was supposed to be devoted to *systemic* power. Finally, in the sixth edition, Domhoff devotes little more than a page to the "military-industrial complex," where he asks whether the U.S. military is "separate" from the other sectors of the power elite. The question obviously answers itself: neither Mills nor anyone else would argue that "separation" exists at the summits of power, as that would be logically absurd; total institutional (or ideological) autonomy is impossible at any level, for any sector. Mills wrote that the different realms of elite power were indeed *interwoven*, or integrated. Still, Domhoff implausibly moves ahead, insisting the Pentagon does not in fact "maintain at least some degree of independence from the corporate community."[27] And he is right: the spheres are fully interconnected within a rather cohesive power structure.

All the military contractors, Domhoff argues, are fully integrated into the corporate structure – and, once again, that is true enough. Mills himself never would have contended otherwise. Domhoff adds that "the claim of a separate military-industrial complex [never made] is contradicted by the fact that the defense budget rises and falls in terms of foreign policy crises and military threats."[28] Do these "crises" and "threats" simply fall from the sky, or does the military (and foreign-policy apparatus) have some crucial role to play here? Yes, the budget has been occasionally impacted by international (not to mention *domestic*) events and developments, but the larger truth is that the overall U.S. postwar spending trajectory has been steadily upward, even in years after the Cold War ended. By 2016, military (not "defense") expenditures had reached an all-time high. The "complex," moreover, extends far beyond military contractors to include a vast permanent war system: an empire of bases, a sprawling Pentagon bureaucracy, huge nuclear complex, intelligence system, homeland security apparatus, the war on drugs, and dozens of related federal agencies. Contrary to what Domhoff argues, the military has a far more pervasive influence on American society today than it did in Mills' time.

In his effort to grapple with this issue, Tom Hayden, commenting on Mills' influence in *Radical Nomad* (2006), appears skeptical about any "independent" power of the military. He suggests that Mills' work had indicated the military acted as something of an "autonomous causal force in history" – a departure from Marxism. Hayden writes that "it would be lopsided to insist with Mills on the *independence* of the military elite from the political economy."[29] Such absolute "independence," as noted, is hardly the point. Strangely, Hayden wants to downplay the growth of an *increasingly* militarized economy, society, government, and foreign policy. Perhaps realizing this mistake, Hayden elsewhere actually formulates a view perfectly consistent with that of Mills. Thus: "Perhaps the military indeed has autonomous causal power, but within a framework of value determined in the institutions of the political economy."[30] And, more crucially: "Mills' work was a brilliant effort to elaborate what Marxism knew as the 'superstructure' .... It was Mills' important contribution, and one reflective of the unusual developments of the postwar period, to have seen the relevance of the new institutional agencies of power."[31] Indeed!

From this standpoint, Mills' seminal power studies transcended the antinomies – and limits – of both liberalism and Marxism, though in the end he did appropriate key insights from Marxism (without lapsing into reductionism). At one point in *The Marxists* (1963), Mills could write:

> we do not accept as sufficient the simple view that high economic men unilaterally make all decisions of national consequence. We hold that a simple view of "economic determinism" must be elaborated by "political determinism" and "military determinism"; that the higher agents of these three domains now often have a noticeable degree of autonomy; and that only in the often intricate ways of *coalition* do they make up and carry through the most important decisions.[32]

This would indeed be the historical trajectory of a militarized state-capitalism that Mills was the first to theorize.

In American society the stupendous growth of militarized state-capitalism, legitimated tenuously by a decaying liberal ideology, has meant widespread personal alienation, social atomization, and collective disempowerment. The political consequences of this epic transformation have been enormous – above all for popular movements, which (since the 1970s) have had great difficulty getting and maintaining traction. As elite power solidifies, it seems that society as a whole becomes riddled with new contradictions and challenges; anti-system opposition is bound to weaken or fragment in an atmosphere of fear, anxiety, and escapism, where agencies of far-reaching change (active, collective subjectivity) are so often blocked. By the early twenty-first century American public life had become saturated with false or misleading pursuits of self-activity, characterized by increasing levels of violence and crime, mounting problems of substance addiction, health calamities, and of course severe ecological challenges – all defying effective political solutions within existing political arrangements.

The stranglehold that corporate, government, and military elites have over American society aligns with an outdated liberal ideology stressing rampant self-interest, competition, and endless material growth. Authoritarianism, gross social inequality, poverty, civic violence, war, environmental crisis – none of this has been (or can be) seriously confronted, much less resolved, within a liberal-capitalist framework where "collective goods" remain so thoroughly devalued. Further, elections that are bought and controlled by wealthy business interests and their lobbies – where big issues are ritually trivialized within the corporate media – have become little more than spectacles of big spending, meaningless rhetoric, and false hopes. Party differences have attained little meaning in such a political culture. Here most varieties of liberalism, preaching the values of freedom and individualism, are destined to lead to manifestly illiberal, even despotic, outcomes equivalent to Hobbes' famous state of nature calling fort h an all-powerful Leviathan. Ostensibly libertarian, the ideology readily turns authoritarian, as both the Frankfurt School and Mills had suggested. Concentrated power at the summits is blessed with more flexibility to broaden its domain over the mass of the population.[33]

The Mass Society

The steady advance of modernity is associated with Enlightenment values driven by science, technology, and economic growth leading inexorably to democracy and material betterment for most of the population. That is one side of capitalist rationalization. Yet another side – the darker side – brings forth statism, oligopoly, bureaucracy, and hierarchical social relations, as Weber and the "elite theorists" argued in the early twentieth century. One result was emergence of mass society that, in its diffuseness, conflicted with Marx's well-known view of a flourishing, collectivized, highly-politicized working class prepared, at some point, to overthrow an oppressive system. An amorphous mass society was bound to generate widespread attitudes of despair and futility that, in Gramsci's words, were likely to produce any number of "morbid symptoms."

The concept of a fragmented, atomized society – at odds with prospects for a crystallized proletarian opposition – points toward greater elite maneuverability, a narrowing public sphere, and diminished citizenship. Mills fully anticipated this development in *The Power Elite*, writing that the American public was being transformed into a "society of masses."[34] Mills saw this as the inevitable result of concentrated economic and political power, a condition destined to both *mirror* and *reinforce* authoritarianism. The onset of mass society, he observed, reduced people to manageable objects – not only through commodity production, but through bureaucracy, the media, advertising, and elections. Over time, large-scale depoliticization was inescapable. Against the crushing power of state-capitalism, overwhelming in scope and resources, the "mass" was rendered more impotent than the lore of a model pluralist democracy suggested. Here Mills concluded, some believe prematurely, that the very idea of a public, democratic citizenry had turned into nothing but a sad illusion.[35]

For American politics in the postwar era, structural and ideological convergence at the summits of power corresponded to amorphousness and conformity at the general level of social existence. Thus: "The top of modern American society is increasingly unified and often seems willfully coordinated: at the top there has emerged an elite of power. The middle levels are a drifting set of stalemated, balancing forces: the middle does not link the bottom with the top. The bottom of this society is politically fragmented, and even as a passive fact, increasingly powerless: at the bottom there is emerging a mass society."[36] This profoundly undemocratic trajectory was systematically reinforced by expansion of the warfare state, Mills writing: "It is not only within the higher political and economic, scientific and educational circles that the military ascendancy is apparent. The warlords, along with fellow travelers and spokesmen, are attempting to plant their metaphysics firmly among the population at large."[37] He added: "American militarism, in fully developed form, would mean the triumph in all areas of life of the military metaphysic, and hence the subordination to it of all other ways of life."[38]

One source of this predicament would be media culture or the culture industry – a motif that Mills, as we have seen, took from the Frankfurt School. As this sector developed to keep pace with the stupendous growth of markets, it meant that attitudes, beliefs, and choices would be shaped increasingly by opinion-making processes able to manipulate and distort what became known as "public opinion." Social and political consciousness would thereby be "managed" by the ruling interests – a concept further embellished by Wolin in his book *Democracy, Inc.* (2007) Mills wrote: " ... with the increased means of mass persuasion that are available, the public of public opinion has become the object of intensive efforts to control, manage, manipulate, and increasingly intimidate."[39] Wolin would refer to this phenomenon as "managed democracy," reflecting the vast ideological resources available to elites – resonant with Gramsci's earlier concept of hegemony and Marcuse's later theory of one-dimensionality. In slightly more mechanistic fashion, Mills at one point argued that opinion-makers in American society were little more than "transmission belts" for elite interests and agendas.[40] And those interests and agendas were firmly shared at the top, especially when it came to crucial economic and global issues.

For Mills, "mass society" coexisted with a psychology of routine, order, and conformity consistent with an authoritarian politics. Here liberalism came to represent a detached form of thought devoid of political meaning, outmoded but still available for purposes of elite legitimation. Mills observed that "If, as a rhetoric, liberalism has become a mask of all political positions, as a theory of society it has become irrelevant, and in an optative mood, misleading."[41] Ideological agreement was so solid at the summits that one could speak of an all-encompassing "liberal consensus," easily meshing with the aforementioned "higher immorality," Mills noting: "Within the corporate worlds of business, war making, and politics, the private consciousness is attenuated – and the higher immorality is ritualized."[42] This explained the famous postwar "bipartisan support" for U.S. foreign ventures – though the sixties would see considerable slippage of this consensus, when the Civil Rights, antiwar, and new-left protests would loudly disturb the popular quietism of American society.

To the degree elite power and mass society are interwoven, that dialectic under conditions of capitalist modernity deserves more attention that it generally receives. In Mills' words: "The rise of the power elite ... rests upon, and in some ways is part of, the transformation of the public in America into a mass society."[43] To be sure, we find in this context a proliferation of groups and identities but, given how detached these groups and identities are from mass politics, they wind up impotent, lacking any real leverage or agency. For Mills, in fact, the very idea of coherent social formations within contemporary mass society – a premise shared by liberalism and Marxism alike – is nothing but a "fairy tale."[44] On the main issues in particular (the economy, foreign policy) the modern citizenry has little if any significant input, minor relevance. At this juncture tyranny – social just as much as political – gains strength from a multiplication of identities engulfed in conformity, a thesis articulated long ago by John Stuart Mill in *On Liberty*.[45]

Writing primarily about 1950s American society, Mills commented: "In all modern societies, the autonomous associations standing between the various classes and the state tend to lose their effectiveness as vehicles of reasoned opinion and instruments for the rational exertion of political will."[46] Here again concentrated forms of economic and governmental power served to assimilate and neutralize all intellectual dissent and political opposition. It is worth noting that Mills formulated these ideas well in advance of a colonizing media culture shaped by movies, TV, and the Internet. The very fact that ruling elites might have their *own* interests and agendas fully apart from the general population renders democratic prospects close to unthinkable.

In the decades since Mills set forth these ideas, the gap between ruling interests and subordinate masses has only widened. That dynamic, moreover, has been strengthened by widening elite reliance on the political spectacle of elections, party competition, and campaign advertising. Thus: "The spectacle of an efficient elite maintaining its authority and asserting its will over the mass by rationally calculated use of irrational methods of persuasion is the most disturbing nightmare of mass democracy."[47]

If mass society during Mills' time gave rise to greater personal alienation and disempowerment, it was also bound to produce attempts, mostly furtive, at recovery of subjectivity, including oppositional forms of self-activity. Such attempts have taken any number of forms: psychological, social, cultural, political. Addressing this dynamic within the context of historical fascism (specifically Nazism), theorists like Erich Fromm, Wilhelm Reich, and Adorno sought to frame a connection between deepening personal alienation and the rise of fascism. In *Escape from Freedom*, Fromm wrote that authoritarian politics – for Europe at least – emerged in great measure from individual pursuit of meaning and empowerment through a higher power. With older bonds of family and community loosened or destroyed by modernity, the "solution" for those seeking solidarity and purpose was found in a newer source of identity. In Germany that meant a strong leader, party, or state, energized by a transformative ideology. "Empowerment" would come through some version of the party/state built on the emotional appeals of nationalism or, better, a virulent nationalism, and this meant fascism in such countries as Italy and Germany.[48]

After the legacy of Mills, few more recent writers have explored deeply authoritarian tendencies of contemporary American politics with the historical and theoretical breadth of Sheldon Wolin. In *Democracy, Inc.*, Wolin, following Mills, harbors no illusions about earlier U.S. history or the Founders whose reputed contributions to constitutional democracy have been wildly overblown across the ideological spectrum. In fact the Constitution, more than anything, laid the groundwork for centralized government and elite rule, a document revealing contempt for the democratic capacities of ordinary people – expressions of a pre-democratic era in which all forms of domination, later contested, were taken for granted.[49] Nor does Wolin entertain comparable myths about later American development, even taking into account struggles for democratization that were set in motion by a wave of popular movements: labor, populist, suffragist, black liberation, and others.

Taking analysis of power relations well beyond the mainstream, Wolin sets out to demolish fictions of a political system that from the outset barely concealed its darker legacy, behind the façade of a God-ordained national destiny. This was a country whose ruling elite, after all, presided over slavery, genocidal destruction of native populations, a ruthless capitalism, and perpetual colonial wars – all at a time of drastically restricted suffrage. Later, as democratic politics vastly improved, capitalist rationalization would give rise to an enlarged corporate, imperial, and globalized power structure that would in many ways clash with the requirements of political democracy.

Turning to the immediate post-World War II era, Wolin asks whether democracy even of the minimalist kind had much future at a time of expanding corporate, state, and military power aligned with the elite drive toward "full-spectrum" world domination. He reluctantly concludes that "One cannot point to any national institution that [today] can be accurately described as democratic ...."[50] Congress, the presidency, court systems, parties, bureaucracies, corporate workplaces, schools, universities – all these arenas of public life have been hierarchical, lacking widespread citizen participation. As for elections, voting turnout has rarely surpassed 50 percent in national elections and has often descended below 20 percent in local balloting. Power at the summits has grown so concentrated, along with mounting inequalities in wealth and income, that few commentators nowadays pause to take notice.

A decisive turning-point for Wolin was the expanded "power imaginary" of World War II and its aftermath: full-scale war mobilization, nuclear politics, a superpower agenda, the security state, and rise of a war economy have all extended the boundaries of power, making a shambles of the Constitution and fueling both statist and corporate authoritarianism. The classical liberalism of free markets, small government, and local autonomy had with the Cold War begun to lose whatever efficacy it possessed, even while opinion-leaders continued to celebrate its virtues. A new "power imaginary" meant, above all, an energized superpower agenda, global expansion, and solidification of corporate-state power – al consistent with the process of capitalist rationalization. As Wolin notes, the most novel aspect of this historic shift was its *immense scope*, beyond what the U.S. had earlier advanced as a colonial, interventionist nation driven by a morally-righteous nationalism. Thus: "Virtually from the beginning of the nation the making of the American citizen was influenced, even shaped by, the making of an American imperium."[51]

This "power imaginary" did not overturn but rather deepened and extended longstanding American oligarchical traditions. Here Wolin seems to be building on the central argument of Mills' *The Power Elite*, except that in *Democracy, Inc.*, flirting with the concept of "totalitarianism," Wolin ends up fixing attention on a behemoth more awesome and frightening than could even be found in Mills. As with Mills, Wolin's critical dissection of the American power structure is most illuminating when exploring the dialectic between superpower politics and domestic authoritarianism – a trend more fully explored in chapter seven. He sees the appearance of "managed democracy" where popular governance steadily declines in the face of capitalist rationalization, a phenomenon more visible in the post-9/11 milieu where terrorism (and the response to it) has functioned to legitimate the war economy and security state. In this setting "Terror is both a response to empire and the provocation that allows for empire to cease to be ashamed of its identity."[52] Constraints on power easily vanish in such a spatially and temporally limitless struggle. A global crusade against episodes of anti-Western terrorism allows the imperial state to cloak its power in the wounded innocence of avenging victim – raising comparisons with the sort of "palingenetic" ultra-nationalism that fueled classical fascism.[53]

The specter of a vengeful superpower armed with a doomsday military arsenal squaring off against purportedly deadly enemies calls forth a Hobbesian state of nature where the threat of chaos and anarchy is countered by a massive, all-powerful Leviathan. After all, the logic of imperial domination dictates repeated military interventions, political subterfuge, global surveillance, maximum elite flexibility, and "bipartisan" consensus – all signposts of steadily narrowing democratic politics. Wolin describes a postwar system more or less congruent with this Hobbesian scenario. At a time when familiar defining characteristics of the liberal state atrophy, the system gradually and almost imperceptibly acquires a new identity as "inverted totalitarianism," an order built on the deepening and solidifying of *existing trends*. It may well be the case that, as the revitalized "power imaginary" reshapes the public landscape, the old liberal ideals – democracy, free markets, limited government – will take on greater urgency, all the more so as those ideals become more detached from political reality.

The problem of shrinking political discourse, while consistent with Mills' analysis of "mass society," also closely echoes Marcuse's thesis of "one-dimensionality," though for Marcuse the problem was explained as a function technological rationality, discussed earlier by Horkheimer, Adorno, and other Frankfurt School theorists. Advanced industrial society, in Marcuse's view, was becoming an administered order beneath its liberal-democratic pretenses, all the while subverting critical thought and oppositional politics. Thus: "By virtue of the way it has organized its technological base, contemporary industrial society tends to be totalitarian. For 'totalitarian' is not only a terroristic political coordination of society, but also a non-terroristic economic-technical coordination which operates through the manipulation of needs by vested interests. It thus precludes the emergence of an effective opposition against the whole."[54] Marcuse concluded that "one-dimensional thought is systematically promoted by the masters of politics and their purveyors of mass information. Their universe of discourse is populated by circular, self-validating hypotheses which, incessantly and monopolistically repeated, become hypnotic definitions of freedom."[55]

Wolin, for his part, extends and reinvigorates the legacy of Mills at a time when an authoritarian and imperial state – however undermined by recurrent economic crises – shows few signs of weakening. Like Mills, Wolin theorizes a novel integration of state, corporate, and military power for postwar America, and like Mills he shows how mass political inertia is thoroughly interwoven with authoritarian politics. As noted, however, Wolin goes beyond Mills in his attention to ideology and culture within the legitimating process, crucial at times of sharpening crisis, as conventional thinking begins to lose hold. Wolin dismantles political myths that appear increasingly detached from everyday social reality. Wolin's dystopic view of American politics reflects a system of militarized state-capitalism that Mills had more broadly analyzed several decades earlier.

No doubt sooner than he might have realized, Mills wrote the obituary of a modern liberalism overridden by corporate, state, and military power. It would be the task of later critics of American politics to elaborate this trajectory in greater detail: Marcuse, Wolin, Chris Hedges, Michael Parenti, a few others. As Hedges writes in *Death of the Liberal Class* (2010): "What endures is not the fact of democratic liberalism but the myth of it. The myth is used by corporate-power elites and their apologists to justify the subjugation and manipulation of other nations in the name of national self-interest and democratic values." He adds: "The anemic liberal class continues to assert, despite ample evidence to the contrary, that human freedom and equality can be achieved through the charade of electoral politics and constitutional reform. It refuses to acknowledge the corporate domination of traditional democratic channels for ensuring broad participatory power."[56]

The gulf separating liberal platitudes and actual political realities that Mills so brilliantly deconstructed has only widened across the decades; indeed oligarchical structures have become ever more authoritarian and globalized. In Hedges' view:

> The inability of the liberal class to acknowledge that corporations have wrested power from the hands of citizens, that the Constitution and its guarantees of personal liberty have become irrelevant, and that the phrase *consent of the governed* is meaningless, has left it speaking and acting in ways

that no longer correspond to reality. It has lent its voice to hollow acts of political theater, and the pretense that democratic debate and choice continue to exist.[57]

As Mills had anticipated, the American political system is in no way friendly (or open) to genuine social reforms, much less radical change – that is, whatever happens to challenge ruling interests and agendas. The corporate-state and its myriad institutions is expertly designed to block anti-system forces, Hedges commenting:

> The liberal class cannot reform itself. It does not hold within its ranks the rebels and iconoclasts with the moral or physical courage to defy the corporate state and power elite. The corporate forces that sustain the media, unions, universities, religious institutions, the arts, and the Democratic Party oversaw the removal of all who challenged the corporation and unfettered capitalism.[58]

While Hedges indicts the major parties for shamelessly "colluding" with oligarchical power, in actuality the problem is less *collusion* than an organic confluence of dominant interests embedded in the twin processes of capitalist rationalization and corporate globalization.

The power elite of Mills' day has in the decades since attained a global presence that no observer of the early postwar era could have anticipated. Critics such as Leslie Sklar (*The Transnational Capitalist Class*), David Rothkopf (*Superclass*), William Robinson (*Global Capitalism and the Crisis of Humanity*), and Peter Phillips (*Giants*) have charted the rise of an international power elite that dwarfs twentieth-century conditions. By 2020 there were roughly 400 "super elites" at the top of the global pyramid where 17 financial conglomerates were managing some $41 trillion in networks of interlocking capital – a stupendous concentration of wealth centered in North America, Europe, and a few Asian nations.[59]

This vast concentration of wealth and power means the richest 1 percent of the world population controls nearly half of all planetary wealth, while the top 30 percent control 95 percent of all wealth and resources. Put differently, a total of 2,043 billionaires hold $7.67 trillion in available wealth, reflecting a network of obscene (and surely unsustainable) economic inequalities.[60] These are the elites attached to the World Economic Forum, with firm leverage at the World Bank, International Monetary Fund, and World Trade Organization. Phillips adds: "They personally know or know of each other, do business together, hold significant personal wealth, share similar educational and lifestyle backgrounds, and retain common global interests. Nearly all serve on the boards of directors of major capital investment firms or other major corporations and banks."[61]

Global elites were simultaneously presiding over roughly $255 trillion in global wealth and resources at a time when more than 2 billion people (of more than 7 billion) were living in extreme poverty, tens of millions on the verge of starvation. Such wealth, increasingly concentrated in the sectors of finance and technology, happens to coincide with the sharpening ecological crisis and mounting threat of resource wars among nations and corporations, on a planet of shrinking natural materials. Anticipating such a nightmarish future, many countries in the world are currently (in 2020) devoting massive new resources to their military forces, including nuclear weaponry that has already brought some nations closer to all-out war.

So long as huge transnational corporations and banking networks dominate the landscape, hopes for enlarged citizen participation will be diminished. At this juncture the fiction of human "progress" emerging from the combined processes of industrial development, scientific advance, and technological innovation simply ignores the exploitation, repression, violence, and war associated with the darker expressions of modernity. In Hedges' words: ".... corporations are not concerned with the common good. They exploit, pollute, impoverish, repress, kill, and lie to make money. They throw poor families out of homes, let the uninsured die, wage useless wars to make profits, poison and pollute the ecosystem ... and crush all popular movements that seek justice for working men and women."[62]

What Mills in his most imaginative moments could not have foreseen was the degree to which the power elite would preside over an ecological crisis possibly leading to global catastrophe. In the 1950s, of course, imminent disaster resided in the threat of nuclear annihilation. While that fear has not vanished, today it appears to have been superseded by fears of environmental destruction so extreme that planetary survival has been thrown into question, Hedges writing: "The human race is about to be abruptly reminded of the fragility of life and the danger of hubris. Those who exploit human beings and nature are bound to an irrational lust for power and money that is leading to collective suicide."[63] He concludes, with appropriate sense of urgency: "Our mediocre and bankrupt elite, concerned with its own survival, spends its energy and our resources desperately trying to save a system that cannot be saved."[64] Were Mills around today, he could not have phrased the matter more succinctly – or more ominously.

Notes

1 C. Wright Mills, *The Sociological Imagination* (New York: Oxford University Press, 1959), p. 129.
2 Ibid.
3 Ibid., pp. 149–150.
4 Ibid., p. 150.
5 Ibid., p. 166.
6 C. Wright Mills, *The Power Elite* (New York: Oxford University Press, 1956), p. 5.
7 Ibid., p. 7.
8 Ibid., p. 8.
9 Ibid., p. 9.
10 Ibid., p. 23.

11 Ibid., p. 165.
12 Ibid., p. 171.
13 Ibid., p. 185.
14 Ibid., p. 202.
15 See Seymour Melman, *The Permanent War Economy* (New York: Simon and Schuster, 1985), and Fred Cook, *The Warfare State* (New York: Collier Books, 1964).
16 Mills, *Power Elite*, p. 355.
17 Ibid., p. 360.
18 Ibid., p. 361.
19 Ibid., p. 235.
20 Ibid., p. 276.
21 C. B. Macpherson, *The Life and Times of Liberal Democracy* (New York: Oxford University Press, 1977), pp. 89–92.
22 Mills, *Power Elite*, p. 274.
23 Ibid., p. 343.
24 G. William Domhoff, *Who Rules America?* (New York: McGraw-Hill, 2010), ch. 2.
25 Ibid., p. xiv.
26 Ibid., p. 218.
27 Ibid., p. 39.
28 Ibid., pp. 39–40.
29 See Tom Hayden, *Radical Nomad: C. Wright Mills and His Time* (Boulder, CO: Paradigm, 2006), p. 132.
30 Ibid., p. 133.
31 Ibid., p. 133.
32 C. Wright Mills, *The Marxists* (New York: Dell, 1962), pp. 12–13.
33 For Mills' prescient analysis of "mass society," see *Power Elite,* pp. 315–324.
34 Ibid., p. 302.
35 Ibid., ch. 12.
36 Ibid., p. 324.
37 Ibid., p. 219.
38 Ibid., p. 223.
39 Ibid., p. 310.
40 Ibid., p. 317.
41 Ibid., p. 336.
42 Ibid., p. 343.
43 Ibid., p. 297.
44 Ibid., p. 300.
45 See John Stuart Mill, *On Liberty* (Cleveland: Meridian Books, 1962), pp. 129–130.
46 Mills, *Power Elite*, p. 310.
47 Ibid., p. 78.
48 See Eric Fromm, *Escape from Freedom* (New York: Avon Books, 1969).
49 On the waning of Constitutional powers in the face of new challenges, see Sheldon Wolin, *Democracy, Inc.* (Princeton, NJ: Princeton University Press, 2008), ch. 1.
50 Ibid., p. 17.
51 Ibid., p. 18.
52 Ibid., p. 19.
53 On the theme of palingenetic nationalism, see Roger Griffin, *The Nature of Fascism* (London: Routledge, 1991).
54 See Herbert Marcuse, *One-Dimensional Man* (Boston, MA: Beacon Press, 1964), p. 3.
55 Ibid., p. 14.
56 See Chris Hedges, *Death of the Liberal Class* (New York: Nation Books, 2010), p. 8.
57 Ibid., pp. 9–10.
58 Ibid., p. 14.

59 Peter Phillips, *Giants* (New York: Seven Stories, 2018), pp. 29–30.
60 Ibid., p. 27.
61 Ibid., p. 29.
62 Hedges, *Death of the Liberal Class*, p. 17.
63 Ibid., p. 194.
64 Ibid., p. 201.

6
CAPITALISM, TECHNOLOGY, POWER

This book focuses on how modern capitalism has managed to increase its domination over the public landscape since World War I and, more emphatically, across the post-World War II era. Put differently, theoretical and political attention is fixed throughout on the widening challenges faced by oppositional (especially anti-system) movements in settings where ideological hegemony has taken its firmest hold. Both Lenin and Gramsci, as we have seen, were among the first to grasp this problem as an obstacle to revolutionary change. Crucial expectations of classical Marxism, its hopes fixated on the industrial proletariat, have been negated in great measure by the incessant workings of capitalist rationalization fueled by technology as one locus of power.

By late twentieth century and into the new century, this process has given rise to what might be labeled advanced techno-capitalism.[1] While this system was first theorized more than a century ago, nowadays technology as a broadening system of domination has come to shape and reshape the economy, government, military, culture, education, and the entire sphere of communications. Early Marxists obviously could not have anticipated this development, much less a globalized corporate-state form of capitalism within which it is embedded. And they could not have imagined the enormous roadblocks it would pose for anti-capitalist movements and parties. Today, of course, we have seen how oppositional politics – Socialists, Communists, Greens, others – have uniformly suffered the fate of deradicalization even while the modern crisis intensifies.

The main features of techno-capitalism can be located at the center of capitalist rationalization, driven increasingly by an integration of economic and political interests that define the rise of state-capitalism. Technology in this milieu intersects with virtually everything – material productivity and growth, workplace efficiency and controls, education, the military, corporate globalization, media culture. One ideological cornerstone of this system is technological rationality, first theorized by Weber and later more fully explored by the Frankfurt School.

Twentieth-century capitalism in the U.S. gave rise to a novel system – militarized corporate-state-capitalism, a departure from anything preceding it, whether classical liberal capitalism, social democracy, Soviet-style Communism, or fascism. Technological rationality would be central to this new matrix of power, which only gained momentum across subsequent decades. To understand this system, as Mills was the first to recognize, demanded theoretical categories far removed from those furnished by classical Marxism, or in fact reconstituted versions of the tradition. At this juncture, ideological hegemony would rest increasingly upon technological rationality, mediated through the culture industry that had become so integral to mass society.

Capitalism and Technology

In their classic *Dialectic of Enlightenment*, Adorno and Horkheimer had (in the 1940s) set forth arguments leading up to Marcuse's seminal work of two decades later. The authors viewed modernity – above all capitalist modernity – as a source of domination shrouded in false Enlightenment claims of social progress: freedom, democracy, prosperity. Instead of (or alongside) such "progress," the developmental pattern was leading to an administered order in which liberal democracy survived as little more than a political façade. Adorno and Horkheimer wrote that this apparatus "turns into an instrument of rational administration by the wholly enlightened as they steer society toward barbarism," for "enlightenment is as totalitarian as any system." They added: "A technological rationale is the rationale of domination itself. It is the coercive nature of society alienated from itself."[2]

In such a society modern forms of domination include not only enlarged state functions but corporate interests that have taken control of an increasingly rationalized public realm. This dynamic was imperfectly captured by Marx's heralded theory of commodity fetishism or Lukacs' later theory of reification, as these were based more strictly on market (or exchange) relations that, while still present, had been superseded by more pervasive and authoritarian forms of control. The first theorist to fully appreciate this aspect of modernity was Gramsci, writing in "Americanism and Fordism" during the 1930s (part of his *Prison Notebooks*), where he extended his concept of hegemony to transformation of the capitalist workplace. As Gramsci framed capitalist rationalization, with the U.S. ever at the forefront, workers had become atomized and pulverized by the workings of assembly-line technology, where they were subjugated by management and turned into helpless robots or "trained gorillas."[3]

For post-World War II American society, techno-capitalism is shaped by the growth of technology as both structural and ideological force. In *One-Dimensional Man*, Marcuse depicts technological rationality precisely as a system of integration and control, a phenomenon that reinforces the broad matrix of domination with special roots in advanced capitalism. One result has been growth of a new authoritarian politics, yet another the closure of critical thinking and radical opposition. Marcuse writes: "In the medium of technology, culture, politics, and the economy merge into an omnipresent system which swallows up or repulses all alternatives." It follows that, for modern capitalism, technology is nothing less than fully constitutive of the rhythms and flows of everyday life. Thus: "Today domination perpetuates and extends itself not only through technology but *as* technology, and the latter provides the great legitimation of expanding political power, which absorbs all spheres of culture."[4]

Though rarely discussed, Marcuse had earlier (in the mid-1950s) theorized Soviet development along similar lines in *Soviet Marxism*. In the USSR history had revealed fatal shortcomings of Marxist theory – or, put differently, showed how economic rationalization in a bureaucratic-centralist setting required newer categories of analysis. Marcuse wrote that the Soviet system was built on full-scale mobilization of human, material, and technological resources for distinctly political ends.[5] In Soviet society "technological progress and mass production shattered the individualistic forms in which progress operated during the liberal era."[6] In this context theory (or "Marxism-Leninism") winds up ritualized as a form of official state ideology: "Soviet Marxism here shares in the decline of language and communication in the age of mass societies."[7] In other words, the trajectories of East and West under a regimen of technological rationalization shared far more in common than standard Cold War discourses had assumed.

After his extended study of Soviet politics, Marcuse concluded that for Marxism, theory no longer corresponded even vaguely to actuality, to any rendering of historical concreteness. Even more problematic, "In its ossified form, emptied of its meaning which had been critical of and antagonistic to the established society, the ideology became a tool of domination."[8] Here Marcuse's analysis of a Soviet society in the midst of accelerated economic development would anticipate the very conditions of advanced capitalism laid out in *One Dimensional Man*. In both cases technology served to establish new foundations for elite rule through expanded social and ideological control.

Back to American society, Marcuse took up the familiar Frankfurt discourse linking technological rationality, mass culture, and consumerism. A passage from *One Dimensional Man* seems to address this ensemble of relations:

> The capabilities (intellectual and material) of contemporary society are immeasurably greater than ever before – which means the scope of society's domination over the individual is immeasurably greater than ever before. Our society distinguishes itself by conquering the centrifugal social forces with technology rather than terror, on the basis of an overwhelming efficiency and an increasing standard of living.[9]

While a sweeping process of rationalization that winds up propelling growth and efficiency is ultimately "irrational" in its disastrous larger consequences, it nonetheless serves to legitimate the system."[10]

At times Marcuse appeared to retain faith in Marxism, yet his general body of work refuted that: the power of capitalist rationalization was simply too overwhelming, too stifling to permit continuation of older modes of thought – or of politics. In *One Dimensional Man* he complained that, "confronted with the total character of the achievements of advanced industrial society, critical theory is left without the rationale for transcending the society."[11] Not only had the modern proletariat become fully integrated into the matrix of domination, basic theoretical categories inherited from the Marxist classics had become worn out, obsolete. The prospects for qualitative change (as opposed to liberal reformism) had become effectively blocked in a world ruled by technological rationality.

Beyond that impasse, modern capitalist society itself has grown increasingly authoritarian, even "totalitarian," given that even mild forms of dissent had been systematically undermined, or in fact irrelevant even where permitted. Thus: "In this society, the productive apparatus tends to become totalitarian to the extent to which it determines not only the socially needed occupations, skills, and attitudes, but also individual needs and aspirations. It thus obliterates the opposition between the private and public existence, between individual and social needs."[12] Read politically, such passages demonstrate the corrosive effects of capitalist rationalization working beneath the structures and processes of constitutional democracy. Like Mills, Marcuse believed that electoral politics as normalized in the U.S. and Europe could never be a useful vehicle of radical change; the status quo defies all transcendence of its structures and values.

Here again Marcuse depicts a convergence of corporate-state capitalism and Soviet Communism beneath the superficial differences and rival ideological claims – at odds with the Cold War mythology of the period. Such heretical views were denounced by gatekeepers of the political and media establishments, wedded to the epic conflict between "democracy" versus "totalitarianism," that is, between good and evil. In both systems, according to Marcuse, technological advance brought increased material abundance along with uneven development and heightened domination.[13] In both cases, moreover, the observable result was "authoritarian ritualization of discourse."[14] Under such conditions it was likely that Marxist theory would collapse of its own insufficiency: "The reality of the laboring classes in advanced industrial society makes the Marxian 'proletariat' a mythological concept; the reality of present-day socialism makes the Marxian idea like a dream."[15] Not only Soviet Marxism, but "Western" variants of Marxism had lost their conceptual vitality.

With postwar stabilization of capitalism in the West, the problem faced by general populations everywhere was that of *systemic domination*. It was as if, after so many decades of capitalist rationalization, the majority of people ended up bound to Weber's "iron cage" – ideologically if not socially. The deep system of controls available to ruling elites had grown more invasive over time, more irreversible. With proletarian opposition everywhere now weakened if not eviscerated, the question for many turned on prospects for a newer source of negation. In Marcuse's words: "How can the administered individuals – who have made their mutilation into their own liberties and satisfactions, and thus reproduce it on an enlarged scale – liberate themselves from themselves as well as from their masters? How is it even thinkable that the vicious cycle be broken?"[16] At this juncture, the epic struggle to overturn domination would require an entirely new historical subject – or, in Gramsci's terminology, an "historical bloc" comprised of diverse social forces.

In *Counterrevolution and Revolt*, Marcuse would later elaborate on his pessimism about a class-based revolution: "Socialism no longer appears as the definite negation of capitalism."[17] In reality, for the U.S. at least, there was had developed a stronger mass base for *fascism*: "The country possesses economic and technological resources for a totalitarian organization immeasurably greater than Hitler's Germany ever had."[18] At the point Marcuse famously located a "substratum of the outcasts and outsiders, the exploited and persecuted of other races and other colors, the unemployed and unemployable." One great advantage of this approach was "their opposition hits the system from without and is therefore not deflected by the system."[19]

That opposition would ostensibly take shape in the "Great Refusal" – a stratagem, if it can be called that, loosely grounded in the 1960s new left and counterculture. Here and elsewhere Marcuse recognized not only the historic impotence of liberalism but, more centrally, the decline of mass Socialist and Communist parties in Europe. While the Great Refusal could be situated in elements of the new left, that too would be rather problematic. In *Counterrevolution and Revolt* he commented, with seeming resignation, that "at the present stage [early 1970s], the New Left is necessarily and essentially an *intellectual* movement, and the *anti*-intellectualism practiced in its own ranks is indeed a service to the Establishment."[20]

This indispensable "service" to the power elite would signal a return to the familiar pessimism of the Frankfurt School. That same motif would later be restated in the concept of "artificial negativity" in the work of Paul Piccone.[21] In Piccone's view, the totally-administered society had so rationalized and homogenized the system as to require occasional injections of "artificial negativity" as an "internal control mechanism" to keep the political order from stagnating. The result was a more legitimated and stabilized capitalist system that long ago had managed to domesticate new forms of social conflict.

The McDonaldized Society

There is of course nothing new about capitalist rationalization of the workplace – or of modern society in general. Fordism, or Taylorized mass production, go back to the 1890s in the U.S. as well as a few other industrializing countries. As noted, this mechanism allowed ruling elites to stave off disruptive class conflict and further consolidate power. Science, technology, bureaucracy – these resources were employed in the service of efficiency and control. While capitalism has grown increasingly corporatized and globalized over many decades, the main components of rationalization have scarcely disappeared.

What might be viewed as Fordist domination of the labor process anticipated far-reaching changes in production and work relations beyond what Weber theorized after 1900 and Gramsci had in mind during the 1930s. Such writers as Harry Braverman (*in Labor and Monopoly Capital*) and Richard Edwards (in *Contested Terrain*) during the 1970s would extend Gramsci's fragmentary work in "Americanism and Fordism," describing the system as even more authoritarian and repressive than had been typical of earlier types of Fordism.[22] In this harshly coercive milieu the degree of proletarian subjectivity, or agency, needed to revolutionary action would be difficult, if not impossible, to reach.

By the 1970s capitalism had become fully rationalized in the U.S. and Europe, based mainly on control mechanisms embedded in technological innovation, going well beyond the realm of production itself. Class relations had grown more regulated, institutionalized, and contained. Modes of domination as such were now further routinized, both structurally and ideologically, indicative of concentrated power, oligopolistic markets, economic globalization, and technological advance. Within such an order various surveillance functions – electronic monitoring, eavesdropping, tracking, and so forth – would begin to expand as part of a hyper-rationalized matrix of production and consumption. Government and corporations would further merge within a framework of planning and coordination.

This fortress, unprecedented in scope, has taken capitalist rationalization to new heights, with ever more sophisticated modalities of control. George Ritzer, for example, has written extensively on the more recent spread of "McDonaldization" – that is, growth of the fast-food economy and its replication across the society, remaking production, work, consumption, food habits, even medicine.[23] The McDonald's regimen has for decades represented a metaphor for stepped-up regulation and standardization of daily life. The food industry has built a workforce that is poorly paid, subject to weak nonexistent labor protections, powerless, subject to technological forces where management exercises nearly total control over the minds and bodies of its employees. By 2020, the McDonaldized workplace had surveillance so ubiquitous, so effective, as to be taken for granted.

This same technological apparatus has extended from fast foods to retail operations (Wal-Mart, K-Mart), coffee shops (Starbucks), health services, and higher education to supposedly meet the digital age. Echoing and updating Gramsci, Ritzer observes: "Instead of expressing their human abilities on the job, people are forced to deny their humanity and act like robots."[24] Advanced forms of surveillance – Internet monitoring, GPS tracking, mobile technology, public cameras, facial recognition devices – are more intrusive everywhere along the public terrain. The older Fordist and Taylorized systems nowadays seem rather antiquated. Data collection on virtually everything has become routine for personal records, Internet transactions, banking, travel, health information, and so on. The rise of Idematics and similar corporate surveillance has only streamlined what is best described as an Orwellian process.

Ritzer's seminal work was deeply influenced by Weber, who would appreciate McDonaldization as the ultimate expression of capitalist rationalization, writing: "The fast-food restaurant has become the model of rationalization. Although it has adopted elements of rationalization pioneered by its predecessors, it also represents a quantum leap in the process of rationalization."[25] McDonald's thus embellishes the power of nonhuman technology – tools, machines, knowledge, rules, procedures – to maximize its power over humans. With the spread of robotics, employees are forced to surrender their autonomy and subjectivity to the whole apparatus of domination.[26] In contrast to Marcuse's emphasis on technological rationality – that is, essentially a form of ideology – for Ritzer the impact on workers (and others) is more the consequence of *structures*.

In the McDonald's world of routinization, human contact is to be minimized, regulated. For the consumer, moreover, the fast-food culture perfectly fits the rhythms of a suburban, mobile, dispersed population, where the extent of everyday decision-making is reduced. It also converges with the ascendancy of media advertising within a dynamic mass-consumer society.

Elsewhere Ritzer refers to the rapid growth in advanced capitalism of new means of consumption – namely, "cathedrals of consumption" such as casinos, theme parks, sports extravaganzas, shopping malls, cruise ships, more recently superstores like Amazon and Wal-Mart. All this corresponds to differing forms of economic rationalization, laid out in *Enchanting a Disenchanted World*, meaning: "As is the case with religious cathedrals, the cathedrals of consumption are not only enchanted, they are also highly rationalized."[27] Effectively favoring the Frankfurt School over Marxism, Ritzer writes: "American society is now better characterized by consumption than production."[28] Put differently, the factory has been supplanted by fast-food outlets and shopping malls as centers of daily life and, therefore, of consciousness formation, the linkage supplied by technology: "It is probable that technological change is the most important factor in why it is that we are now witnessing the ascendancy of the new means of consumption."[29]

For Ritzer, McDonaldization and the cathedrals of consumption illustrate a phase of capitalism associated with technological innovation, suburbanization, and physical mobility tied to the rise of automobile culture and the corporate media. The social consequences, as both Mills and Marcuse had emphasized, include a more rigid social and ideological conformity even in the midst (nowadays) of identity politics and "multiculturalism." Though Ritzer directs little of his analysis toward politics, the historical reverberations of McDonaldization seem inescapable: trends work steadily to defeat prospects for radical change.

The Mass-Surveillance Order

The intensifying process of capitalist rationalization has meant, first and foremost, heightened forms of domination – over the workplace, over society, over nature. Nowhere has this process been more fully played out than in postwar American society, though a few other industrialized systems have been catching up. Given this trajectory, who could be astonished at the expansion of a surveillance society without historical precedent in its scope and consequences. George Orwell to the contrary, the contemporary American power structure dwarfs earlier totalitarian regimes in its enormous capacity for social and ideological control.

As previously indicated, that power structure is unique, with no clear antecedent – a form of militarized state-capitalism developed nowhere else in the world. Its global presence, its constant pursuit of wealth, resources, and power effectively dictates a warmaking machine and an authoritarian state. It also guaranteed the demand, or need, for a surveillance order beyond anything historically imagined. By early twenty-first century this system was firmly entrenched, a dominant (though often unacknowledged) force in American life, its constituent elements ubiquitous: the NSA, FBI, CIA, DEA, DHS, and Pentagon to name the crucial sectors. Giant communications and technology corporations became fixtures of that system. We have arrived at what Maureen Webb has labeled the "corporate-security complex" vital to an imperial foreign policy.[30]

There is nothing paradoxical or illogical about this behemoth. Indeed, with the growth of technological surveillance, personal tracking, and Internet monitoring we have reached a point where the most intrusive controls face few ethical, social, or political constraints; it is all about the command of unfettered elite power. Webb comments: "In the fray of all the activity ... corporations are constantly pushing the envelope of social control by technological means – egging on governments to embrace bigger, newer, more expensive and more intrusive systems of social control."[31] What Ritzer describes for workplace rationalization extends to the war making apparatus and security state, now worldwide in scope. Only an authoritarian state with vast technological power can sustain great superpower ambitions insofar as ruling elites, in Webb's language, "need to maintain tight control at home in order to extract the political, material, and human resources they need for their [imperial] project and, at the same time, to avoid being overwhelmed by dissent and popular unrest."[32]

To fully grasp the role of mass surveillance in the U.S., a useful point of departure is the NSA (National Security Agency), dramatized in the 2014 Oscar-winning documentary *Citizenfour*, directed by Laura Poitras with NSA defector Edward Snowden once at the center of an ongoing international saga. The reality of a draconian security apparatus in the U.S. had by then become rather common knowledge. Less well known was the historical context of such an enormous threat to human freedom, privacy, democracy, and indeed social change – above all, the spectacular growth of a warfare state beginning in World War II and spanning the decades of the Cold War and then a new era of regime-change interventions in the Middle East and elsewhere. Since 1945 this global fortress has evolved with little resistance among either elites or masses. Nowadays it includes no fewer than 17 federal agencies along with hundreds of state and local agencies involved in homeland security, surveillance, covert operations, war on drugs, military interventions, and ordinary law enforcement. It is strongly aided and abetted by the Big Tech sector of corporate capitalism.

When interviewed in *Citizenfour*, Snowden commented: "We are building the biggest weapon of oppression in the history of mankind." A pressing question for the current era: could this system have already grown beyond the capacity of mortal humans to understand, much less counter or overturn? Could it represent a fatal blow to hopes in the U.S. or other advanced capitalist countries for sustaining anything close to a democratic politics, much less transformative change? Put differently, could humanity even begin to effectively confront challenges such as global warming so long as the surveillance order remains intact?

According to such writers as James Bamford (in *The Shadow Factory* and elsewhere) and Glenn Greenwald (in *No Place to Hide*), the aggressive NSA has been engaged in nonstop secret monitoring and tracing of both American citizens and others around the world, with little if any accountability, based on generally questionable (if at times persuasive) rationale of imminent foreign threats to national security or "democracy" (as was claimed during the Russiagate hoax).[33] As *Citizenfour* pointed out, the post-9/11 U.S. surveillance network vacuums up billions of electronic transactions *daily*, capable of locating millions of people via cell-phone activity, social media interactions, facial recognition devices, and GPS coordinates. The NSA in turn shares its voluminous information with such agencies as the FBI, CIA, DEA, and IRS, along with multiple layers of state and local police agencies.

The NSA itself is nowadays involved with corporate giants, especially those in the Big Tech sector. It works closely with business interests like Microsoft, Verizon, AT&T, Apple, and Google – all crucial to the smooth functioning of American (also global) communications technology. The Agency produces massive watch lists, identifying (in 2015) as many as a million potential "threats" entered into the Terrorist Identities Datamart Environment (TIDE). For such purposes the NSA maintains acres of super-computers, its mission going back to 1952 and best detailed in a series of books by Bamford, starting with his classic *The Puzzle Palace* and including *Body of Secrets* and *A Pretext for War* along with the previously mentioned *The Shadow Factory*.[34]

The NSA continues to collect many billions of telephone items and computer data from around the world, much of it from (theoretically exempt) American citizens, part of an unparalleled system of Metadata collections known only to ruling elites. The threat this poses not only to ordinary freedoms and privacy but to virtually any form of dissent and protest – crucial to the work of social movements and citizens organizations – should be obvious, as it was to both Snowden and the filmmakers of *Citizenfour*. While such "deep state" surveillance technology serves elite domination, that state of affairs has, sadly, has met little opposition in Congress, the media, academia, or elsewhere. Moreover, as we shall see, the Democrats (allied with media outlets) thoroughly relied on such operations to carry out their sabotage of the Trump presidency starting in spring 2016.[35]

Driven by a tightening merger of dominant interests – corporate, government, military, media – this power apparatus has taken on an existence of its own, feeding a system of integrated domination. Aside from the work of Bamford and Greenwald, recent books that explore this politics of surveillance include Bob Scheer's *They Know Everything about You*, Bruce Schneier's *Data and Goliath*, Anthony Gregory's *American Surveillance*, and Peter J. Hasson's *The Manipulators*.[36]

Modern technology, as Frankfurt School critics, George Orwell, and such writers as Jacques Ellul and Langdon Winner long ago predicted, always had the potential to be turned into an instrument of repression. Could the system now have reached that potential? In fact that system already surpasses, in certain ways, earlier fascist and Stalinist modes of terror and propaganda. Here Greenwald writes: "Technology has now enabled a type of ubiquitous surveillance that had previously been the promise of only the most imaginative science fiction writers. Moreover, the post-9/11 American veneration of security has created a climate particularly conducive to abuses of power."[37] That assessment, in the modern era of Washington "deep state" resurgence, turns out to be something of an understatement.

The contribution of media culture to this authoritarian nightmare cannot be stressed enough. Integral to the success of the American political class. The media establishment long ago stopped performing simple tasks of information and entertainment. The most respected outlets (starting with the *New York Times* and *Washington Post*) have been converted into tools of outright propaganda in partnership with agencies of the "deep state." Greenwald notes: "Those who thrive within the structure of large corporations tend to be adept at pleasing rather than subverting institutional power. It follows that t hose who succeed in corporate journalism are suited to accommodate power. They identify with institutional authority and are skilled at serving, not combating, it."[38]

Whether this is a prime example of Orwellian totalitarianism is yet another matter. In his classic *1984*, Orwell envisioned a tyranny rooted in a matrix of government surveillance, public manipulation, state propaganda, and perpetual warfare – a system referred to as INGSOC that would be firmly under the control of a well-organized party elite. Such a tyranny would be maintained under the auspices of Big Brother, dedicated to little beyond the accumulation of power (also wealth) for its own sake. Orwell's main protagonist was Winston Smith, working for the notorious Ministry of Truth and charged with carrying out nonstop propaganda, surveillance, and police work. The novel served to popularize the term Orwellian, which over time came to signify official deception, crude manipulation, and brainwashing in the service of a totalitarian state that looked very much like Stalin's USSR. That state would permit no dissent, criticism, protest, or other forms of opposition.

Orwell's fictional country of Oceania was indeed based on the Soviet Union, hardly surprising since *1984* was written just as the Cold War was gaining momentum. According to Orwell – and a legion of Western social scientists and journalists – totalitarian power corresponded to a life of abject misery for the great mass of people, living in the midst of scandalous elite privilege and power. Most citizens of Oceania were condemned to a life of two-way telescreens, those in control able to monitor their every move. All public space was under the watchful eye of the Thought Police: the slightest indication of dissent was to be met with merciless governmental controls, arrests carried out for the flimsiest of infractions. Orwell, a dedicated anarchist, was deeply influenced by Spanish leftists during the Civil War, the work of Leon Trotsky, and Orwell's own life-changing experience during the 1930s Spanish events. The great horrors of Stalinism, slowly revealed during the same time period, became the main source for Big Brother and *1984*.

Orwell's great work became part of the Western struggle against "totalitarianism," then located mainly in the USSR though ostensibly applicable to Nazi Germany and other fascist regimes. This found epic representation in another of Orwell's books, *Animal Farm*, Hannah Arendt's *Origins of Totalitarianism*, and such Hollywood films as *The Manchurian Candidate, Enemy of the State, V for Vendetta*, and *The Hunger Games* sequence, where we encounter an impoverished, powerless mass of people facing monolithic state power controlled by a tiny group of sadistic power-mongers, a system the creators seemed to associate with "state socialism." A harsh critique of totalitarianism has been advanced by a wide spectrum of morally-charged opponents of authoritarian statism: anarchists, Trotskyists, liberals, conservatives, social democrats. Of course Orwell's book has done much legitimate this critique, its popularity just as strong today as during the peak of Stalin's power during the 1940s and 1950s.

In fact these critics were completely off the mark – and remain so today: the metaphor "1984" amounts to a largely worthless model for understanding present-day surveillance and, more pertinently, modern power structures. The Orwellian reference suffers from failure to deal with the general system of domination of which intelligence and surveillance operations are simply one part. This view of totalitarianism was always mechanistic and ahistorical, framing Big Brother as something imposed externally, in the dead of night. To the contrary, power structures within modern capitalism have evolved more or less organically through a complex historical process drive by capital accumulation, technological rationalization, corporate globalization, and (for the U.S.) an expanding war economy and security state that, as mentioned, goes back to World War II. This system was hardly imposed by some evil outside force but has rather matured domestically within a specific historical framework.

As Mills emphasized in the *Power Elite*, we have here not so much a monstrous, all-powerful Big Brother but an historic merger of corporate, government, and military (along with media) power – all within the gradual maturation of modern capitalism. The issue of propaganda, so crucial to Orwellian discourse, is riddled with assorted myths and partial truths: Orwell's crude rendering fails to capture what is actually situated within capitalist modernity, where mass media, popular culture, and the larger communications terrain profoundly impacts the general society, transforming large areas of mass consciousness in the process. The newer reality is not to be confused with state-organized brainwashing that has rarely been effective, whether during fascism and Nazism or Soviet-style Communism. As noted, this point was stressed by Marcuse in *Soviet Marxism*, where he explored the futility of an official, ritualized state ideology. The Orwellian model always suggested a mechanistic, crude, lifeless view of how popular beliefs and attitudes are formed.

For many years the American surveillance system has conducted its business with few impediments or limits all the more so after 9/11 and the stepped-up war against terrorism, which eventually gave way to media-generated anti-Russia hysteria. The targets have been many: foreign countries, suspected terrorist groups, drug traffickers, dissident intellectuals. Rarely, however, have massive intelligence resources been turned against competing election campaigns, yet that was precisely the case when the Trump campaign and presidency was targeted for sabotage, then impeachment, by deep-state operations loyal to Barack Obama starting in early 2016 – a crusade that desperately (and futilely) sought out high "crimes" year after year.

Trump's most unforgivable problem, beside his improbable ascent to the White House, was his promise to end Middle East wars and seek closer relations with Russia to fight jihadic terrorism and contain a nuclear arms race. This was too much for the Democrats, neocon foreign-policy establishment, deep-state agencies, and the corporate media run by such interests as Comcast, AT&T, and Amazon, all closely tied to Big Tech. Their overwhelming ambition was to isolate and marginalize Russia, perhaps with longer-term aspirations of regime change. Here Putin had to be demonized as a dictatorial, imperialist monster. Angered, powerful figures in the outgoing Obama administration unleashed the permanent Washington bureaucracy to get Trump removed from office, aided and abetted by the corporate media. These elites settled on an evidence-free collusion theory, many going so far as to accuse Trump of being "Putin's agent" or a "Russian asset." When that failed, charges revolved around Trump's supposed scheme to get the Ukrainians involved in a corrupt maneuver to influence the 2020 election.

While the Ukraine pretext also uncovered no wrongdoing on Trump's part, the ensuing impeachment proceedings did serve to immobilize his presidency, forcing the U.S. to adopt a more hostile stance toward Moscow (including stepped-up economic sanctions). Since 2017 American/NATO destabilizing activities in eastern Europe have been on the upswing. Meanwhile, a new Cold War accompanied by rampant domestic McCarthyism has only worsened international tensions while degrading political discourse in Washington and across the country. The anti-Russia hysteria that poisoned the public landscape is extensively covered by Don Kovalik in *The Plot to Scapegoat Russia* and Stephen F. Cohen's *War with Russia?* [39]

At a time when Russia was being routinely assaulted for "destroying American democracy," it was actually the Democrats (along with their deep-state and media enablers) who set out to illegally reverse the 2016 election outcome. To carry out such an unprecedented plan, Washington elites seemed entirely prepared to provoke Russia to the edge of nuclear exchange – a war that could have meant the end of planetary civilization. Relying on phony charges and a dishonest Special Counsel, Trump's fanatical enemies sought out every conceivable transgression as a pretext for what can only be described as a domestic coup. There is abundant evidence that, not only corporate media outlets but elements of Big Tech participated in the plot. Writes Gregg Jarrett in *The Russia Hoax*, after exhaustive research on the plot: "The greatest peril to democracy today is not a foreign force but the abuse of power from within."[40]

A similar scheme was hitched nearly two decades earlier, when the deep state (notably the CIA), neocons, Pentagon, and the media orchestrated a propaganda war justifying President George W. Bush's disastrous invasion of Iraq. Then, of course, the propaganda revolved around Saddam Hussein's supposed stockpile of weapons of mass destruction – indeed his supposed imminent threat to the U.S. homeland. Throughout this fraudulent orchestration of criminal military intervention, the CIA and NSA famously combined to gather "incriminating sources of information," even using the United Nations mission in the Middle East to do so.[41] The result was one of the most destructive ventures in U.S. history.

Back to everyday life: over the past two decades sophisticated U.S. surveillance technology has gotten only more rationalized and refined with each passing year. One could argue that this phenomenon now constitutes a dominant feature of advanced industrial society. For a superpower like the U.S. such development has been unavoidable – its elites requiring nothing short of full-spectrum information. This apparatus, as we have seen, routinely collects, analyzes, and stores data on tens of millions of people in the U.S. and around the world. Public cameras, GPS systems, tracking operations, infrared sensors, and drone activities are by 2020 a routine feature of everyday life in American society. So-called "eye-in-the-sky" coverage is virtually inescapable, whether in workplaces, public buildings, streets, vehicles, or for the Internet and social media. Drone surveillance has become increasingly ubiquitous, its costs having dropped considerably. Public resistance to such invasion of privacy and freedoms is often invisible, especially as the majority of people are clueless about its origins and consequences. The problem is that not only do such "deep state" agencies as the NSA and CIA work in total secrecy, so to do many of their corporate partners.

Big Tech Oligarchy

The twenty-first century has seen the rise of a corporate sector like nothing before it in history – a sector with increasingly *global* reach. The rapid ascent of high-tech giants – Microsoft, Google, Facebook, Amazon, Twitter, Apple, etc. – is a development that in

2020 would be hard to over-state. Though Marcuse was able to identify crucial theoretical categories of this development, he could not have imagined it astonishing scope and repercussions. At this juncture capitalist rationalization appears to be reaching its zenith, expanding well beyond the framework of Fordism and Taylorism, or even Orwellian narratives. One difference regarding Big Tech is that its chieftains view their own brand of technological rationality as uniquely liberating – a domain of free expression, open interaction, intellectual creativity, and political empowerment, endowing Silicon Valley (and its many kindred locales) with a special historical trajectory. Many high-tech elites go further, embracing their work as noble, even spiritual.

The reality is that the technology giants are in the process of remolding every sphere of life within advanced capitalism. In certain ways the Silicon Valley template turns out to have more in common with McDonaldization than its propagandists will ever admit. With the Internet, social media, and other sectors of the new technology, we are dealing with a globalized oligopoly able to shape the worldwide flow of markets, communication, knowledge, and decision-making. Beneath all the libertarian pretenses we encounter just the opposite – concentrated economic power, social manipulation, political conformism, a willingness to shut down dissident views. In fact Big Tech would have far more in common with Marcuse's "one-dimensionality" than with the familiar open-society claims of Mark Zuckerberg (Facebook), Jack Dorsey (Twitter), and Jeff Bezos (Amazon). These CEOs do, however, celebrate multiculturalism and identity politics associated with present-day progressivism and embraced fully by liberal Democrats.

As of 2020 the U.S. was home to 15 of the world's top 20 tech corporations, though China was rapidly catching up. Many of these interests have close ties with the Pentagon, deep state, and other leading government sectors. Here the very idea that workers, consumers, or the general public have much control over the flow of global resources and transactions is a sad myth: these giants are virtually unaccountable to any state or public source – a situation worsened to the extent tech firms operate within their own bubble, and where they are globalized. Matters worsen further, as Hasson argues in *The Manipulators*, as the corporate culture famously becomes one of arrogant conformism and intolerance.[42]

In the U.S., above all, the rapid ascent of social media has created something of an enlarged but distorted public square – a manipulated center of everyday discourse that *appears* to reduce barriers of historical separation. Such vehicles as Facebook, YouTube, Twitter, and Amazon are nowadays routinely used by the vast majority of Americans. Zuckerberg for one has repeatedly described his domain as a source of "tools for good."[43] While secular, the terrain of social media is thoroughly dominated by liberal ideology and particularly identity politics where arbitrarily defined "hate speech" is targeted, safe spaces protected, and censorship (notably of conservative views) increasingly common. Sophisticated algorithms are employed to regulate or delete "inappropriate content," usually with little recourse. All discourse is thoroughly monitored and tracked by large teams of censors.

Google alone, with yearly revenues surpassing that of nearly 70 countries, has the unchallenged technological capacity to accumulate, process, store, and utilize information with few limits or regulations. The corporation follows its own strict rules and procedures, some fully or partially hidden from view. Surveillance activities at Google, enabled by its vast global presence, are increasingly devoid of effective public oversight or monitoring. Close ties between Big Tech and the intelligence apparatus tighten in the absence of government accountability or media transparency. Never before has a corporate stratum enjoyed more power over the public landscape. While leading figures at Google, aligned with YouTube and its five billion videos accessed daily, like to champion diversity, there is precious little diversity of *thought* with ideas closely monitored for content. Hasson describes Big Tech as a "politically correct monoculture," a parody of leftwing campus culture.[44] Its many ideological gatekeepers work diligently to protect the liberal establishment from assorted "false claims" and "offensive content" – that is, political challenge.

In the case of Facebook, where 43 percent of Americans reportedly get their news and information, "hate speech" and other supposed forms of "extremism" are likewise searched out and often deleted. Zuckerberg, aided by a vast army of "fact checkers," has said the corporation aspires to be an "arbiter of truth," yet the criteria are completely subjective. The supposed emphasis on "quality news sources" never deterred Facebook from daily promotion of the fact-free Russiagate hoax over four years. It seems that ads showing Trump as a mass-murdering tyrant colluding with Russian agents never violated Zuckerberg's prohibition of "fake news" or "hate speech." Meanwhile, thousands of reports from sources like CNN, *The Daily Beast*, and *HuffPost* could be routinely posted without the slightest consideration of "provocative content" or the gatekeepers' resources noted above.

By 2020, Twitter was becoming more or less central to public discourse in the U.S. and around the world. There were more than 75 million subscribers, many of them daily participants in vigorous but ostensibly "healthy conversations." Twitter interactions were said by managers to be guided by "authoritative criteria," though as elsewhere the standards were vague and unevenly enforced. In theory there was no political bias or partisanship, but that is hardly the case, as Hasson points out.[45] In fact the outlet is staffed almost entirely by passionate liberal Democrats intent on banning all expressions of "hate speech," "violent discourse," and "conspiracy theories." It turns out that these "standards" are applied regularly only to conservatives. At Twitter, it turns out, so-called "bad-faith" actors fell into just one (conservative) ideological camp.

With onset of the Trump presidency the social media sector of the Internet was converted into what Hasson describes as an "all-encompassing censorship regime."[46] At every outlet aggressive censors monitor political speech with great vigilance, always in the guise of protecting "cultural diversity" and weeding out all manifestations of "hate speech." While such violent groups as Antifa get abundant free space and favorable coverage, conservatives with no violent history are routinely targeted by "fact checkers" and other authoritarian monitors.

In spring 2020 the rapid spread of the COVID-19 pandemic across the world opened space for stepped-up technological surveillance – typically, of course, under the pretext of health concerns. Indeed new forms of monitoring and tracking of the general population were gaining heightened legitimacy, if not urgency. James Kilgore in *Truthout* writes that "the lethal coronavirus has come along just in time to become the great enabler of a world in which big tech increasingly takes over the functions of government."[47] In American society particularly there has been a move by political and medical elites to "blend" carceral electronic monitoring with coronavirus quarantine management."[48] Smartphone-based apps were beginning to replace the ankle shackle, facilitated by BI, the largest electronic monitoring company in the U.S. One prototype of this move is Israel-based SuperCom, already marketing its quarantine (or lockdown) management software to the U.S. and many other countries. Such tech giants as Google and Apple have become deeply involved in this medical-driven surveillance.

The problem of mass surveillance can only worsen in coming years, a point central to Shoshana Zuboff's massive volume *The Age of Surveillance Capitalism*, which illustrates the historic linkage of economics, technology, and surveillance. This system, she argues, has turned profoundly undemocratic, embracing authoritarian controls with relatively few restraints. Thus: "Surveillance capitalists know everything about us, whereas their operations are designed to be unknowable to us. They accumulate vast domains of new knowledge from us, but not for us. They predict our futures for the sake of others' gain, not ours. As long as surveillance capitalism [is] allowed to thrive, ownership of the new form of behavior modification eclipses ownership of the means of production as the fountainhead of capitalist wealth and power in the twenty-first century."[49]

As Zuboff amply shows, surveillance technology is firmly rooted in the process of capitalist rationalization. She writes: "Surveillance capitalism employs many technologies, but it cannot be equated with any technology. Its operations may employ platforms, but these operations are not the same as platforms. It employs machine intelligence, but it cannot be reduced to those machines. It produces and relies on algorithms, but it is not the same algorithms." There are always "puppet-masters that hide behind the curtain …."[50] And those "puppet-masters" amount to a "priesthood in charge of oversight and control." Such power manages to "exceed the historical norms of capitalist ambitions, claiming dominion over human, societal, and political territories that range far beyond the conventional institutional terrain of the private firm or market." This is nothing short of a "coup from above."[51]

A pressing question today, in light of new realities, is whether a modern citizenry has become trapped in something akin to a fortified "iron cage" of oligarchical rule, technological domination, and mass surveillance. That could mean, in the end, the triumph of a power elite far beyond what Weber, the "elite theorists," Mills, or the

112   Capitalism, Technology, Power

Frankfurt School could have imagined during the twentieth century. In fact both Weber and Marcuse, in quite different ways, more than hinted at such a possibility – reflected in warnings of an "administered society" or new "totalitarianism." Here again we face the specter of authoritarian rule strengthening beneath the façade of liberal-democratic politics. Entirely unforeseen by Marx and later Marxists (with the partial exception of Gramsci) this post-Orwellian world would deal a crushing blow to human subjectivity and collective agency throughout contemporary social and political life. Its harsh consequences for any possible working-class insurgency going forward seem much too obvious to require further elaboration.

Horkheimer long ago reached the pessimistic conclusion that an authoritarian and repressive society can endure for a long and terrifying period. In *Dialectic of Enlightenment*, Horkheimer and his colleague Adorno ultimately arrived at a similar point in their intellectual evolution. Referring to the false promises of Enlightenment rationality, they concluded: "The paradoxical nature of faith ultimately degenerates into a swindle, and becomes the myth of the twentieth century; and its irrationality turns it into an instrument of rational domination by the wholly enlightened as they steer society toward barbarism."[52] Could this passage have amounted to the most profound critique of modern industrialism and the technological order it has bequeathed?

Given the seemingly insurmountable wealth, power, and sheer force now available to ruling elites, it is surely worth considering whether Horkheimer and Adorno might indeed be correct, despite the familiar celebrations of "diversity" and "multiculturalism." The historical examples of fascist tyranny remain fresh enough, not to mention the long postwar trajectory of militarism and imperialism associated with U.S. power. At present we encounter scattered efforts to recover subjectivity in a thoroughly administered world, but these have all too often become emaciated, futile, more a source of despair than of hope. Could we in the most highly-industrialized (also most surveillance-driven) society ever, have wound up subjected to a reign of hyper-technological rationality where even the most vigorous struggles for social change are easily negated – or might novel, more urgent political solutions be identified somewhere on the horizon? Where can modern humanity find genuine social and political leverage in an age of militarized state-corporate domination?

Notes

1 On the development of techno-capitalism, see Douglas Kellner, *Critical Theory, Marxism, Modernity* (Baltimore: Johns Hopkins University Press, 1989), ch. 7.
2 Horkheimer and Adorno, *Dialectic of Enlightenment*, p. 121.
3 Antonio Gramsci, "Americanism and Fordism," in *Selections from the Prison Notebooks*, pp. 309–310.
4 Herbert Marcuse, *One Dimensional Man*, p. 158.
5 Herbert Marcuse, *Soviet Marxism* (New York: Vintage Books, 1956), p. 35.
6 Ibid., p. 67.

7 Ibid., p. 72.
8 Ibid., p. 75.
9 Marcuse, *One Dimensional Man*, p. x.
10 Ibid., p. xiii.
11 Ibid., p. xiv.
12 Ibid., p. xv.
13 Ibid., p. 42.
14 Ibid., p. 101.
15 Ibid., p. 189.
16 Ibid., pp. 250–251.
17 Herbert Marcuse, *Counter-Revolution and Revolt* (Boston: Beacon Press, 1972), p. 4.
18 Ibid., p. 25.
19 Marcuse, *One Dimensional Man*, pp. 256–257.
20 Marcuse, *Counter-Revolution and Revolt*, p. 32.
21 See Paul Piccone, "The Politics of Artificial Negativity," *Telos* no. 25 (1972).
22 Harry Braverman, *Labor and Monopoly Capital* (New York: Monthly Review Press, 1974), and Richard Edwards, *Contested Terrain* (New York: Basic Books, 1979).
23 See George Ritzer, *The McDonaldization of Society* (Thousand Oaks, CA: Pine Forge Press, 2000).
24 Ibid., pp. 30–32.
25 Ibid., p. 39.
26 Ibid., p. 107.
27 George Ritzer, *Enchanting a Disenchanted World*, p. 9.
28 Ibid., p. 28.
29 Ibid., p. 31.
30 See Maureen Webb, *Illusions of Security* (San Francisco: City Lights, 2007), p. 195.
31 Ibid., p. 202.
32 Ibid., p. 206.
33 See Glenn Greenwald, *No Place to Hide* (New York: Metropolitan Books, 2014), ch. 3.
34 See especially James Bamford, *A Pretext for War* (New York: Anchor Books, 2005), pp. 307–325.
35 For an excellent debunking of the Russiagate fiasco, see Gregg Jarrett, *The Russia Hoax* (New York: HarperCollins, 2018).
36 The most thorough, critical, and recent of these books is Peter J. Hasson's *The Manipulators* (Washington, D.C.: Regnery, 2020).
37 Greenwald, *No Place to Hide*, p. 2.
38 Ibid., p. 233.
39 See Dan Kovalik, *The Plot to Scapegoat Russia* (New York: Skyhorse Publishing, 2017), and Stephen F. Cohen, *War with Russia?* (New York: Skyhorse Publishing, 2019). One of the eminent Soviet and Russian scholars of the past several decades, this would be Cohen's final book; he died of lung cancer in September 2020.
40 Jarrett, *Russia Hoax*, p. xv.
41 On the scandalous role of U.S. intelligence agencies in the prelude to the war against Iraq, see Bamford, *A Pretext for War*, especially pp. 386–389, and Dilip Hiro, *Iraq* (New York: Nation Books, 2002), ch. 6.
42 See Hasson, *The Manipulators*, p. 3.
43 Ibid., p. 17.
44 Ibid., p. 53.
45 Ibid., p. 88.
46 Ibid., p. 169.
47 James Kilgore, "Big Tech is Using the Pandemic to Push Dangerous New Forms of Surveillance," *Truthout* (June 22, 2020), p. 4.
48 Ibid.

49 Shoshana Zuboff, *The Age of Surveillance Capitalism* (New York: Public Affairs, 2019), p.11.
50 Ibid., p. 16.
51 Ibid., p. 21.
52 Horkheimer and Adorno, *Dialectic of Enlightenment*, p. 20.

7
THE MILITARY BEHEMOTH

For several decades the greatest impediment to world peace – not to mention democracy and, more imminently, ecological sanity – has been the enormous reach of American imperial and military power. More specifically, that refers to the perpetual use of U.S. armed forces in the service of global supremacy, a trajectory inherited from World War II. The idea that Washington elites have been dedicated to a nonviolent world order, national sovereignty, and universal human rights has belonged to the most preposterous myths. Since 1900, and more distinctly since 1945, the U.S. has been ceaselessly dedicated to superpower domination aligned with expansionist beliefs of a benighted, entitled, "indispensable" nation. And indeed by the third decade of the twenty-first century the U.S. retains that unique status, though now increasingly contested at a time of Chinese ascendancy.

In 2020 Washington maintained bases in over 100 countries, was involved in several armed conflicts or proxy wars, had spent many trillions of dollars in Middle East interventions since 2001 alone, and devotes more than one trillion dollars yearly to nourish its insatiable war machine. Meanwhile, Pentagon war planners maintain a nuclear arsenal of several thousand warheads and dedication to unprecedented modernization of its facilities and weaponry. Often neglected is the fact this swollen warfare state contributes an estimated 2 percent of the total world carbon footprint. Constraints on further growth of the military behemoth – whether from Congress, the media, of popular forces – remain virtually invisible. On the contrary, pressures toward future military buildup are sure to intensify as geopolitical and resource conflicts gather momentum.

Recent efforts to criticize or oppose this system are ritually met with ridiculous charges of "isolationism," as if such a posture were even remotely possible in a thoroughly globalized network of economic and political power. References to "isolationism" can refer only to particular forms of military intervention, Andrew

DOI: 10.4324/9781003197461-8

Bacevich writing: "Isolationism is a fiction, bandied about to divert attention from other issues. It is a scare word, an egregious form of establishment-sanctioned fake news. It serves as a type of straightjacket, constraining debate on possible alternatives to militarized American globalism, which has long since become a source of self-inflicted wounds."[1] The long absence of an antiwar movement in the U.S. merely compounds this predicament.

With all its vicissitudes – and failures – one cannot help but observe a certain political *continuity* in U.S. foreign policy and military behavior since World War II. Reading Mills' *Power Elite*, written in the 1950s, this point is difficult to escape: the contours of an imperial juggernaut were set in motion during and after the war. As Mills observed: "Alongside the corporate executives and the politicians, the generals and admirals … have gained and have been given increased power to make and to influence decisions of the gravest consequence."[2] After noting that war had become an endemic feature of American life, Mills added: "It is not only within the higher political and economic, scientific and educational circles that the military ascendancy is apparent. The warlords, along with their fellow travelers and spokesmen, are attempting to plant their metaphysics firmly among the population at large."[3] That project has succeeded admirably, thanks to all the "fellow travelers" and "spokesmen" situated among the military contractors, lobbyists, and media propagandists.

Mills was, of course, referring to the extensive militarization of both the political and the larger culture, sources of ideological support for continuous imperial ventures. Public opposition to U.S. interventions, volatile at times (as during the Vietnam and Iraq wars), has never produced much durable impact. What Mills wrote many decades ago still resonates: "American militarism, in fully developed form, would mean the triumph in all areas of life of the military metaphysic, and hence the subordination to it of all other ways of life."[4] For the power elite, this development confers enhanced freedom of action, a more flexible reign, for they "have come into command of instruments of rule quite unsurpassed in the history of mankind."[5]

By the twenty-first century, disparate sectors of the power structure had converged around an imperial stratagem designed to sustain U.S. superpower hegemony in a more competitive setting – not only the Pentagon but intelligence agencies, Wall Street, Big Tech, and corporate media. Both Republicans and Democrats came to share an aggressive, militarized foreign policy – that is, an essentially neocon strategy. With ascendancy of the Clintonites during the 1990s, in fact, it was the Democrats who could increasingly be described as the "War Party."[6] Theirs was a project of ambitious globalization involving Middle East wars, hostility to Russia, and increased reliance on the "deep state," meaning a reinvigorated NSA, CIA, and FBI among other federal agencies. For the Clintonites and their allies, this meant vigorous pursuit of world domination behind an ideological façade of "humanitarian intervention," progressive social goals, and above all identity politics. Their calling card would be the disastrous adventures in the Balkans, Iraq, Afghanistan, Libya, and

Ukraine. Their "idealism" was grounded in new manifestations of American exceptionalism and, with it, militarism.

The New Imperial State

Postwar consolidation of the warfare state gave rise to an imperial order with a power and scope unrivalled in human history, embedded in a power structure extending far beyond the presidency or executive branch as such. This apparatus was rooted in a dynamic constellation of forces – economic, political, cultural, global – that has pushed American society steadily toward consolidated elite power over succeeding decades. The implications for popular access to decision-making, for a viable democracy, cannot be overlooked. Authoritarian statism and oligarchical rule have been central to American life since World War II, an era marked by the development of military Keynesianism, vital to postwar economic growth. Although foreign ventures have brought new risks and costs to society as a whole, for corporate elites they have meant new sources of wealth and power, dynamic mechanism of capital accumulation. Today more than ever state power and the war economy are tightly interwoven.

In the aftermath of World War II, the greatest spectacle of death and destruction in history, terminated by the atomic bombing of Japan, would take on new meaning in a society where military power was now closely tied to growth, modernity, and progress as well as national identity and projections of world supremacy. Science and technology would likewise be crucial to U.S. geopolitical ambitions. New episodes of warfare – in Korea, Indochina, Central America, the Balkans, Middle East – all built on deceit and secrecy, would ultimately take on a veneer of routine and normalcy.

What Mills had earlier defined as the "military metaphysic" became integral to postwar American life – a phenomenon mostly taken for granted, rarely debated. The 2020 military budget (for the Pentagon, intelligence agencies, homeland security, veterans programs, etc.) easily surpassed one trillion dollars, exceeding peak Cold War levels of 1965 and 1985. This surpassed the *combined* expenditures of other, ostensibly hostile nations: China, Russia, Iran, North Korea. At this point, moreover, the U.S. remained the only country in the world with a sprawling armed forces presence outside its borders, including nuclear deployments in Europe and elsewhere, naval operations on every ocean, a string of fortified bases adjacent to Russia, Iran, and China, and dozens of CIA and NSA sites as launching pads for surveillance, covert operations, and proxy wars. Any strictly "defensive" rationale for such extravagant use of human, technical, and natural resources has never been convincingly set forth. Meanwhile, Washington was responsible for as many as 10 million deaths (and several times that many wounded) in the three biggest postwar military campaigns – Korea, Indochina, Iraq.

The warfare state is now such a deeply institutionalized sector of American society that ideological supports have been more or less automatic, among both elites and the general population, Democrats and Republicans alike. This strong consensus was disturbed only briefly, at the time of the Vietnam War when the peace movement raised fundamental questions about U.S. foreign policy. Aside from brief interludes of antiwar protest (as before the Iraq war in 2003), U.S. military interventions have continued, often for many years, largely undeterred by popular opposition. By 2020, in fact, American involvement in Afghanistan was nearing its *twentieth* year. One reason lies in the ongoing strength of American nationalism. A deeper explanation can be found in the vast material benefits derived by corporations and much of the workforce from military Keynesianism, a system that also generates super-profits for hundreds of Pentagon contractors and subcontractors long vital to the war economy.

As the warfare state has become so widely entrenched, opposition to it has been nearly virtually impossible to mount, much less sustain. In the U.S. antiwar protests have typically focused on immediate events (that is, wars) rarely confronting the *structural* features of the war economy, security state, nuclear complex, or empire of bases. Protests typically come and go, leaving all the systemic foundations intact. On this point Seymour Melman has persuasively argued: "A peace movement in such a society can no longer limit itself to criticism of direct military combat. For this is no isolated condition but rather the continuous consequence of the dominant rule of the war-making institutions in public life."[7] To have lasting reverberations, therefore, antiwar mobilizations would have to target the main centers of power – something that has never happened, even during the turbulent Vietnam War years.

Meanwhile, the authoritarian character of military institutions and culture has produced a steady erosion of liberal-democratic politics – the same dynamic identified by Mills, who as noted described a ruling elite as infected with a "higher immorality."[8] Concentrated elite power would characterize what Robert J. Lifton later called the "superpower syndrome," with its emphasis on nuclear weaponry.[9] That "syndrome" would thrive in a newer context – the global ecological crisis – that would be marked by accelerated resource wars. From 1945 to the present, an expanding nuclear complex would endow Washington with doomsday military force.

From Communism and the Soviet threat to jihadic terrorism, the postwar years have witnessed a perpetual recycling of wars against demonic enemies, presented as a threat to freedom, democracy, and national security. The American war machine has always thrived on a continuous supply of monsters, especially those with dark skins, mostly inhabitants of Asia, Latin America, and the Middle East. Here, as part of a twisted historical logic, sophisticated technowar celebrated by the superpower and the menace of villainous enemies has been tightly interconnected, the former needed to extinguish the latter and to justify its existence. The more "savage" the enemy, the clearer the rationale for all-out warfare in the legacy of a Good War that destroyed fascism.[10]

Such political demonization is filtered through a complex propaganda network involving the federal government, military, media, think tanks, and public relations firms. All-out military combat has its origins in the World War II pursuit of total victory against the Japanese. With few hard rules of military conduct, the line separating combatants from civilians effectively vanished, the U.S. seeking revenge for the "treachery" of Pearl Harbor, John Dower observing: "In the course of the war in Asia, racism, dehumanization, technological innovation, and exterminationist policies became interlocked in unprecedented ways."[11] In this historical ontext, with the notion of noncombatants rendered obsolete, a policy of mass destruction could more easily embraced, close to what Dower labels "idealistic annihilation."[12] Here the entire Japanese population amounted to a monolithic enemy, eligible to be targeted with terror bombing and, finally, the atomic incineration of Hiroshima and Nagasaki.

Across U.S. history, no event brought more power and legitimation to the imperial state than the Japanese attack on Pearl Harbor – essentially a "Godsend," as Dower put it, bringing Washington into World War II.[13] That event – and lesser ones to follow – would enable ruling elites to turn chaos into order, defeat into victory. Military action was typically framed in the political culture as entirely reactive, justified, "defensive." Decades after Pearl Harbor, the 9/11 terrorist attacks served that very ideological function, in effect another "Godsend." If, as Michael Rogin has argued, such political demonology (first targeting Native Americans) engages the very core of American politics, nowadays it more fully resonates with the comforting myth of a noble superpower facing yet another foreign evil. Rogin has suggested that U.S. national identity had eventually morphed into something akin to an "imperial self" confronting a multitude of "alien" threats.[14]

With the warfare state having solidified its presence, strong currents of authoritarianism, militarism, and imperialism could more likely be reinforced. Here the ideological syndrome Roger Griffin identifies as basic to earlier fascist regimes has seemingly resurfaced within American society at least since the 1990s, as suggested by such critics as Chris Hedges and Sheldon Wolin.[15] A unification of corporate oligarchy, the state, and military readily follows, undergirded by the superpower ethos. For the U.S., moreover, militarism has profoundly reshaped mass consciousness, while mortal enemies (now Russia, Iran, and North Korea) stimulate elite vigilance. All this has set limits are set to elections, legislative work, government policy-making, and media discourse.

World War II gave birth to a national security state that, by 1950, had become shrouded in secrecy, as executive control of information flows grew vital to expanded intelligence, surveillance, and military operations. From the early 1950s onward, every worldwide Communist advance – real or manufactured – helped fuel the growth of federal power. Certain "war measures" in place during the 1940s would be extended throughout the Cold War, Gary Wills commenting: "If everything is an emergency, all power is emergency power."[16] With literally millions of classified documents, collected and processed by the Pentagon, CIA, NSA, and FBI, the storehouse of hidden communications was sure to proliferate with each passing year, no matter who occupied the White House. U.S. military adventures routinely took place in the absence of significant Congressional or public input – and we have seen how there were many such adventures. As Washington chose to exercise its self-proclaimed "right" to intervene freely around the world, it would clearly need a more powerful, globalized state apparatus.

With the onset of World War II, capitalist rationalization and the warfare state developed more or less in unison. Scientific and technological innovation extended from the Manhattan Project to the nuclear complex, space exploration, security buildups, and later such breakthroughs as robotics, Artificial Intelligence, satellites, and drones. For the U.S., at least, modernity would be understood in the form of international military supremacy, translated into new sources of domination and violence on a world scale. The imperial state, increasingly at odds with the requirements of political democracy and ecological sustainability, has flourished from one president to the next, one crisis to the next, one enemy to the next.

The Doomsday Threat

The military-industrial apparatus that took shape during and after World War II would take multiple forms: war economy, security state, empire of bases, nuclear complex, first stirrings of a militarized society. All this would exert a powerful influence on the postwar trajectory of U.S. foreign policy – an influence still felt today.

The general significance of what might be called Bomb Power can hardly be overstated: after 1945 it would emerge as a vital source of American global supremacy. Ruling elites soon began to rely heavily on a sophisticated nuclear complex to assert not only domination but *omnipotence*, a "Godlike" force. Writing in *Superpower Syndrome*, Lifton noted: "More than merely dominate, the American superpower now seeks to control history."[17] He added: "A superpower must not only be dominant in the nuclear arena but such dominance becomes a focal point of its self-definition."[18] In confronting a series of postwar geopolitical crises – the Soviet challenge always uppermost – the American tendency would be to upgrade or modernize its nuclear capacity. And indeed the U.S. managed to keep in front of all nuclear competitors throughout the Cold War era and beyond.

The Bomb created by the Manhattan Project was seen by scientific and military experts as possibly the greatest triumph of modern technology, changing the world forever. The Project had given rise to a vast community of scientific and technical workers located at 30 research and production sites in the U.S., Canada, and Britain, along with three "secret sites" (Los Alamos, Oak Ridge, Hanford) where the nuclear complex thrived. More than 30,000 military and civilian people were employed at the Project, the first major step toward full-blown technowar. When the Atomic Energy Commission (AEC) was formed in 1946 – the year of the Bikini test – the American nuclear establishment had already become a fixture of the warfare state.[19] Merging expertise from government, the military, corporations, and academia, the nuclear complex reinforced the trend toward concentrated power. Secrecy here, along with a disabled Congress, meant that supports for a massive arsenal would be maintained as a matter of bipartisan consensus, reinforced by Cold War ideology. An overblown "power imaginary" (Wolin's term) ensured that the warfare state would follow an authoritarian path, the Bomb now having forever transformed U.S. history, politics, culture, and foreign policy.

Atomic supremacy gave Washington strategic cover for many of its postwar armed interventions, and perhaps several of its *non-military* interventions. Behind every U.S. move the threat of mass always lurked. A rapidly-modernizing arsenal – by the early 1960s the U.S. had accumulated nearly 10,000 warheads – provided new sources of military investment, R & D, technological development, and corporate super-profits. Once the Soviets and Chinese were able to build their own nuclear capabilities, this dangerous logic would be further solidified. An exaggerated Soviet menace in fact helped drive U.S. nuclear ambitions well into the 1980s.

As atomic politics gave rise to a new power mystique in Washington, what might be described as a weapons oligarchy came to shape American national identity after World War II.[20] The new scientific-military elite would modernize super-weapons with seemingly little regard for risk or expense – a problem that would surface with the Nuclear Non-proliferation Treaty (NPT) in 1968. The general culture at the Pentagon and foreign-policy establishment stood opposed to limits and constraints when it came to development of nuclear weaponry. The nuclear complex has long been centered at three major labs – Sandia and Los Alamos in New Mexico, Livermore in California. Thousands of scientists, technicians, and managers are given elevated status, generous salaries, and a special niche in the political order, an elite community that Helen Caldicott labels a "scientific bomb cult."[21] This is a setting where design and production of doomsday weapons is viewed with patriotic enthusiasm, even aesthetic wonder. The prospect of hundreds of millions of civilian deaths is ritually concealed within esoteric techno-strategic discourse and game-theoretical models championed by social scientists from diverse backgrounds, flourishing regardless of what party occupies the presidency.

Since 2000 the Bush, Obama, and Trump administrations have followed a treacherous path of nuclear "modernization," all the while threatening Iran over its (so-far peaceful) nuclear energy program and looking for ways to "neutralize" the North Korean arsenal. Obama for one entered the White House with a promise to reverse the global arms race, which should have meant significant cutbacks in weaponry as well as facilities. Obama's oft-praised Berlin speech of June 2013 called for a "world without nuclear weapons," starting with reductions in deployed warheads below Cold War levels, building on the bilateral START treaty with Russia which stipulated cuts in U.S. battlefield warhead totals from 5,000 to 1,500 by 2020.

By the time Obama left office in 2017, however, Washington was slated to spend $350 billion over a decade for ongoing nuclear development – improved research labs, weaponry, delivery systems, command-and-control operations. That amount could reach a staggering one trillion dollars by 2030, a scheme eagerly advanced by Trump in 2017. Uranium enrichment activities were under way at several locations around the country. Streamlined warheads were being designed at Y-12 sites in New Mexico and Tennessee, including fresh cycles of "replacement bombs" such as the B61–12 warheads. These refinements have allowed the U.S. to make inflated claims about reducing warhead totals while the overall deployments lose little, if any, in total firepower. Conforming to NPT statutes limiting nuclear modernization is scarcely an issue for Pentagon managers, as insatiable demands of the warfare state and corporate profiteers like Raytheon, Lockheed-Martin, and Northrop-Grumman easily take precedence. Before leaving office, Obama ordered 12 new ballistic missile subs along with 400 new or refurbished land-based missiles.

Pentagon obsession with global nuclear supremacy nowadays goes beyond its peak at the height of the Cold War, geared to its modernizing agenda, continued first-use doctrine, wide international deployments, and various "contingency" plans for using nukes against designated targets. Dictated by joint U.S./NATO priorities, increasingly directed at Russia, Europe today hosts the largest concentration of nuclear weapons on earth. Hundreds of warheads are dispersed, operational within the U.S./NATO scheme of preemptive first-strike, meaning first-launch option. Washington has stationed B61 bombs (tactical warheads) in Germany, Belgium, Holland, Italy, and Turkey. (These "smaller" nukes are still at least 13 times more powerful than the Hiroshima bomb.) Newly deployed B61–12 warheads amount to what the Federation of American Scientists calls "all-in-one nuclear bombs on steroids" – simultaneously more usable and more explosive.

For many years the U.S. has shamelessly found ways to advance both nuclear modernization and deployments to benefit geopolitical objectives – the NATO project being just one example. In his book laying out the approach of the Commission on Weapons of Mass Destruction, Hans Bix long ago expressed his fear of possibly horrendous consequences of NPT violations by leading nuclear states.[22] For the past decade or more, the same question continues to resurface: how can nuclear proliferation be contained when atomic outlaws such as the U.S. routinely privilege their own military priorities over universal rules and norms? Unfortunately, the U.S. has a long tradition of abrogating such rules and norms, of setting its own course in world politics. While the U.S. all too often transgresses NPT protocols, various efforts to convince Israel, Pakistan, and India (all non-NPT members) to adhere to the NPT have gone nowhere. Blix pointed out that "Convincing states that do not need weapons of mass destruction would be significantly easier if all U.N. members practiced genuine respect for existing [U.N.] restraints on the threat and use of force."[23]

The WMD Commission report stressed that "Any state contemplating replacement or modernization of its nuclear weapons systems must consider such action in the light of all relevant treaty obligations and its duty to contribute to the nuclear disarmament process. As a minimum, it must refrain from developing nuclear weapons with new military capabilities or for new missions." The report added: "Every state that possesses nuclear weapons should make a commitment not to deploy any nuclear weapons, of any type, on foreign soil."[24] For many years the U.S. regarded its leaders as entitled to sidestep NPT statutes prohibiting modernization and proliferation, consistent with the ideology of national exceptionalism and contempt for the ideal of universality.

Presently the most urgent of questions necessarily arises: is the threat of nuclear holocaust greater now than at any point in the past? As we face deepening global challenges – ecological crisis, resource wars, intensified geopolitical strife – the logical response here must be an emphatic "yes." Thus in January 2017 the familiar Doomsday Clock was advanced to two-and-a-half minutes before midnight, the biggest threat level in more than 30 years – a level that has yet to decline. The madness of a nuclear arms standoff continues exactly when prospects for genuine arms control seem hopeless, and when the NPT is being torn to shreds by the U.S. and other leading nuclear states. When it comes to the precarious condition of atomic politics, the world is emphatically moving in the wrong direction. As for the U.S., it retains a few thousand warheads in several countries, pursues modernization of its arsenal, assists outlaw nations, provides several NATO countries with sophisticated warheads, prepares to militarize space, and represents the greatest obstacle to reversing the arms race.

In his provocative book *The Doomsday Machine*, Daniel Ellsberg writes that American plans for general nuclear war remain firmly in place, a reality kept from the general population. As Washington targets Russia with trigger-ready nukes close to that nation's borders, its strategic operations prone to false alarms and accidents, prospects for nuclear Armageddon would seem to heighten by the day, Ellsberg commenting: "The basic elements of American readiness for nuclear war remain today what they were almost 60 years ago: thousands of nuclear weapons remain on hair-trigger alert, aimed mainly at Russian military targets including command and control, many near or in cities." While this untenable state of affairs is officially claimed to be for armed deterrence, "that widely-believed public rationale is a deliberate deception."[25]

Ellsberg writes that devastation from a U.S. first-strike on Russia would bring an immediate 275 million deaths, with another likely 325 million deaths six months later – a total of 600 million even before radiation fallout is taken into account. Even worse, such an attack would create massive firestorms in dozens of cities on both sides, smoke lasting for many years and enveloping the planet, blocking sunlight, and lowering annual temperatures. That would soon destroy the food harvests worldwide, bringing probable total starvation within a year.[26]

Against this horrifying backdrop, Washington has never renounced the first-use doctrine, which U.N. resolutions (rejected by the U.S.) proclaim is "the gravest crime against humanity." Nor has the U.S. relaxed its aggressive, threatening posture toward Russia. According to Ellsberg, "... virtually any threat of first-use of a nuclear weapon is a terrorist threat."[27] The problem with any "nuclear exchange" is that the death and destruction cannot be limited in terms of either space or time; Doomsday would be the inevitable result, its impact almost certainly total. Meanwhile, public awareness of such a threat within American society is nonexistent. Military information is scarcely available, there are no debates, and Congress itself is completely out of touch, seemingly disinterested. We have a policy of "utter madness," with no meaningful change – no moves toward arms control – in sight.

Such nuclear madness, in great part inherited from U.S. military strategies (e.g., the terror bombing of cities) adopted during World War II, now appears so thoroughly accepted within elite culture that imminent change is rather unlikely, especially given the irrational hostility toward Russia. At the same time, the nuclear complex has for decades done so much to reinforce and embolden authoritarian and militaristic features of the modern American power structure.

Permanent War?

Nothing presently hovers more menacingly over the American (indeed global) landscape than worsening relations with Russia – more accurately, the threat of thermonuclear holocaust. Thanks almost entirely to U.S. maneuvers since the early 1990s, proponents of a new Cold War turning into a that war that might spell the end to planetary life can hardly be dismissed, especially in the wake of the Russiagate saga waged by a cabal of neocon warmongers: the deep state, Democratic Party, military contractors, establishment media. The very idea that Vladimir Putin's Russia intervened in American politics to swing the 2016 presidential election outcome in favor of Donald Trump has surely poisoned U.S.–Russia relations for years, perhaps decades.

This unyielding conflict between two nuclear powers is nothing new, of course, its origins going back to the Bill Clinton presidency. That turbulent history includes a series of belligerent moves by Washington to "isolate" Russia, some even hoping to precipitate regime change in Moscow: steady eastward march of NATO to Russian borders, imposition of economic sanctions, recurrent U.S. military threats, armed forces exercises, and placement of nuclear warheads close to Russia, plot to carry out regime change in Ukraine during 2014, nonstop anti-Russian propaganda in the U.S. media. The Ukraine coup against a democratically-elected president was the latest in a series of neocon-organized regime changes – Serbia, Afghanistan, Iraq, Libya – leading up to moves against Syria and Ukraine. In the fanciful realm of American foreign policy, it seems the imperial state has arrogated to itself special "rights" and entitlements to overthrow governments it opposes. In fact only the U.S. appears to possess (and act upon) that "right."

The Russiagate fiasco, fanned nonstop by the mainstream media, sanctimoniously accused the Russians (the evil Kremlin) of precisely what the U.S. has long practiced with abandon – interfering in the political life of foreign nations. For Washington, of course, such "interference" has extended far beyond electoral meddling, to include the armed overthrow of weaker governments – Korea, Vietnam, Laos, Cambodia, Iran, Guatemala, Chile, Panama to name several. And U.S. intervention in Russia throughout the 1990s and beyond, including efforts to illegally swing the 1997 presidential election in favor of Boris Yeltsin, is widely known though little condemned.

Russiagate, it turns out, involved not only unhinged propaganda directed against Moscow but, more crucially, a plot to overthrow Trump's presidency – that is, internal "regime change" driven by some of the usual deep-state suspects (CIA, FBI, NSA). The idea was to short-circuit Trump's promise to end Middle East wars and initiate a new era of cooperation with Russia, thoughts deemed intolerable to the neocons now ruling the U.S. foreign-policy establishment and its media outlets. Efforts to derail closer relations with Russia for rather small political objectives seemed especially irrational given the overwhelming logic favoring a U.S.–Russia partnership: taking on such threats as nuclear war, arms proliferation, climate change, and jihadic terrorism. Establishment hatred of Russia, fueled by a litany of lies, myths, and distortions, would easily carry the day within a badly-deteriorating political culture.

After a series of failed investigations consuming vast human resources, it was easy enough to see that Russiagate had been a fraud from the outset: no evidence indicated that the Trump campaign or administration had ever "colluded" with Moscow, or that Russians had any impact on the 2016 election. As Stephen Cohen writes in *War with Russia?*, it was actually a matter of "Intelgate over Russiagate," a scandal more directly involving the Washington intelligence apparatus than Putin's Russia.[28] These operators were perfectly willing to push the U.S. closer to nuclear warfare with Russia in order to set up a pretext for impeaching Trump.

What made Russiagate so different was both the ferocity and mendacity of unprecedented political and media attacks on a sitting occupant of the White House. Never before had a president been loudly denounced as an agent of a foreign power, indeed as a "traitor" (in the words of former CIA Director John Brennan, working on CNN) without even a shred of evidence. One of Trump's mortal sins? Daring to actually meet with the Russian leader in Helsinki during July 2018 – an encounter that scarcely deviated from standard political behavior. Russiagate made it impossible for Trump to conduct ordinary international diplomacy, a predicament much worse than during the McCarthyism outrages of the 1950s (that were quickly delegitimated). As Cohen writes: "American elites themselves have made Russiagate the number-one threat to U.S. national security, not Russia."[29]

Some highly-respected liberal outlets – *New York Times, Washington Post, HuffPost*, CNN, MSNBC, *Daily Beast* – were so brazen in their attacks that even minimal codes of honesty and consistency were thrown out the window. History was either forgotten or dismissed. The most consequential actions emanating from the White House were ritually blown out of proportion. Editions of the *Times* or *Post* might contain six or seven lengthy articles bashing Trump, often for doing nothing beyond what predecessors had regularly done. In Cohen words: "The media's combined loathing for Trump an 'Putin's Russia' has produced, as we have seen repeatedly, on of the worst episodes of malpractice in the history of American journalism."[30]

Trump's election revealed as never before the tight convergence of Democrats, the deep state, and establishment media, bringing to light all the desperate fear-mongering. The *Times* took on this propaganda mission with special zeal, identifying Russian hackers at every Internet site, those hackers' amazing power to swing an American election nothing short of miraculous. It was surely the best example ever of post-fact journalism. Trolls at the Internet Research Agency in St. Petersburg were said by the *Times* to have targeted all 50 states with devastating impact across social media, yet those postings (in 2016) amounted to only a few thousand in a sea of 33 *trillion* entries total. Obviously the *Times* was never able to demonstrate that he supposedly backward and incompetent Russians managed to alter even a few votes, even assuming that was their intent.

The post-election atmosphere of anti-Russia hysteria was such that even mundane and generally routine meetings with "the enemy" were described as criminal, treasonous – beyond the mania earlier associated with FBI Director J. Edgar Hoover. Representative Adam Schiff denounced even mild critics of Russiagate as Kremlin "agents" and "spies," bereft of minimal evidence yet still embellished by Democratic hacks at CNN and elsewhere. Here the silly vilification of Vladimir Putin, again entirely fact-free, had no ethical limits across the establishment media. Putin was described alternatively as a "KGB thug," most fearsome dictator in the world, white supremacist, fascist, friend of the "oligarchs" (the very same business elites championed by the Clintons, Bush, and Obama presidencies). Putin was ritually depicted as a xenophobic tyrant who, like the Stalinists, is bent on "military aggression."

While Putin clearly had authoritarian learnings, he did handily win open elections and worked with a strong national legislature (Duma), his days working as an intelligent agent – a role blown out of proportion in Washington and the mainstream media – long past. He presided over one of the dynamic multi-ethnic states in the world. As for fascism, this most laughable of charges quickly vanishes against the historical setting of epic Russian struggles precisely *against* fascist tyranny, while it was the U.S.-sponsored Ukraine coup in 2014 that elevated neo-Nazis to power. Concerning Putin's "imperial" ambitions, here again it is the American demonizers who stand guilty of what they so loosely attack the Russians. The stubborn reality is that Moscow has long been on the *defensive*, above all since collapse of the Soviet

Union in 1991. U.S./NATO forces have been deployed along vast stretches of western Russia, a threat that would never be tolerated by the U.S. (for example, a Russia-orchestrated coup in Mexico or Canada). The economic sanctions program alone can be viewed as a form of economic warfare.

The new Cold War fostered by Democrats in partnership with the CIA, FBI, CNN, and others has not only degraded the political culture but taken the world perilously closer to nuclear war. Facing off against the hated Russians has indeed become something of a neocon fantasy, not to mention a convenient rationale for Hillary Clinton's defeat. Deep-state operatives like James Clapper, William Comey, and John Brennan have worked to exacerbate conflict with Russia, behaving as if the old Communist regime were still around, or that the Russians can compete militarily with the U.S. at one-fifteenth the budget. The precise origins of Russophobia are complex, requiring far more analysis than can be provided here. What seems especially pertinent is the disgraceful readiness of American elites to push the world to the brink of nuclear catastrophe for petty electoral advantage.

The despicable role played by the media in this saga would be difficult to exaggerate. Owned and managed by such corporate entities as AT&T, Comcast, and Amazon, all closely aligned with the intelligence apparatus, this sector of the power structure fostered nonstop ideological hysteria –from Russophobia to Russiagate – designed to delegitimate and then nullify the Trump presidency. A siege mentality swept the public sphere, any critical views fiercely denounced and, where possible, canceled. Elite hatred of all things Russia prevailed across print journalism, cable news, academia, even Congress, a sad return to the "higher immorality" that Mills had viewed as central to elite behavior.

As Russiagate revealed elite manipulation at its most extreme, a drastic turn toward authoritarianism seemed imminent. Never before had the subversive forces of the CIA and FBI been so evident, so transparent in the frenzied attempt to remove Trump from office – no doubt clearing the way for more neocon-orchestrated wars in the Middle East and perhaps beyond. Never in U.S. history had one party so brazenly utilized intelligence agencies to spy on its opposition. Beyond any flagrant "abuse of power," this sordid episode revealed just how far the Washington power structure has become removed from the sphere of democratic politics.

The Age of Technowar

Since World War II U.S. imperial power has steadily expanded through continuous scientific and technological modernization, made possible by the world's largest industrial system. A foundation of "technowar" was built from massive human, material, and technological mobilization of resources. Its first impetus came from the Manhattan Project, of course, but there were plenty of other innovations: missiles, aerial bombing, jet aircraft, radar, new communications and surveillance methods, to name the most important. We know that the all-important electronic dimensions of warfare came into vogue after 1941. The later introduction of computer technology, with its multifaceted purposes, would serve to further rationalize every aspect of military life, along with more recent advances such as robotics, AI, satellite technology, and aerial drones.

The idea of technowar could be associated not only with birth of the nuclear age but a uniquely strategic approach: preference of maximum force, use of weapons of mass destruction, more recently forms of distance combat. Unlimited saturation bombing of cities in Germany and Japan during 1944 and 1945 ultimately laid the foundations for the atomic destruction of Hiroshima and Nagasaki, then for later conventional aerial attacks on Korea and Indochina, all with enormous civilian casualties. Technology found its greatest advantage in systematic aerial warfare, referred to by John Dower as the "irresistible logic of mass destruction."[31] In this context all talk of morality or even "limits" of warfare was routinely brushed aside.

Thanks to more efficient techniques of aerial bombardment, it could be said that the very psychology of mass destruction enabled its proponents to ignore the horrific consequences of their actions. For many, advanced weaponry was regarded as a blessing, an instrument of freedom and democracy, even peace. That happened to be the case for those who worked on the Manhattan Project, as it would be for those who staffed the postwar American nuclear complex. If such weaponry was developed for noble causes, then it would surely be unthinkable *not* to use it in combat, in circumstances where national security might be at stake. More to the point, it turned out that ruling elites were delighted to have such unbelievable war powers at their disposal. It could even be a thing of aesthetic beauty, Dower writing: "Like any piece of complex engineering, the war machine itself could be perceived as a marvelously functioning system deserving of aesthetic appreciation."[32]

It is possible to identify five distinct forms of mass-destruction weaponry available to modern war planners – atomic, chemical, biological, economic (massive sanctions), conventional (aerial terrorism). It is not widely known that the U.S. is the only nation to have both developed and *used* all of those, from World War II to Korea, Indochina, and Iraq. Millions of civilians as well as combatants have been killed, tens of millions more wounded – a barbaric legacy of imperial warfare spanning seven decades. Meanwhile, for the U.S. we have the largest armed forces apparatus in history, always prepared for new instances of technowar.

The rapid growth of American intelligence and surveillance operations since the late 1940s coincides with the larger proliferation of federal agencies – among them the CIA, NSA, DEA, and DHS – that regularly partner with corporations, law enforcement, and foreign entities. Most of these work in secrecy, have little public accountability, and cast a larger than generally-known presence across the political terrain. Advances in communications technology endow this system with virtually limitless capacity to collect, store, process, and interpret data related to most arenas of public (even private) life. The imperial state furnishes a rationale for the most active security apparatus on the planet, located not only at the Pentagon but at an ensemble of federal agencies, Big Tech, corporate lobbies, think tanks, and universities.[33]

The most wide-ranging of these agencies has long been the CIA, created by President Truman in 1947 as part of the National Security Act coinciding with onset of the Cold War. Its special modus operandi includes worldwide clandestine operations – usually to either support friendly governments or overthrow "unfriendly" ones. The CIA has for many years been the subject of enterprising journalistic and scholarly research that has brought much of its shadowy and nefarious work to light.[34] At times the CIA has functioned as something akin to the president's clandestine army, responsible to no one beyond the White House. Chalmers Johnson notes that "The CIA belongs as much to the president as the Praetorian Guard once belonged to the Roman Emperor."[35] Its mission relies on every tool available: political assassination, death squads, sabotage, surveillance, drone attacks. It has conducted military operations, espionage, insurrection, and regime change in such countries as Guatemala, Iran, Nicaragua, Panama, Chile, Iraq, Yugoslavia, and Ukraine.

Technowar as embraced by the Pentagon and CIA is nowadays driven by computer systems that enhance battlefield integration by means of sophisticated operations like robotics, AI, and drones. The Defense Advanced Research Projects Agency (DARPA), set up in 1958, has been crucial to the continuous rationalization of warfare, beneficial to both the military proper and security state. The U.S. easily leads the world in military-related R&D, much of it located at universities, drawing from the contributions of physics, chemistry, engineering, and aeronautics. Some labs and research sites also depend heavily on such disciplines as media and communication studies, where computer science underlies virtually everything. Technowar points toward a more information-oriented battlefield – even a reformulation of the battlefield itself – to include global surveillance, cyber-security, and cyber-warfare not to mention space technology.

Technological change in the converging fields of aviation, robotics, computer science, surveillance methods, and weapons development has given rise to widening uses of drone warfare by Washington since 2000 for lethal objectives in Pakistan, Iraq, Afghanistan, Yemen, Somalia, and most likely Iran. Managed jointly by the Pentagon and CIA, drone operations are preferred for their supposed efficiency and precision – also their minimization of American casualties. After many years of unmanned aircraft strikes by the U.S., the reality has been one of repeated, sometimes random civilian killings. Drones have thoroughly impacted how intelligence is gathered and combat operations are conducted.[36] Where such intervention has violated a nation's sovereignty, as is typically the case, the transgression of international law evokes little response in the corridors of elite power, or in the media.

Drone warfare has some great advantages: it is relatively cheap, risk-free, mobile, and (in many cases) efficient for strictly defined purposes. Its casual and routine use, on the other hand, threatens to make armed combat all the easier. Here Peter Singer notes: "Robots may entail a dark irony. By appearing to lower the human costs of war, they may seduce us into more wars."[37] Medea Benjamin shows how the widespread use of Predator drones facilitated U.S./NATO regime change in Libya. In April 2011 President Obama approved the use of such drones, armed with Hellfire missiles to attack Moamar Qaddafi's headquarters in Tripoli, a prelude to his capture and murder. Obama insisted he did not need Congressional approval since this was confined to aerial combat and thus required no ground troops, meaning of course no American casualties. As Benjamin notes, "Libyan ground forces couldn't exchange fire with machines that targeted them from 50,000 feet."[38] At the same time, dozens of *Libyans* were killed and wounded during the many strikes.

Drones, while integral to the practice of technowar, hardly qualify as weapons of mass destruction. They do, however, offer the specter of omnipotent power – a form of power derived from spectacular advances in modern science and technology. As Lifton emphasized, such technowar was at the core of the superpower ethos involving the struggle for geopolitical domination. Beyond drones, Prospects for some type of "apocalyptic violence" were endemic to the superpower mythology, potentially leading all the way to nuclear war, Lifton observing: "Apocalyptic violence becomes the ultimate form of collective regeneration. We may say that death is totalized, is focused upon as the source of this regeneration and the decisive indicator of apocalyptic achievement."[39] If imperial power is deemed to be under siege, facing an imminent threat – possibly a replay of the Pearl Harbor syndrome – could a future replay of Russiagate create a pretext for all-out war?

The postwar rise of the U.S. to leading superpower status brought untold strength but also new vulnerability – the latter tested by Soviet competition and the later jihadic terrorist challenge. Writes Lifton: "For a nation, its leaders, or even its ordinary citizens to enter into the superpower syndrome is to lay claim to omnipotence, to power that is unlimited, which is ultimately power over death." That power, it follows, could only be made possible by the most sophisticated military technology. Lifton adds: "At the heart of the superpower syndrome then is the need to eliminate vulnerability that, as the antithesis of omnipotence, contains the basic contradiction of the syndrome."[40] In the end, "nuclear weapons lie at the core of superpower status. Large stockpiles of such weaponry ... provide an apocalyptic dimension to projections of force and threatened destruction."[41]

The great scope, and destructive force, of modern technowar has not dissuaded ruling elites from their warlike ways. The enormous cost in human life and material resources scarcely matters when the "higher immorality" comes into play. Viewed against the backdrop of what Dower calls a "depersonalized megamachinery," imperial warfare ends up a normalized feature of American politics, all the more so where it can be distant, remote.[42] Reflecting on the "aesthetics of mass destruction," Dower mentions "the satisfaction that came from operating a mammoth political and industrial bureaucracy, whatever its purpose might be. When the purposes were deemed noble [as in the American case] such technocratic seductiveness might be heightened, but these gratifications were intensified by the serpent's eye of unrestrained violence itself. Visualizing hell on earth does not preclude finding it attractive."[43] Here we can see, in extreme form, the military consequences of capitalist rationalization.

Meanwhile, the warfare system and security state have become such fixtures of American public life that any real departure from a global, interventionist militarism seems implausible – not to mention its authoritarian consequences. We have a nation – and not only its elite stratum – that remains fully addicted to war, with risks and outcomes nowadays veering toward doomsday. This is not strictly a question of economic interests or geopolitical agendas, although these obviously matter, but goes to the very essence of American political and media cultures.

Notes

1 See Andrew Bacevich, "American Imperium," *Harper's* (May 2016), p. 29.
2 C. Wright Mills, *The Power Elite*, p. 171.
3 Ibid., p. 219.
4 Ibid., p. 223.
5 Ibid., p. 23.
6 On the evolution of the Democrats in the United States as the new "war party," see Diana Johnstone, *Queen of Chaos* (Petrolia, CA: CounterPunch Books, 2016), ch. 7.
7 Seymour Melman, *The Demilitarized Society* (Montreal: Harvest House, 1988), p. 42.
8 Mills, *The Power Elite*, p. 343.
9 See Robert J. Lifton, *The Superpower Syndrome* (New York: Nation Books, 2003).
10 On the Good War in U.S. militarism and popular culture, see Carl Boggs and Tom Pollard, *The Hollywood War Machine*, second edition (New York: Routledge, 2016), ch. 5.
11 John Dower, *War without Mercy* (New York: Pantheon, 1986), p. 93.
12 John Dower, *Cultures of War* (New York: W.W. Norton, 2010), p. 252.
13 On "Pearl Harbor as Godsend," see Dower, *Cultures of War*, ch. 6.
14 Michael Rogin, *Ronald Reagan the Movie* (Berkeley: University of California Press, 1986), p. 284.
15 On historical developments favoring American fascism, see Chris Hedges, *American Fascists* (New York: Free Press, 2006); Sheldon Wolin, *Democracy, Inc.* (Princeton, NJ: Princeton University Press, 2008); and Carl Boggs, *Fascism Old and New* (New York: Routledge, 2018).
16 See Garry Wills, *Bomb Power* (New York: Penguin Press, 2010), p. 133.
17 Lifton, *Superpower Syndrome*, p. 3.
18 Ibid., p. 130.
19 Wills, *Bomb Power*, pp. 45–46.
20 Lifton, *Superpower Syndrome*, p. 135.
21 Helen Caldicott, *The New Nuclear Danger* (New York: The New Press, 2002), p. 15.
22 Hans Blix, *Why Disarmament Matters* (Cambridge, MA: MIT Press, 2008).
23 Ibid., p. 73.
24 Ibid., p. 49.

25 See Daniel Ellsberg, *The Doomsday Machine* (New York: Bloomsbury, 2017), p. 12.
26 Ibid., p. 17.
27 Ibid., p. 333.
28 See Stephen F. Cohen, *War With Russia?* (New York: Skyhorse Publishing, 2019), pp. 152–157.
29 Ibid., p. 158.
30 Ibid., p. 159.
31 See Dower, *Cultures of War*, p. 223.
32 Ibid., p. 270.
33 Nick Turse, *The Complex* (New York: Henry Holt and Col, 2008), p. 35.
34 See Chalmers Johnson, *Nemesis* (New York: Henry Holt and Co., 2006), p. 95.
35 Ibid., ch. 3.
36 On the larger impact of drone warfare, see Medea Benjamin, *Drone Warfare* (New York: OR Books, 2012).
37 Cited in Benjamin, *Drone Warfare*, p. 148.
38 Benjamin, pp. 149–150.
39 Lifton, *Superpower Syndrome*, p. 22.
40 Ibid., p. 129.
41 Ibid., p. 130.
42 Dower, *Cultures of War*, p. 269.
43 Ibid.

8
THE ROAD TO ECOSOCIALISM?

It is now well more than a century since Marx and Engels last wrote anything for posterity. Much has changed across that expanse: capitalism still exists, in many ways stronger than ever, but has undergone transformations that nineteenth-century theorists could not have fully anticipated. Far removed from the era of classical political economy, capitalism has grown steadily more corporatized, more oligopolistic, more statist, more technological, more integrated, above all more *globalized*. (It is not enough to say that Marx and Engels were *aware* of such tendencies when, in fact, their work never systematically incorporated them.) While still beset with potentially explosive contradictions, the modern world system nonetheless appears more solidified, less vulnerable to revolutionary challenge owing to its integration, adaptability, and *scope*. Neither a more diversified and less proletarianized working class nor political forces once ideologically aligned with (a generally reformist) Marxism nowadays offer a viable threat to elite power. The yawning gulf separating classical theory (liberal or Marxist) from modern capitalist reality is hardly to be blamed on writers of that period; they were, like other mortal intellectuals, working within certain historical parameters.

The New Global Landscape

As the present ecological crisis worsens by the day, its reversal calls for a reckoning with global capitalism before it is too late to save planetary life as we know it. Climate change and related problems, the result of ceaseless economic growth, rampant urbanization, fossil-fuel driven warming, and resource wars brings humanity ever closer to imminent catastrophe. The current threat far transcends anything that some Marxists might have associated with "metabolic rift." The path to theoretical clarity and political strategy will now have to follow a far different course than anything derived from the Marxist classics. It is one thing to argue for eliminating "private property" or "commodity production" in favor of a socialized economy, yet another to strategically confront the most intimidating power structure ever known, one embedded in sprawling fortresses of corporate, state, and military interests. It is one thing to imagine a "proletarian revolution," yet another to forge a complex, shifting, multi-class bloc of oppositional forces capable of taking on world capitalism. It is one thing to anticipate a natural upsurge of "revolutionary consciousness" among workers (or others), yet another to subvert expanding forms of ideological hegemony, bureaucratic hierarchy, and technological control precisely designed to block such consciousness. It is one thing to fantasize about an epochal "reunification" of humans and nature, yet another to begin transforming a globalized regime that spends trillions of dollars to protect its wealth and power while continuing its destruction of the natural habitat.

Such considerations align with a radically altered public landscape, not only for the economy but for state governance, class relations, culture, and ecosystems. The very *expanse* of this challenge is nearly incomprehensible, today magnified by the persistent threat of both conventional warfare and nuclear doomsday scenarios that classical Marxism could not have foreseen. Some limits of Marxism were identified long ago, dramatically revealed by the Bolshevik Revolution. Lenin had shown that revolutionary politics would have to fight the twin pressures of economism and spontaneism, an injunction that, however, would later be generally forgotten. "Western Marxism" came to occupy a certain intellectual niche within modernizing European societies, but after World War II that tradition (mired as it was in pessimism) failed to generate any lasting *political* alternative. It fell victim to what Russell Jacoby would characterize as the "dialectic of defeat."[1] Postwar consolidation of capitalist power – aided immeasurably by effective mechanisms of institutional and ideological control – eroded hopes for proletarian revolution and, ultimately, impaired the very efficacy of (even reconstituted) Marxist theory.

Meanwhile, the grand scheme of a "liberation of productive forces" was rapidly turning into an ecological nightmare, at the very time politics was proving inadequate to the challenge. The postwar European Socialist and Communist parties quickly turned into reformist, loyal oppositions, "catch-all" organizations with little concern for environmental issues. In the world we now inhabit, moreover, the kind of ecological politics needed to help lift humanity from impending disaster will not derive much inspiration from the Marxist classics. With the natural habitat already pushed beyond capacity, as basic resources (notably land and water) are increasingly unable to meet worldwide demands, no exit from the crisis is thinkable without genuine constraints on economic growth – and that includes a wasteful, destructive, cruel meat-based food system. The road ahead will depend, among other things, on sharpening critical analysis of the nexus corporate power, agribusiness, resource utilization, and food consumption – issues only sporadically addressed within the Marxist tradition. An ecological model of development, to date advanced politically only by the

European Greens, cannot be undertaken without the spread of vigorous anti-system movements, requiring the kinds of change in mass consciousness the industrialized world has never seen. The logic of capitalist rationalization would have to be pierced. Here Murray Bookchin writes: "What we tragically lack today – primarily because instrumentalism tyrannizes our bodily apparatus – is the ability to sense the wealth of subjectivity inherent in ourselves and in the non-human world around us."[2] In my opinion, failure to address the submerged problem of speciesism is likely to doom any ecosocialist project, John Sanbonmatsu arguing: "… to affirm a socialism without animal liberation is to affirm a civilization based on continual antagonism with the rest of nature."[3]

Against a background of intensifying class strife and political turbulence, Antonio Gramsci saw ideological contestation – as a cornerstone of revolutionary change, Chantal Mouffe writing: "Antonio Gramsci must be the first theorist to have undertaken a complete and radical critique of economism, and it is here that the main contribution to the Marxist theory of ideology lies."[4] Gramsci, as we have seen, followed Lenin's devastating critique of economism and spontaneism, Lenin having argued that a theory so crippled (shown in the case of Eduard Bernstein and the Russian Mensheviks) would severely constrict the range of political action. Both Lenin and Gramsci nurtured their revolutionary outlooks in the tracks of earlier anti-system intellectuals – Herzen, Chernyshevsky, and Nechaev in Russia, Labriola in Italy.[5] Those outlooks retained a sharp distinction between revolution and reform, socialism and liberalism.

One lesson to be retrieved from the legacy of Lenin and Gramsci – indeed from history itself – is that social change typically occurs in defiance of rigorous or predictable schemas, especially when it comes to revolution. Their work signaled a sharp turn from the theoretical primacy of economics, a shift generally associated with the Comintern that both Lenin and Gramsci helped establish in 1919. They believed, credibly enough at the time, that without a vanguard party socialism would simply remain a utopian ideal. (Contrary to received wisdom, the autocratic Tsarist system that Lenin and the Bolsheviks faced offered considerably *less* political challenge than would be the case for later corporate-state systems.) Domestic oppositional groups, movements, and parties would be condemned to isolation, where in the end they were not crushed and defeated, as in Italy. Reformism could secure better wages and social conditions, but on the larger political terrain would be easily neutralized. It was similarly true that workers and their allies might not be ready to pursue risky, disruptive anti-system change – a chasm the Bolshevik leadership and its cadres were eagerly prepared to fill. Many decades after Lenin and Gramsci passed from the scene, amidst a worsening ecological crisis, it seems worth asking whether such a political strategy – in effect a revolution from above – might be the best option where the life and death of billions of people might hang in the balance.

At this juncture the old Marxist view of imputed revolutionary consciousness falls dismally short of the new political imperative. In their provocative book

Climate Leviathan, Geoff Mann and Joel Wainwright call for a radical departure from political normalcy, at a time when few mass counter-forces are visible. They write: "On political and existential grounds … the left needs a strategy – a political theory, one might say – for how to think about the future."[6] One problem, noted previously, is that ideological legacies inherited from the past now appear exhausted, whether referring to Communism, social democracy, liberalism, or anarchism. As for liberalism, it currently serves as the main legitimating belief-system for capitalist power, while social democracy has failed to seriously address ecological issues. Communism, such as it is, remains far too closely identified with authoritarian power grown increasingly bureaucratic and conservative to be nowadays taken seriously as a political alternative.

Fixated on this very predicament, Mann and Wainwright argue for what might be considered a (somewhat moderated) variant of Jacobinism – an outcome they believe even now inheres in what they call "planetary sovereignty," or "world government," a system with enough leverage to render binding, global, life-and-death decisions. They note that the world system is already well along a path to Climate Leviathan, "because the further consolidation and expansion of extant power structures would seem to be the only structures of scale, scope, and authority even close to adequate to the challenge of climate change."[7] Precisely how this Leviathan might be taken to the next level, however, is never clearly indicated. The "planetary sovereignty" Mann and Wainwright have in mind would ideally intersect with a new green Keynesianism, or international Green New Deal. Waiting patiently for *history* (or the gradual unfolding of systemic contradictions) to generate political solutions adequate to the ecological threat would be futile, no more realistic than waiting for a proletarian revolution. If no radicalized mass constituency is likely to emerge from conventional electoral activity, what then? Could such a departure suggest it is time to revisit, in modified form, the creative Jacobinism of Lenin and Gramsci?

We know from abundant evidence that if the ecological crisis is not reversed within the next two or three decades, it could be too late. We face not only the unparalleled threat of global warming – hotter temperatures, rising sea levels, desertification, agricultural calamities – but a chilling future of sharply declining natural resources. The capacity to produce enough food for the existing world population of 7.7 billion, much less a probable *10 billion* by 2050, can be entertained only as sheer fantasy. In the dystopic future we face the prospects of violent geopolitical strife over natural resources and arable land loom increasingly large. Meanwhile, the dark side of globalization proceeds at an ever more frenzied pace, driven by worldwide economic and technological change that seems beyond the current human capacity to solve, or even grasp.

Despite recurrent promises to "save the Earth," those at the summits of global power continue full-speed ahead: record economic growth (though rudely interrupted in 2020 by the disease pandemic), heavy reliance on fossil fuels, expanded meat-based food consumption, stepped-up military preparedness to meet new zones of geopolitical conflict. Short of revolutionary change, humanity will remain hostage to a few hundred transnational corporations and financial institutions, the majority of those based in the U.S., Europe, and China. We live in a world where the richest 1 percent of humanity obscenely controls more than half the world's wealth, while the top 30 percent owns fully 95 percent of the wealth. As of summer 2020, the world's total wealth was close to $255 trillion, nearly two-thirds based in the U.S. and Europe. As Peter Phillips writes, capital remains located in the hands of fewer than 400 global elites, their "common ideological identity being engineers of capitalism, with a firm belief that their way of life and continuous capital growth is best for all of humankind."[8]

None of these corporate giants or allied governments has shown much indication to alter course, their empire of many trillions of dollars in wealth and resources basically non-negotiable – or in any way reformable. Before the 2020 virus-driven downturn, annual worldwide utilization of oil, gas, and coal was on the *upswing* by roughly 2 or 3 percent. Goals set by the 2015 Paris Accords, on the whole voluntary, were being only sporadically met as those nations most responsible for the worsening carbon footprint (U.S., China, Japan, India, Russia) on the whole continue along the merry path to oblivion. Given the ecologically-ruinous logic of modern corporate power, the path to disaster is most likely to be interrupted by systemic collapse, at which point the planet will probably be unlivable.[9]

On this point Wallace-Wells aptly concludes the world will soon face the old Hobbesian diktat of authoritarian state power where "the people give up their liberty for protection offered by a king. Global warming suggests the same bargain to would-be power-mongers: in a newly-dangerous world, citizens will trade liberties for security and stability and some insurance against climate deprivation." He adds that "a new form of sovereignty will not be national but planetary – the only power that could plausibly answer a planetary threat."[10] This would of course bring elevated meaning to the primacy of politics.

Facing such crisis, global counter-forces are nowadays best described as weak to nonexistent: the radical-ecological potential of major progressive groups seems elusive at best. We notice ecosocialist ideas scattered about here and there, but one looks in vain for a viable ecosocialist *politics*. Environmental groups proliferate across the landscape, yet typically remain on the margins of political relevance. Workers, for their part, veer from apathetic to hostile when facing big ecological problems, noteworthy in their opposition to the various Green New Deals proposed in the U.S., Europe, and elsewhere. As political stakes mount, prospects for revolutionary change recede.

A Modern Jacobinsm?

In the nearly forgotten lexicon of Lenin and Gramsci, an answer might be found in political mechanisms strong enough to dispatch ruling elites and launch an ecological path forward – that is, return to an "external element" or vanguard force, with a strategic eye on gaining state power. That could be a future wellspring of radicalized *mass* opposition, not its substitute as might be assumed. For Mann and Wainwright, that "element" is alternatively framed as "Climate Leviathan," "Climate X," and "planetary sovereign." (For this writer, a modified Jacobin concept seems more fitting than Leviathan, typically understood more as rule-giver or arbiter than *transformative* agent.) Jacobinism suggests, now as before, an historic revitalization of politics. Mann and Wainwright argue that their version of "sovereign" is congruent with an already hyper-globalized order, the ecological crisis itself being worldwide in scope. The familiar utopian idea of world governance was once held not only by generations of Marxists and Communists but by visionary progressives like Bertrand Russell, Albert Einstein, and Linus Pauling, all in their day most alarmed by the threat of nuclear war.[11] Nowadays, in fact, the threat is dual: nuclear doomsday *and* ecological disaster.

The discussion of Jacobinism has a long – often confusing – history within (and outside) the Marxist tradition. For Marx himself, the reference invoked fearsome images of dictatorship, conspiratorial activity, even terrorism – more than anything, abject failure on the part of revolutionaries. By imposing a (premature) "political solution" on civil society, it subverted the organic flow of historical forces and recalled the disaster of Bonapartism during the French Revolution. Jacobinism came to signify a mechanistic, authoritarian politics considered either dangerous or illusory, a trap that happened to ensnare Marx's contemporary Louis Blanqui (and the League of Communists). Blanqui, like Bonaparte, was ready to force a political revolution before its time, side-stepping the need for gradual proletarian buildup. Here the supposed futility of Jacobinism was explained by its addiction to state power that, soon enough, would become a tyrannical end in itself.

Viewed differently, Jacobinism can be located as a moment of social (and ecological) transformation achieved through the instrument of state power – that is, revolution from above.

Historically, this type of change required an ensemble of conditions for success: wartime chaos, struggle against foreign enemies, collapse of elite legitimacy, tightly organized revolutionary opposition, a multi-class political coalition. In its Leninist expression, overthrow of the established order took place only in countries that had not yet undergone very high levels of industrialization, starting with Russia. Contrary to Marx, Jacobinism in these circumstances generally won state power not through a Bonapartist coup but rather by means of sustained popular mobilization – witness Yugoslavia, China, Vietnam. The mostly peasant masses were central to this political drama. There is no reason to believe that any modern-day "Climate Jacobin" could advance without such a developed "national-popular" component, to use Gramsci's phraseology, especially within advanced capitalism.

Marx's view, as we have seen, affirmed the primacy of economics – an approach later stood on its head by Lenin and Gramsci. Their Jacobinism self-consciously avoided that label – or its equivalent, Bonapartism – but did embrace the primacy of politics, including some reliance on an "external element." Across the twentieth century, it turns out, historical change would in crucial ways work against Marx and for the rough equivalent of Jacobinism – for better or worse. One point is that it is no longer true that the political apparatus of capitalist society is simply an extension of the economy, if indeed that was ever the case. For most societies, state power has its own logic, its own historical dynamics, its own center of gravity – all reinforced by the stupendous growth of military power and continuous wars, later reinforced by the ascendancy of intelligence networks and surveillance operations. This is no mere "superstructure." At the same time, if the state constitutes its own nucleus of power, for highly-industrialized societies we have seen a tightening merger of corporate, state, and military interests along lines theorized by Mills in *The Power Elite*. It follows that, within the matrix of state-capitalism, the role of markets in commodity production shares dominance with broadening *institutional* reach, an historic function of capitalist rationalization.

Gramsci's Politics Revisited

The great importance of Lenin's theoretical contribution cannot be overstated, yet it remains no more than a point of departure. In his flagrant break with Marxist orthodoxy – in his emphasis on the immediacy of revolution – the Russian architect of Jacobinism had overcome three (related) ideological impediments during his stewardship of the Bolsheviks: spontaneism, scientism, economism. His vigorous embrace of revolutionary organization and ideology meant the primacy not only of politics but of a disciplined group of professional cadres prepared to win state power on the road to socialist transformation. For that historic task sustained mass support would require organizational cohesion and ideological direction. Neither the proletariat nor any other class force alone was capable of such revolutionary efficacy. No historical processes or economic laws would suffice – and for Lenin the October Revolution itself provided evidence of such political truth. Here we have a crucial step toward modern Jacobinism in both theory and practice.

Leninist revolution, and the Communist revolutions that followed (in China, Yugoslavia, Vietnam) under the banner of "Marxism-Leninism," depended on the overthrow of existing class and power relations. It departed from the prevailing social-democratic model based on a gradual, evolutionary process through parliamentary, electoral, and trade-union activity –that is, a "majoritarian" revolution thought to be more consistent with Marx's own approach. A new (imputedly proletarian) political order was brought into being from above, Jacobin-style, that in time generated party-state rule best described as bureaucratic centralism. The well-known historical result was Soviet Communism and later kindred authoritarian systems of the twentieth century.

Writing into the 1930s, Gramsci arrived at a form of Jacobinism believed to be more compatible with the developmental complexities of advanced capitalism – a system Italy was then approaching. (We know too that Gramsci had already become aware of how, under Stalin, the USSR was destroying hopes for a truly liberating socialism.) Capitalism in the West meant higher levels of industrialization, a broadened and more diverse proletariat, an educated population, the elevated significance of culture and ideology. From this standpoint, Gramsci's vague notion of a cultural revolution understood as preceding the conquest of state power, a "national-popular mobilization," could be viewed as the strategic basis of a democratic transition from capitalism to socialism. It would be surely far less statist and authoritarian than Lenin's original Jacobinism. Nearly a century after Gramsci's epic theorizing in the *Prison Notebooks*, however, it is worth noting that no such revolution (proletarian or otherwise) has occurred in the West or anywhere else. At this juncture the efficacy of Gramsci's creative departure remains impossible to conclusively judge. At the same time, Gramsci did share with Lenin (as well as Luxemburg and Lukacs) an uncompromising revolutionary outlook aligned with contempt for liberal-democratic institutions.

From a contemporary vantage point, it is not clear just how an even modified Jacobinism might define a modern politics of ecosocialism, even at a time when the stifling limits of competing approaches – anarchism, social democracy, liberal reformism, Soviet-style Communism – cannot be ignored. The historical record offers little inspiration for radical change. As for Jacobinism, it does obviously advance a political way out of the global crisis – one that recognizes the futility of electoralism and parliamentarism as these forms are nowadays constituted. Mann and Wainwright fully acknowledge that no "solution" to the crisis is thinkable in the absence of urgent, radical, global action. Liberal democracy, for its part, has been maintained for the very purpose of blocking, or negating, such change. At this juncture a modified Gramscian Jacobinism is at least theoretically consistent with an anti-system strategy. The question we now face is whether such a "climate Jacobin" might allow for even a modicum of democratic politics.

Gramscian theory as outlined in the *Prison Notebooks* effectively transformed Lenin's vanguard party into something of a "modern prince" grounded in a confluence of Machiavelli and Lenin, moderated by distinctly Italian figures of Labriola and Benedetto Croce, whose "ethico-political" sensibility permeates the *Notebooks*. Prince-like features are worth stressing: the primacy of politics, popular mobilization, ideological consent, creative leadership. Thus: "But what Machiavelli does is to bring everything back to politics – i.e., to the art of governing men, of securing their permanent consent, and hence of founding 'great states'."[12] In terms theorized by Croce, the historical outcome would be formation of an "ethico-political" order that might today be labeled "socialism." In Gramsci's view, this process would be driven by a type of "catharsis," that is, an historic shift from the economic/corporate phase to one of political renewal. That transition would appear to be a precondition nowadays for reversal of the global crisis.

How might a political option so manifestly undemocratic as "Climate Jacobin" be seriously entertained within modern liberal-democratic societies, especially taking into account the anticipated fierce resistance across the ideological spectrum? After all, no contemporary political outlook – liberalism, conservatism, socialism, Greens – would nowadays want to question, much less jettison, universal faith in democracy, or promote an authoritarian regime calling forth the Bolshevik or Soviet legacy – even if facing imminent descent into barbarism. Yet we have Mann and Wainwright stating: "Democracy as we know it (especially its hegemonic liberal variety) seems profoundly inadequate to the problems that lie ahead, and to imagine that democracy in another form is going to fix things takes what many might justifiably see as an increasingly ludicrous leap of faith."[13] This fresh but unsettling viewpoint actually gains more than a little credence once we consider that political systems of most advanced industrial societies currently fall well short of inflated democratic claims. Corporate and state power, interwoven in the U.S. with swollen military, intelligence, military, and law enforcement sectors – backed by well-funded lobbies, think tanks, and commercial media – work tirelessly to impede real change, and here with few exceptions they have been remarkably successful. Here the role of the American warfare state, both domestically and globally, would be difficult to exaggerate.[14]

The Grand Illusion

If party-state rule, or bureaucratic centralism, has been the historic success of Leninist Jacobinism, it might be worth pondering whether yet another mode of statism could facilitate transition to a post-capitalist society. We have seen how earlier capitalist systems compatible with traditional liberalism and socialism have, across the industrialized world, more or less seamlessly evolved into advanced state-capitalism along lines theorized by Austro-Marxism and some Frankfurt School writers. The question here is whether state-capitalism rooted in a merger of big corporate and governmental power might lay the structural and ideological groundwork for ecosocialist prospects. Against the backdrop of globalized oligarchical rule – in the midst of unprecedented ecological crisis – the path forward seems riddled with too many roadblocks to allow for much optimism.

There is, however, a coherent argument to be made, following such earlier theorists as J. A. Schumpeter and Rudolf Hilferding, not to mention the Austro-Marxist Karl Renner, who believed that industrialized capitalism as such might pave the way toward socialism in the absence of dramatic crisis or collapse. Drawing on Marx, Weber, and others, advocates of an evolutionary alternative to Bernstein and the reformists focused on the historic consequences of progressive rationalization: economic planning, technological advance, bureaucratic hierarchy, expanded state power, institutionalization of class conflict. When taken over by a new, more enlightened ruling stratum this system could be redirected toward radical, egalitarian priorities without any Jacobin conquest of state power. To the degree that these economies had already experienced high levels of socialization, visible in the welfare state, widening labor reforms, and broadened public infrastructures, the road to an entirely new form of socialism could now be paved.

This evolutionary pattern was no doubt seductive when first theorized roughly a century ago – and even today seems worth revisiting. It did not mean historical contradictions and crises identified by classical Marxism has simply vanished. On the contrary, they remained but were attenuated by the effects of capitalist rationalization, much as Weber and most "Western Marxists" had anticipated. Those very contradictions and crises would in fact help drive further development, this time potentially leading toward socialism. The most appealing element of this "strategy" would seem to be its viability, its efficacy in a setting where large-scale revolutionary violence – not to mention its likely authoritarian consequences – was definitely an outcome to be avoided.

At the same time, whether such a transition could ever be realized on a planetary scale is highly problematic – as indeed would be the prospects of creating a sustainable, ecological model of development within such a top-heavy, integrated system of power. The idea of a gradual socialization of capitalist economies, central to Bernstein's dream of a unified socialist Europe, has in the end given rise to something else: welfare-state capitalism. Even should it open new progressive vistas, however, such a protracted, uneven historical process will obviously fall short of urgent, radical change demanded by the global crisis. During the 1980s a few European Green parties did address this imperative, looking to merge party and movements within an ecological politics, but they soon yielded to the incessant pressures of deradicalization, following the postwar trajectory of European Socialists and Communists. Viewed thusly, historical efforts to sidestep Jacobinism have so far met with universal futility.

Traversing the Modern Impasse

U.S. ascendancy to leading superpower status after World War II profoundly altered the global landscape in every way. Since 1945 perpetual warfare has been the norm for a nation credibly described as "addicted to war." In Bruce Gagnon's words: "The corporate oligarchy in Washington has used space-based technologies to spy on us and to direct all warfare on the planet … The Pentagon has the largest carbon footprint on the planet but, sadly, there is little acknowledgement of that fact by most climate-change groups, which illustrates the 'off-limits' nature of the growing military domination of our society."[15] Sadly, neither this reality nor the dangerous U.S. nuclear complex merits attention from "ecological Marx" protagonists. Daniel Ellsberg writes in *The Doomsday Machine* that American war planners continue to secretly prepare for "all-out nuclear war –an irreversible, unprecedented, and almost unimaginable calamity for civilization and most life on earth …" That unthinkable outcome would mean, according to Ellsberg, at least 600 million dead, the virtual end of agriculture, mass starvation, and final descent into oblivion.[16]

Meanwhile, on the terrain of political action, it is nowadays hardly controversial to say that electoral arrangements have never been friendly to radical change, while as noted leftist parties in advanced capitalism have suffered ongoing and irreversible deradicalization. In the present milieu, no major party – aside briefly from the European Greens – has managed to inject urgent ecological priorities into the electoral arena. Whatever Marx's influence on modern ecological thought – rather limited, as I have argued – ecosocialist ideas have not gotten very far. Hopes of fusing ecological and socialist goals *as a political project* remain just as elusive today as they were in the 1970s, when the concept first emerged.

As might be expected, Mann and Wainwright stress the *political* limits of classical Marxism, clearly one linchpin of their shift toward "climate Leviathan." For them, reversing the crisis would spell the end of globalized corporate-state power, including the modern incarnations of imperialism and militarism. Existing international organizations (International Monetary Fund, World Trade Organization, World Economic Forum) would have to be transformed, more probably jettisoned. Economic growth would be drastically reduced, the agriculture/food complex would turn toward plant-based foods, fossil fuels would be phased out, public goods and services would expand, national armed forces would be sharply reduced and confined to domestic borders. Those changes could lay the groundwork for some variant of ecosocialism.

While such an alternative would be truly transcendent, it could be realized even if Marx and Engels never wrote a single book. It is nowadays possible that classical Marxism might present more of an ideological barrier than catalyst moving forward. Any durable marriage of socialism and ecology – viewed by some as a form of "radical political ecology" – demands, as it must, a break with the system of globalized power. In Lowy's words: "The central premise of ecosocialism … is that nonecological socialism is a dead end and a nonsocialist ecology cannot confront the present ecological crisis."[17] Nothing within this historic shift would require a proletarian revolution, scientific materialism, sustained material growth, or theoretical emphasis on the primacy of economics. The biggest unresolved question today, as in the past, is one of *political strategy* – and here too the texts of Marx and Engels offer some help, but on the whole little inspiration or guidance.

No doubt the Marxist tradition has deepened our critical understanding of early capitalism; the theoretical debt to Marx and Engels here is immense, but for contemporary purposes it is more sharply limited. As we enter the third decade of the twenty-first century, the theory – whatever its scientific claims – falls dramatically short in terms of both historical analysis and political vision. Meanwhile, the expanse between theory and reality continues to widen. A thriving ecosocialism, in whatever form it appears, will have to confront a wide panorama of global challenges, including the ever-present dangers of resource wars, militarism, and nuclear apocalypse, if anything resembling a "green agenda" is to be secured.

To this point Victor Wallis writes, in *Red-Green Revolution*: "Militarism, expansionism, and environmental plunder are all of a piece, and find their fullest expression in U.S. policies. An essential task for both environmental and peace activists is to join forces, as the demands of each group reinforce those of the other."[18]

Whatever the strategy, a vigorous revitalization of politics will be the *sine qua non* of planetary survival, considering that the crisis has so far eluded decisive human intervention. Economic analysis for such purposes is obviously indispensable, but hardly sufficient. As mentioned, we have no scientific laws that could rigorously decipher, much less predict, modern political behavior. On this point Mann and Wainwright observe: "... beyond an appreciation of the scientific consensus on climate change, it is not clear that scientific literacy is necessary to grasp the political-economic transformations required. The political problems we face cannot be fixed by simply delivering science to the masses. If good climate data and models were all that were needed to address climate change, we would have seen a political response in the 1980s."[19] They continue: "Planetary sovereignty stands as in some ways it always has, as the completion of modernity. Though it presents itself as a defense of life and civilization, planetary governance cannot countenance democracy."[20] Is democracy as we have come to know it these past two centuries now approaching obsolescence?

In modern liberal-democratic societies, any "solution" that invites authoritarianism, or Jacobinism – even where it might be understood as staving off planetary disaster – will understandably provoke fears of Stalinist tyranny. That many societies in the West and elsewhere have already fallen into various authoritarian tendencies, including ever more intrusive surveillance technology, should matter, but possibly will not. As Mann and Wainwright comment: "Democracy is not majority rule and has little to do with the vote. Rather, democracy exists in a society to the extent that everyone could rule, could shape collective answers to collective questions. No nation-state today meets this criterion."[21] Turning to American society in particular, the situation is today all the more laden with obstacles, starting with a corporate-state behemoth defended by the largest military apparatus ever known. Under such conditions, a Jacobin-inflected ecosocialism might at least offer prospects of a more rational, more peaceful, more sustainable planetary habitat.

Notes

1. Russell Jacoby, *The Dialectic of Defeat* (London: Cambridge University Press, 1981).
2. Murray Bookchin, *Ecology of Freedom* (Palo Alto, CA: Cheshire Books), p. 279.
3. Sanbonmatsu, in *Critical Theory*, p. 31.
4. See Chantal Mouffe, "Hegemony and Ideology in Gramsci," in Mouffe, ed., *Gramsci and Marxist Theory* (London: Routledge & Kegan Paul, 1979), p. 170.
5. On the great influence of nineteenth-century radical intellectuals on the development of Bolshevism, see Adam B. Ulam, *The Bolsheviks* (New York: Collier Books, 1965), chs. 2, 3.

6 Geoff Mann and Joel Wainwright, *Climate Leviathan* (London: Verso, 2018), p. 130.
7 Ibid., p. 173.
8 Peter Phillips, *Giants* (New York: Seven Stories Press, 2018), p. 29.
9 This point is further developed elsewhere. See Carl Boggs, "The Grand Illusion," *CounterPunch* (January 22, 2020).
10 Wallace-Wells, *Uninhabitable Earth*, p. 192.
11 Mann and Wainwright, *Climate Leviathan*, p. 127.
12 See Gramsci, "The Modern Prince," in *Selection from the Prison Notebooks*, pp. 167–168.
13 Mann and Wainwright, *Climate Leviathan*, p. 182.
14 See Carl Boggs, *Origins of the Warfare State* (New York: Routledge, 2017).
15 Bruce Gagnon, "Addicted to Weapons," in Helen Caldicott, ed., *Sleepwalking to Armageddon* (New York: The New Press, 2017), p. 37.
16 Daniel Ellsberg, *The Doomsday Machine* (New York: Bloomsbury, 2017), p. 17.
17 Lowy, *Ecosocialism*, p. xi.
18 Victor Wallis, *The Red-Green Revolution* (Toronto: Political Animal Press, 2018), p. 194.
19 Mann and Wainwright, *Climate Leviathan*, p. 7.
20 Ibid., p. 191.
21 Ibid., p. 176.

SHELDON WOLIN: A TRIBUTE

The recent passing of Sheldon Wolin (on October 21, 2015) at age 93 marks a farewell to one of the most preeminent intellectual figures the political science discipline has known. More than strictly a political theorist, or political scientist, Wolin had for decades exerted a unique influence within and outside academia, working to the very end of his life. I was fortunate enough to know Wolin when I was graduate student in his political theory courses at U.C., Berkeley in the mid-1960s – courses that permanently shaped my own intellectual and political trajectory. It was in those courses – along with Wolin's elegant writings – that I would arrive at a broadly historical and conceptual understanding of politics not limited to the realm of parties, elections, and legislative decisions. Absent that influence, my educational development would have been something altogether different, and substantially less, than what is has been.

The deep resonance of Wolin's teaching, writings, and other contributions would be magnified by the upheavals of the time. It might be said that Wolin's seminal work intersected with experiences and motifs of the 1960s, especially at Berkeley, where he was at the forefront of struggles for a revitalized politics linked to protests that would spill beyond the boundaries of "normal," routinized political life. Wolin was a powerful voice during (and after) those turbulent years when radical change, fueled by hopes for participatory democracy, seemed to be on the near horizon. The power structure, both institutionally and ideologically, both societal and academic, was widely seen at the time as a lifeless bureaucratic machine detached from any semblance of democratic politics – a phenomenon given expression by the Free Speech Movement and Mario Savio's galvanizing, now-famous speeches. From the FSM (fall 1964) onward, Wolin – along with colleagues Michael Rogin, John Schaar, Hannah Pitkin, and Norman Jacobson – worked tirelessly to energize university life and, with it, the broader political

DOI: 10.4324/9781003197461-10

terrain. Those energies would profoundly alter the lives of many students, teachers, and activists, then and later. What in the end Wolin and his colleagues bequeathed was an ethos of democratic engagement in its most vibrant and all-encompassing forms.

For Wolin, mainstream American politics was largely dysfunctional, ossified – cut off from the sphere of popular interests and demands – a far remove from ceaseless establishment praise for the wonderful virtues of constitutional democracy. In actuality, an entrenched power structure coexisted with an ideological rigidity that political scientists helped legitimate through their "scientific" methodology and interest-group pluralism that worked against social change, a vibrant citizenry, and genuine democratic participation. Wolin believed that moments of historical crisis and insurgency (as during the 1960s) called for a creative, revitalized politics embedded in a community of interests – public values – sharing little in common with a politics reduced to a congeries of private interests, a view generally embraced across the discipline. Such "pluralism," of course, only masked the larger apparatus of domination that characterized American politics. It turned out that the hegemonic outlook of a supposedly *political* discipline was rather useless in facing epic challenges posed by the Civil Rights movement, the Vietnam War, and myriad campus-based protests.

Never a Marxist, never an anarchist, never one to systematically engage the work of the Frankfurt School and Critical Theory, Wolin was nonetheless a radical in the fullest and best sense of the term, his life and work driven by a deep critical spirit insisting that we probe beneath the surface of conventional beliefs and methods – a sensibility again ideally suited to the 1960s, which questioned (and frequently overturned) so much of what had been taken for granted. In fact Wolin, often collaborating with Schaar (in the pages of the *New York Review of Books* and elsewhere), explored the political reverberations of the 1960s in ways rarely matched elsewhere.

Wolin's classic *Politics and Vision*, which shattered pretensions of scientism, positivism, and pluralism that the vast majority of political scientists held so dearly, has had an enduring influence on widening circles of faculty and students (myself included). The book is one I have found myself revisiting over the years, for its probing and original interpretations of the Greek theorists, Hobbes, Machiavelli, Rousseau, Marx, Lenin, and others. Though critical of Marxism, Wolin leveled particularly savage attacks on both classical and modern liberalism (and by extension capitalism), as sources of a diminished public sphere, feeble citizenship, and rampant corporatism. These early critiques were the basis of later, in some ways more systematic and elaborate, formulations in his 2007 work *Democracy, Inc.*, where he debunked familiar claims that American politics is synonymous with democratic norms and practices. (I reviewed this book for the June 2009 issue of *New Political Science*.)

From *Politics and Vision* through his writings on the 1960s, editorship of the journal *Democracy* (early 1980s), and *Democracy, Inc.*, Wolin's intellectual energies were directed toward a rebirth of American politics grounded in an open and dynamic public sphere, deep citizenship, broadened access to governing institutions, and collective decision-making. Such rebirth demanded (and still demands) a far-reaching break with ingrained approaches to the study of democracy itself, which are rife with truncated concepts and resonant myths fully at odds with dynamic citizen participation. For a brief time, at least, the 1960s pointed toward exactly this kind of radical shift, yet the broader and longer American trajectory has clearly favored an ideological narrowing, social disaggregation, and political authoritarianism. In *Democracy, Inc.*, for example, Wolin constructs a rather dark picture of American politics linked to the expansion of corporate power, global interventions, and militarism. That identifiable motif would be finally, and extensively, explored in his wide collection of essays titled *Fugitive Democracy* (2016), where he reflects on the contributions of disparate theorists, from Hobbes to Marx, Weber, the Frankfurt School, and John Rawls.

In contrast to more celebratory treatments of U.S. history, Wolin held that the governing apparatus was emphatically undemocratic and oligarchic from the outset. In *Democracy, Inc.* he writes: "The American political system was not born a democracy. It was constructed by those who were either skeptical about democracy or hostile to it." (p. 228) Across more than two centuries, moreover, the system has in crucial ways only further deteriorated: "A destructive and common feature of organized science, technology, and capital, and of imperial power and the globalizing corporation, is their distance from the experience of ordinary beings." (p. 132) Within such an order elites have managed to create their own insular, esoteric modes of interaction and communication, leading in many ways to the corruption not only of political activity but of "public ethics," visible in high levels of social inequality, pervasive alienation, civic violence, and foreign wars of aggression.

Postwar anti-democratic tendencies were exacerbated, in Wolin's view, according to an extended "power imaginary" resulting from World War II and its aftermath, notably the Cold War. The American warfare state that emerged from the 1940s gave rise to an enlarged federal government, military Kenyensianism, deepening oligarchy, a new era of foreign expansion, and ultimately the surveillance society. The social sciences essentially followed suit, replicating the basic features of this history. Within political science, a decidedly elitist outlook gained currency owing significantly to the work of Leo Strauss, Samuel Huntington, and their disciples – none of whom were especially shy about revealing their contempt for democracy. By the 1960s, many of their followers were entering the Pentagon, right-wing think tanks, security agencies such as the CIA and NSA, and media punditry, where some remain to this day. A stratum ultimately known as "neoconservatives" would (along with hawkish allies) exert their own political impact as they ascended to positions of institutional power – including the catastrophic 2003 decision to invade and occupy Iraq for purposes of "remapping" the Middle East to suit U.S. geopolitical ambitions. Wolin argued that the

Straussian project in particular, undemocratic and imperialistic to the core, helped advance elitist fantasies of unbridled state power associated with heroic feats and disdain for ordinary political and cultural activity.

Wolin understood the postwar system as resting on a foundation of integrated governmental, corporate, and military power – a framework similar to that advanced in the 1950s by C. Wright Mills in *The Power Elite*, but now given enhanced ideological and cultural definition in *Democracy, Inc*. This relatively novel structure of domination, not to be confused with either corporate liberalism or classic totalitarianism, was sustained by a labyrinthine network of interconnections, Wolin stating:

> The persisting conflict between democratic egalitarianism and an economic system that has rapidly evolved into another inegalitarian regime is a reminder that capitalism is not solely a matter of production, exchange, and reward. It is a regime in which culture, politics, and the economy tend toward a seamless whole, a totality. (p. 269)

Viewed thusly, the power structure inevitably transcended momentary differences that might surface between liberals and conservatives, Democrats and Republicans, especially in the realm of foreign policy where "bipartisanship" has long reigned supreme.

In depicting corporations and the state as interwoven within a tightly shared power arrangement, as "indissolubly connected," Wolin rejected the tired conservative myth that government constitutes a hostile, invasive force against business interests and free markets, while also debunking a familiar leftist assumption that the state is nothing but the handmaiden of giant corporations and banks. In Wolin's phrasing, "Superpower is the union of state and corporation in an age of waning democracy and political illiteracy." (p. 131) The system is managed and controlled at the summits of power to satisfy vital economic, political, and global agendas of a ruling oligarchy; there are no "free markets," and there is no "democracy."

As for the academic culture of political science, Wolin was hardly optimistic regarding its value to the much-needed project of political renewal, above all for a society besieged by mounting economic crisis, authoritarianism, and a destructive foreign policy. Following Mills, political revival was expected to be a function of extended democratization. Such an epic task requires far more than gathering, ordering, and analyzing "data" within a purportedly scientific framework. The theoretical enterprise, for Wolin, meant drawing on the intellectual and political resources of the "demos," mobilized toward a more egalitarian, democratic society.

At the end of *Democracy, Inc.*, Wolin concludes:

> To become a democrat is to change one's self, to learn how to act collectively, as a demos. It requires that the individual "go public" and thereby

help to constitute a "public" and an "open" politics, in principle accessible for all to take part in it, and visible so that all might see or learn about the deliberations and decision-making occurring in public agencies and institutions. (p. 289)

It follows that politics will have to be retrieved from its lifeless embodiment in modern structures (governmental, corporate, academic) of power and endowed with a flourishing "life of common involvements," geared to a vision of the public good and liberated from all forms of domination. That was Wolin's empowering message to the 1960s generation and beyond – an enduring legacy that remains just as vital today.

INDEX

9/11 terrorist attacks 119

absolute historicism 49
actuality of revolution 4, 5, 48, 51
Adorno, Theodor 38, 70, 88; on capitalist rationalization 33–34; on culture industry 72; on Enlightenment rationality 112; on mass culture 73, 74; on modernity 97
advanced capitalism 32, 35, 54, 66, 67, 69; advanced techno-capitalism 96; analysis by Mills 77; and Big Tech 109; cathedrals of consumption 102; and Jacobinism 7, 60, 61, 138, 139–140; and Marxism 10; mass culture 71–75; and technological rationality 97, 98; and war against nature 38
aerial warfare 128
alienated consumption 73
Americanism 28
Anderson, Kevin 12–13
anti-Nazi Resistance movement 53
anti-politics 8, 37, 48
anti-system movements 5, 65, 96, 135
anti-system politics 1, 50, 66, 67, 68, 73
antiwar protests 118
Arendt, Hannah 106
Aronson, Ronald 4, 10
artificial negativity 100
Atomic Energy Commission (AEC) 121
Austro-Marxism 32

authoritarian state 63, 67–71, 73–74, 79–82, 103, 137

Bacevich, Andrew 115–116
Bamford, James 104
Bendix, Reinhard 30
Benjamin, Medea 130
Benton, Ted 41
Bernstein, Eduard 9, 32, 45, 54, 141, 142
Bezos, Jeff 109
Biennio Rosso uprisings 53
Big Tech 107; and NSA 104; oligarchy 2, 108–112
Bismarck, Otto von 32
Bix, Hans 122
Blanqui, Louis 60, 138
Bolshevik Revolution 5, 50–52, 134, 139
Bolsheviks 4, 5, 52, 57, 59, 67
Bomb Power 120
Bonapartism 4, 26, 60, 138
Bookchin, Murray 11, 135
Bordiga, Amadeo 48
Braverman, Harry 101
Brennan, John 127
Brown, Lester 40–41
Bukharin, Nicholai 45, 48
bureaucracy 29–30, 31, 33, 68, 131; bureaucratic centralism 53, 139, 141; power 27, 29, 31; rationalization 24, 33, 35
Burkett, Paul 15
Bush, George W. 108, 121

Caldicott, Helen 121
capitalism 1, 23, 65, 133, 149; advanced 7, 10, 32, 35, 38, 54, 60, 61, 66, 67, 69, 77, 97, 98, 102, 109, 138, 139–140; and alienation of humans from nature 15; American 81; and bureaucratic integration/technological rationality 29; classical Marxist view of 33, 68; and class struggles 25–26, 31, 32; coercive form of 28; commodity process 58, 64; corporate globalization 34–36; corporate-state 2, 96, 99; and domination 63; and ecological crisis 13, 14, 16; economic rationalization 24–30; higher 30, 78; ideological consequences of modern technology 74; ideological control mechanisms of 56; and labor 14; liberal 23–24, 30, 31, 32, 63, 65, 67, 78; Lowy on 12; market-based 9; and Marxism 9, 10, 54; and mass culture 72, 73; and metabolic rifts 13–14; militarized state-capitalism 24, 82, 85, 91, 103; modernity 30–34, 36, 63, 72, 73, 75, 87, 97; and natural world 16–21; organized 32; in Russia 51; and scientific materialism 46; surveillance 111; techno-capitalism 96, 97–100; transition to socialism from 1, 17, 56, 140; transnational 3; and war on nature 36–42; Weber on 25; welfare-state 142; *see also* state-capitalism
Carr, E. H. 52
censorship, social media 110–111
CIA 108, 127, 129
Clapper, James 127
class conflict 25–26, 31, 32, 33, 55, 71, 83
class consciousness 53, 55, 65
classical liberalism 23, 24, 25, 26, 27, 80, 89
classical Marxism 4, 9–10, 11, 19, 36, 44, 55; and Bolshevik Revolution 51–52; and capitalism 33, 68; and class consciousness 65; and economic crisis 71; limits of 38, 143; and scientific materialism 46; as traditional theory 47–48
climate Jacobinism 8, 60, 138, 140–141
Climate Leviathan 6, 136, 138, 143
Clinton, Bill 124
Clinton, Hillary 127
Cohen, Stephen F. 107, 125, 126
Cold War 89, 99, 119, 129, 148
collective subjectivity 48, 58, 64, 66, 68
Collins, Randall 31

Comey, William 127
commodity(ies) 26, 136, 139; exchange 14; fetishism 28, 58, 64, 97; universally-dominant 58, 64
Commoner, Barry 11
Communism 4, 23, 59, 136; council 4; Italian 53, 66; Soviet 5, 7, 99, 139
conscious life-activity 17, 38, 45
consumerism 98
consumption: alienated 73; cathedrals of 102; food 40, 41; idols of 73; mass 73, 74
Cook, Fred 80
corporate journalism 105
corporate media 65, 73
corporate-security complex 103
corporate-state 26, 32, 34, 47, 92; capitalism 2, 96, 99; power 3, 6, 24, 65, 66, 71, 89–90
corporations 80, 81, 83, 91, 93, 137; Big Tech 2, 104, 107, 108–112; corporate globalization 34–36, 46–47; emergence of 27; and military 84; rationalization techniques of 27–28; and social control through technology 103; and state 81, 149; transnational 35, 93, 137
council communism 4
COVID-19 pandemic 3, 111
critical theory 65, 68, 71, 99
Croce, Benedetto 49, 64, 140
cultural revolution 140
culture industry 64, 65, 71–75, 87, 97

deep state 104, 105, 107, 108, 109, 116, 127
Defense Advanced Research Projects Agency (DARPA) 129
demagogic plutocracy 27
democracy 7, 27, 89, 108, 141, 144; liberal 24, 27, 30, 97, 118, 140–141, 144; managed 87, 90
Democrats 104, 108, 109, 116–117, 127
deradicalization 6, 11, 49, 53, 96, 142, 143
dialectical materialism 15, 44, 46, 49
division of labor 31
Domhoff, G. William 83–84
Doomsday Clock 123
Dorsey, Jack 109
Dower, John 119, 128, 130–131
drone warfare 129–130

ecological Marx 11, 12–16, 18, 19–20, 21, 37, 41

Index

economic rationalization 24–30, 33, 41, 98, 102
economism 51, 58, 66, 134, 135
ecosocialism 11–12, 39, 61, 137, 143–144; modern Jacobinism 137–139; progressive rationalization 141–142
edinonachalia (one-man management) 58
Edwards, Richard 101
Eisenhower, Dwight 3, 80
elections: electoral politics 3, 66, 91, 99; and power elite 85–86; U.S. presidential 104, 107–108, 124; voting turnout 89
Ellsberg, Daniel 123, 124, 142
Ellul, Jacques 105
Engels, Friedrich 9, 11, 18, 37, 56, 61, 143; and Bolshevik Revolution 51; and early capitalism 46; and ecology 15, 16; framing of nature 20; on human domination of nature 13; on human-nature relations 19, 21; and Jacobinism 4; and materialism 44, 45; and natural sciences 19; productivism 17–18, 20; and revolutionary politics 54; and speciesism 39; on state 26
Enlightenment 25, 32, 64; and capitalist rationalization 33–34; and class conflict 71; and modernity 28, 86, 97; rationality 9, 19, 112

Facebook 110
fake news 110
fascism 23, 25, 32, 34, 67, 100, 126; and anti-system movements 65; and bureaucracy 29; and domination 63; Italian 28, 33, 69; and personal alienation 88; and rationalization 26, 28, 69; and state-capitalism 33
FBI 127
food politics 40–41
food system 40
Fordism 28, 56, 57, 100, 101
Ford Motor Company 27
foreign policy 84, 116, 118, 120, 124–125, 149
Foster, John Bellamy 13, 15, 16, 44, 48
free markets 24, 35, 58, 64
Fromm, Erich 73, 88

Gagnon, Bruce 142
Gibson, James William 47
globalization 3, 50, 54, 91, 136; corporate 34–36, 46–47, 92; and Democrats 116
global meat complex 39

global warming 136, 137
Google 2, 110
Gorz, Andre 11
Gramsci, Antonio 4–5, 45, 54, 55, 96, 101, 137; on Bolshevik Revolution 50–51; hegemony 57, 87, 97; historical bloc 53, 100; on ideological contestation 58, 135; on ideological domination 56; ideological hegemony 64; Jacobinism 5, 6, 7, 51, 59–61, 138–140; and Lenin 5, 58–59, 140; on Marxism 48–49; on rationalization 28; revolutionary outlook of 58, 135, 140
Great Depression 24, 32
Great Refusal 100
green Keynesianism 5, 136
Green parties, European 6, 135, 142
Greenwald, Glenn 104, 105
Gregory, Anthony 105
Griffin, Roger 119

Hasson, Peter J. 105, 109, 110
hate speech 109, 110
Hayden, Tom 84–85
Hedges, Chris 91–92, 93
Hegel, Georg Wilhelm Friedrich 45, 46
hegemony 56, 57, 65, 73, 87, 97, 116
higher capitalism 30, 78
higher immorality 3, 82–86, 87, 118, 127
Hilferding, Rudolf 31, 32, 33, 141
historical bloc 53, 100
historical materialism 5
historicism 48–49, 77–78
Hobbes, Thomas 6, 86
Horkheimer, Max 38, 47–48, 70; on capitalist rationalization 33–34; on culture industry 72; on Enlightenment rationality 112; on modernity 97
human-animal relations 38, 41
human-nature relations 16–17, 19, 20, 21, 37, 41
human-nature unity 14, 15, 37, 39
Hussein, Saddam 108

idealistic annihilation 119
identity politics 7–8, 102, 109, 116
ideological contestation 58, 135
ideological domination 56, 58, 64
ideological hegemony 57, 64, 65, 66, 72, 74, 97
idols of consumption 73
imperialism 50, 52, 61, 83, 112
imperial state 117–120, 124–125, 129

industrialism 13, 21, 31, 34
International Monetary Fund (IMF) 35
inverted totalitarianism 90
Iraq, invasion of 108, 148
isolationism 115–116

Jacobinism 4–5, 6, 7, 59–61, 66, 136; climate 8, 60, 138, 140–141; Gramscian 5, 6, 7, 51, 59–61, 138–140; and Lenin 51, 60, 138–139; modern 137–139
Jacoby, Russell 134
Jarrett, Gregg 108
Jay, Martin 68, 70–71
Johnson, Chalmers 129

Kautsky, Karl 9, 19, 45, 46, 56
Kellner, Douglas 71
Keynesianism 6, 24, 25, 31, 32
Kilgore, James 111
Kovalik, Don 107
Kovel, Joel 11
Kropotkin, Peter 37

labor 14, 18, 31, 101
labor aristocracy 54
Labriola, Antonio 49, 64, 140
Lenin, Vladimir 9, 48, 56, 59, 67, 96, 134; adoption of Fordism 28; and Bolshevik Revolution 52; and class consciousness 55; critique of economism 58; and Gramsci 5, 58–59, 140; Jacobinism 51, 54, 60, 137, 138–139; on power elite 56; revolutionary outlook of 58, 135, 140; scientific approach of 46; theory of revolution 4; vanguard party 4, 26, 140
Leninism 4, 23, 26, 32, 33, 65; critics of 56–57; and Lukacs 58, 64; and Marxism 4, 51; revolutions 52–53, 139
liberal capitalism 23–24, 30, 31, 32, 63, 78; authoritarian state within 68; sources of control within 67; totalitarian tendencies in 65
liberal democracy 24, 27, 30, 97, 118, 140–141, 144
liberalism 24, 30, 59, 78, 136; classical 23, 24, 25, 26, 27, 80, 89; and Great Refusal 100; and mass society 87; myth of democratic 91; pluralist-elitist model of 81
liberal pluralism 73
Libya 130
Lifton, Robert J. 118, 120, 130
Lowenthal, Leo 73

Lowy, Michael 12, 13, 143
Lukacs, Georg 4, 48, 51, 52, 58, 64, 97
Luxemburg, Rosa 9, 45–46, 57

Machajski, Jan Waclaw 57
Machiavelli, Niccolo 51, 61, 140
Macpherson, C. B. 81
Magdoff, Fred 15
Malm, Andreas 12
managed democracy 87, 90
Manhattan Project 120–121, 128
Mann, Geoff 5–6, 59, 136, 140; on democracy 7, 141, 144; planetary sovereignty 5, 136, 138, 144; on reversal of ecological crisis 143; on science 144
Marcuse, Herbert 67, 102, 107, 112; on advanced industrial society 74, 90–91, 99; and capitalism 33; on class-based revolution 100; on convergence of corporate-state capitalism and Communism 99; Great Refusal 100; on liberal capitalism 65; on Marxism 47, 98, 99; one-dimensionality 28, 74, 87, 90, 91, 109; on Soviet development 98; on technological rationality 34, 64, 90, 97; on technology 74, 98
market-based capitalism 9
market fundamentalism 58, 64
Marx, Karl 2, 3, 9, 44, 61, 77, 143; attention to natural sciences 13, 15, 19, 21, 45; and Bolshevik Revolution 50, 52; on capitalism 54, 68; class-conflict model 25–26; commodity fetishism 58, 64, 97; on conscious life-activity 17, 38, 45; and early capitalism 46; ecological 11, 12–16, 18, 19–20, 21, 37, 41; ecological turn 11, 18, 20; epistemology of 45; framing of nature 20; on globalization 34; and Hilferding 32; on historical development 45; on human-nature relations 16–17, 21, 37, 41; and Jacobinism 4, 59–60, 138; on nature 37, 41; philosophy of praxis 46, 48; problem of separation of humans from earth 13, 20; productivism 17–18, 20, 37; Prometheanism 14; and revolutionary politics 54, 55; species-being 37–38; and speciesism 39; on state 26; theory of metabolism 13–14
Marxism 1–2, 4, 9–10, 26, 47, 65; Austro-Marxism 32; and Bolshevik Revolution 50–51; and capitalism 9, 10, 54; domination of nature 15, 39; and

ecology 10, 11–12, 39; emergence of 49; and gulf between leaders and masses 67; historicization of 49; and Leninism 4, 51; limits of 134, 143; Marcuse on 98, 99; and revolutions 53; as source for oppositional politics 49, 50; theory, shaping of 47
Marxism-Leninism 53, 98, 139
mass culture 71–75, 98
mass society 63, 68, 71–75, 86–93, 97
mass surveillance 102–108, 111
materialism 19, 39, 44–45; dialectical 15, 44, 46, 49; historical 5; scientific 11, 15, 46, 48, 49, 56
McDonaldization 101–102, 109
meat consumption 40, 41
media 65, 72, 73, 74, 87, 105, 127
medical-driven surveillance 111
Melman, Seymour 80, 118
metabolic rift 13–14, 15, 20, 37, 38, 39, 133
Michels, Robert 27, 30, 57, 67, 81
militarized state-capitalism 24, 78, 82, 85, 91, 103
military 27, 78, 87, 93, 115, 141; apocalyptic violence 130; and corporations 84; force, growth of 47; imperial state 117–120, 124–125, 129; independent power of 84; isolationism 115–116; metaphysic 87, 116, 117; militarism 47, 61, 80, 87, 112, 116, 119; nuclear complex 120–124, 128, 130; power 23, 60, 83–85, 91, 117; scientific bomb cult 121; spending 82, 84, 117; technowar 47, 118, 121, 127–131; U.S. intervention in foreign nations 125; U.S.–Russia relations 124
military-industrial complex 3, 80, 84
military Keynesianism 24, 79, 80, 117, 118
Mills, C. Wright 2, 3, 54, 70, 72, 77, 102; on corporations 80; criticism of American power structure 81; and Domhoff 83; and Hayden 84–85; higher immorality 3, 82–86, 87, 118, 127; historicist approach to politics 77–78; and Marxism 82–83, 85; mass society 74, 86–93; military metaphysic 87, 116, 117; political directorate 80–81; power elite 60, 79–82, 83, 84, 106, 116, 149; on public opinion 87; rise of authoritarian state 79–82; on social science 77; on warlords 80, 116
modernity 24, 73, 86, 93, 97; capitalist 30–34, 36, 63, 72, 73, 75, 87, 97; and military 120; and nature 36, 37

"modernization of the worker" 28
Mosca, Gaetano 27
Mouffe, Chantal 58, 135
multiculturalism 82, 102, 109
Mussolini, Benito 24, 26, 32

National Security Agency (NSA) 103, 104
natural sciences 13, 15, 19, 45
nature 20; alienation of humans from 15; ethics of respect for 37; humanized 38; human mastery of 13, 14, 17, 20, 21; human-nature relations 16–17, 19, 20, 21, 37, 41; human-nature unity 14, 15, 37, 39; war on 36–42
Nazism 72
neoclassical economics 24, 30, 31, 35
New Deal 24
nuclear complex 120–124, 128, 130
nuclear modernization 121
Nuclear Non-proliferation Treaty (NPT) 121, 122

Obama, Barack 107, 121–122, 130
O'Connor, James 11
oligarchy 27, 57, 81, 90, 91, 117; Big Tech 2, 108–112; corporate 142; iron law of 67; weapons 121
oligopoly 24, 35, 82, 109
one-dimensionality 74, 87, 90, 91, 109
Oppenlander, Richard 40
oppositional politics 42, 49, 63, 64, 67, 91, 96
organized capitalism 32
Orwell, George 103, 105–107

Pannekoek, Anton 9, 57
Pareto, Vilfredo 27
party-state 26, 28, 33, 52, 88, 139, 141
peace movements 118
Pearl Harbor, attack on 119
Pentagon 79, 80, 84, 115, 122, 129, 142
Phillips, Peter 3, 92, 137
philosophy of praxis 9, 44, 45, 46, 48, 49
Piccone, Paul 100
planetary sovereignty 5, 136, 138, 144
Plekhanov, Georgi 19, 46, 48, 57
Poitras, Laura 103
political quietism 73
political strategy 4, 6, 59, 60–61, 133, 143
political theory 48, 59, 136
Pollack, Friedrich 31, 32, 33, 68–70, 71
power 2, 79; American structure of 81, 103, 117, 124, 127, 147; augmentations,

and postwar America 79; bureaucratic 27, 29, 31; corporate 28, 35, 36, 69, 70, 82, 110, 141; corporate-state 3, 6, 24, 65, 66, 70, 71, 89–90; of culture industry 72; imaginary 89–90, 121, 148; military 23, 60, 83–85, 91, 117; and state-capitalism 32, 33; state 4, 5, 9, 24, 25, 26, 27, 28, 30, 31, 32, 52, 53, 57, 59, 60, 68, 69, 73, 78, 80, 106, 117, 137, 138, 139, 140, 141; superpower 78, 80, 90, 115, 116, 118, 119, 120, 130, 142, 149; and technology 96, 98

power elite 60, 100, 116, 149; Domhoff on 83–84; and ecological crisis 93; higher immorality 82–86; international 92; Lenin on 56; and mass society 86–93; Mills on 79–82, 83, 84, 106; transnational 3; and U.S. Constitution 89; Wolin on 89–90

presidential elections, U.S. 104, 107–108, 124

productive forces 17–18, 19, 134

productivism 11, 16, 17–18, 20, 37, 39

proletariat 17, 19, 41, 75, 99; revolutions 4, 53–54, 65, 66, 134; subjectivity/agency 101; Western 65

propaganda 72, 105, 106, 108, 118–119, 126

public opinion 87

Putin, Vladimir 107, 124, 126

Qaddafi, Moamar 130

rationalization, capitalist 2, 23, 32, 41–42, 57, 135, 139; bureaucratic 24, 33, 35; and class conflict 25–26; darker side of 86; and domination 29, 71, 97, 102–103; dystopic scenario of 33–34; economic 24–30, 33, 41, 98, 102; hegemonic power of 65; McDonaldization 101–102; and Marxism 10, 47; and mass culture 74; and military 47, 131; Pollack on 69–70; and power 89, 90, 92; progressive 141–142; and proletarian revolutions 54; specialists, stratum of 28–29; and surveillance 108, 111; techno-capitalism 96, 97; technological 34, 35, 98; and technology 96, 101, 109, 111; and warfare state 120; Weber 2, 25, 26, 31, 33, 56, 57, 64, 78, 86; workplace 28, 100, 103

red-green politics 11

reformism 54, 59, 66, 75, 135

Reich, Wilhelm 66–67, 88

reification 58, 64, 74, 97

Renner, Karl 141

revolution(s) 3, 52, 53–56, 58–59, 60; actuality of 4, 5, 48, 51; Bolshevik Revolution 5, 50–52, 134, 139; class-based 100; cultural 140; Lenin's theory of 4; proletarian 4, 53–54, 65, 66, 134; revolutionary change 2, 9–10, 18, 45, 51, 52, 135, 137; revolutionary consciousness 4, 51, 54, 59, 64, 135; revolutionary politics 54, 55, 56, 134; revolutionary transgression 6–7; *see also* Jacobinism

Ritzer, George 101–102, 103

Robinson, William 92

Rogin, Michael 119

Roosevelt, Franklin 24, 31, 80

Rothkopf, David 92

Rousseau, Jean-Jacques 37

Russia 51; anti-Russia hysteria 107, 126; Russiagate 110, 124, 125–126; U.S. intervention in 125; U.S.–Russia conflict 124, 127; U.S.–Russia relations 124, 125

Saito, Kohei 41, 44, 54; on capitalism 14; on ecological Marx 11, 12, 13–14, 15, 16, 19–20, 21, 37; treatment of Marx 46

Sanbonmatsu, John 39, 135

Savio, Mario 146

Schaar, John 147

Scheer, Bob 105

Schiff, Adam 126

Schneier, Bruce 105

Schumpeter, Joseph 31, 32, 33, 141

scientific materialism 11, 15, 46, 48, 49, 56

scientific naturalism 15

scientific socialism 19

scientific theory 45

Sex-Pol movement 66

Singer, Peter 130

Sklar, Leslie 92

Smith, Adam 30

Snowden, Edward 103, 104

social democracy 4, 26–27, 31–32, 34, 45–46, 59, 69, 136

socialism 10, 14, 27, 51, 78, 100, 140; ecosocialism 11–12, 39, 61, 137–139, 141–144; scientific 19; state 32, 106; transition from capitalism to 1, 17, 56, 140; and vanguard party 59, 135

social Keynesianism 24, 25, 80

social media 2, 109, 110–111
social psychology 48, 66
Soviet Union 53, 98, 105, 106
species-being 37–38
speciesism 38, 39, 40, 135
spontaneism 46, 51, 58, 134, 135
Stalin, Joseph 46, 105, 106
Stalinism 4, 7, 63, 65, 67, 106
state-capitalism 3, 30–34, 53, 65, 69, 78, 139; and authoritarian state 68, 70; and ecosocialism 141; militarized 24, 78, 82, 85, 91, 103; modern 50; and techno-capitalism 96
state socialism 32, 106
statism 24, 25, 31, 61, 63, 66, 141; authoritarian 69, 70, 106, 117; and capitalist rationalization 30; and liberal capitalism 23; Marx on 26; and World War I 34
Struve, Peter 57
SuperCom 111
super elites 92
superpower syndrome 118, 130
surveillance 101, 102–108, 110, 111, 128

Taylor, Paul 37
Taylorism 27, 28, 56, 57, 58, 100, 101
technological rationality 29, 64, 74, 75, 90, 97, 109
technological rationalization 34, 35, 98
technology 2, 68, 96–97; Big Tech 2, 104, 107, 108–112; and consumption 102; McDonaldization 101–102; and mass culture 72, 74; surveillance 101, 102–108, 110, 111; techno-capitalism 96, 97; technological enterprises 2
technowar 47, 118, 121, 127–131
Terrorist Identities Datamart Environment (TIDE) 104
Togliatti, Palmiro 66
totalitarianism 90, 91, 99; inverted 90; and state-capitalism 33; and surveillance 105–106
trade-union reformism 66
transnational capitalism 3
transnational corporations 35, 93, 137
Truman, Harry 129
Trump, Donald 110, 127; and nuclear modernization 121, 122; presidential campaign (2016) 104, 107, 108; and Russiagate 124, 125–126
Twitter 110

Ukraine coup (2014) 124, 126
United Nations 35
universally-dominant commodities 58, 64

vanguardism 4, 5, 26, 51, 59, 135, 138, 140
Vietnam War 118

Wainwright, Joel 5–6, 59, 136, 140; on democracy 7, 141, 144; planetary sovereignty 5, 136, 138, 144; on reversal of ecological crisis 143; on science 144
Wallace-Wells, David 12, 137
Wallerstein, Immanuel 28–29
Wallis, Victor 144
warfare state 115, 117–120, 141, 148; Mills on 79, 80, 87; and nuclear complex 121, 122; and surveillance 103
war managers 47
Weapons of Mass Destruction Commission 122, 123
Webb, Maureen 103
Weber, Max 3, 27, 54, 68, 77, 101, 112; on bureaucracy 29; on capitalism 25; capitalist rationalization 2, 25, 26, 31, 33, 56, 57, 64, 78, 86; and Hilferding 32; iron cage 29, 99; liberal capitalism 31; and state-capitalism 30; technological rationality 97
welfare-state capitalism 142
Williams, Chris 15
Wills, Gary 119
Winner, Langdon 105
Wolin, Sheldon 6–7, 48, 71, 73, 87, 89–90, 91, 146–150
workplace rationalization 28, 100, 103
World Bank 35
World War I 27, 34, 50
World War II 53, 78–79, 80, 89, 106, 117, 119

Yeltsin, Boris 125
YouTube 110

Zuboff, Shoshana 111
Zuckerberg, Mark 109

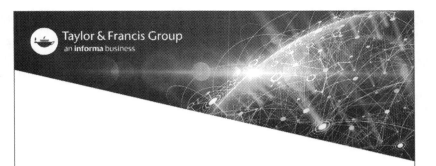

Taylor & Francis eBooks

www.taylorfrancis.com

A single destination for eBooks from Taylor & Francis with increased functionality and an improved user experience to meet the needs of our customers.

90,000+ eBooks of award-winning academic content in Humanities, Social Science, Science, Technology, Engineering, and Medical written by a global network of editors and authors.

TAYLOR & FRANCIS EBOOKS OFFERS:

- A streamlined experience for our library customers
- A single point of discovery for all of our eBook content
- Improved search and discovery of content at both book and chapter level

REQUEST A FREE TRIAL
support@taylorfrancis.com

Printed in the United States
by Baker & Taylor Publisher Services